Ultimate Microsoft Certified Azure AI Engineer Associate (AI-102) Certification Guide

Crack AI-102 Certification by Building Generative AI, Intelligent Agents and Enterprise Azure AI Solutions

Pablo Piovano

www.orangeava.com

First Published: March 2026

Published By: Orange Education Pvt Ltd, AVA®

Address: 9, Daryaganj, Delhi, 110002, India

275 New North Road Islington Suite 1314 London,

N1 7AA, United Kingdom

ISBN (PBK): 978-93-49887-17-6

ISBN (E-BOOK): 978-93-49887-80-0

Scan the QR code to explore our entire catalogue

www.orangeava.com

Get a Free eBook

We hope you're enjoying your recent book purchase! Your feedback is incredibly valuable to us and helps other readers discover books that truly make a difference.

If you found this book useful or enjoyable, we'd greatly appreciate it if you could leave a short review with a 5-star rating on Amazon. Your review supports our work and allows us to reach more learners worldwide.

As a thank-you, we're happy to offer you a **free digital copy of this book** plus a **30% discount code** for your next purchase on our official websites:

www.orangeava.com

www.orangeava.in (For the Indian Subcontinent).

☑ **How it works:**

Leave your review on Amazon, take a screenshot of the confirmation or use the following link to submit the claim and email it to **info@orangeava.com.** Once received the required detail, we will send your rewards within 24 hours, **along with one month free subcription to the book on AVA SkillShelf!**

Claim Form
https://rebrand.ly/4d2477

Thank you for your support–it truly means a lot to us.

Downloading the code bundles and colored images

Please follow the links or scan the QR codes to download the
Code Bundles and Images of the book:

https://github.com/ava-orange-education/Ultimate-Microsoft-Certified-Azure-AI-Engineer-Associate-AI-102-Certification-Guide

The code bundles and images of the book are also hosted on
https://rebrand.ly/636423

In case there's an update to the code, it will be updated on the existing GitHub repository.

Errata

We take immense pride in our work at **Orange Education Pvt Ltd,** and follow the best practices to ensure the accuracy of our content to provide an indulging reading experience to our subscribers. Our readers are our mirrors, and we use their inputs to reflect and improve upon human errors, if any, that may have occurred during the publishing processes involved. To let us maintain the quality and help us reach out to any readers who might be having difficulties due to any unforeseen errors, please write to us at:

errata@orangeava.com

Your support, suggestions, and feedback are highly appreciated.

Dedicated To

My Family,

My Wife, Valeria, for her constant support, patience, and belief in every idea that became a long night of writing.

And to My Daughters, Matilda and Bruna, who remind me every day why curiosity, creativity, and learning truly matter.

I also dedicate this book to the global technical community of Microsoft MVPs and Microsoft Advocates, whose shared passion for technology, open exchange of ideas, and countless conversations at events and meetups continue to inspire growth and collaboration.

OZ Digital, for trusting innovation, supporting professional development, and giving me the opportunity to grow and lead in the field of Artificial Intelligence.

About the Author

Pablo Piovano is the Director of Artificial Intelligence at OZ Digital and a Microsoft Most Valuable Professional (MVP) in Artificial Intelligence (AI), recognized for his contributions to the global AI and cloud community. With more than 15 years of experience in the technology industry, Pablo specializes in designing, implementing, and scaling enterprise-grade artificial intelligence solutions on Microsoft Azure.

Throughout his career, he has worked closely with organizations across multiple industries, helping them adopt AI responsibly and effectively. His expertise spans Generative AI, intelligent agents, knowledge mining, computer vision, document intelligence, and large-scale cloud architectures.

As a Microsoft MVP, he actively contributes to the technical community by sharing knowledge, best practices, and real-world lessons learned through writing, speaking, and collaboration. Pablo works closely with Microsoft MVPs, Microsoft Advocates, and engineering teams, participating in global initiatives and community-driven projects that shape modern AI platforms.

He is a frequent speaker at international conferences and industry events, including Microsoft Build, Microsoft Ignite, and community meetups, where he presents practical guidance on modern AI architectures, Azure AI Foundry, and Generative AI systems.

In his role at OZ Digital, Pablo leads AI strategy and innovation, collaborating with multidisciplinary teams to design solutions that are scalable, secure, and aligned with real business needs.

This book reflects his hands-on experience preparing teams and individuals for the AI-102: Designing and Implementing an Azure AI Solution certification, as well as delivering real-world, production AI systems. His approach emphasizes mastering core concepts, making sound architectural decisions, and applying AI technologies responsibly in enterprise environments.

About the Technical Reviewer

Uma Sesha Sai Chinta is a Generative AI Engineer with strong expertise in building enterprise-grade AI solutions using Microsoft Azure. With nearly four years of experience across AI engineering, automation, and cloud operations, Uma brings a practical and deeply technical perspective to modern AI development. Starting his career in Azure DevOps, he transitioned into the evolving landscape of AI and presently, he specializes in prompt engineering, agent-based architectures, and Retrieval-Augmented Generation (RAG) pipelines.

In his current role at Accenture, Uma focuses on designing AI agents, crafting effective prompts, evaluating model behavior, and orchestrating multi-step intelligent workflows. His hands-on experience spans Azure OpenAI, Cognitive Search, vector databases, evaluation frameworks, and AI-driven automation on enterprise platforms. This blend of cloud foundations and applied AI engineering enables him to bridge reliability, scalability, and real-world problem solving.

Driven by curiosity and a passion for innovation, Uma continues to explore how generative AI, intelligent agents, and automation can transform business operations, and accelerate digital transformation across industries in today's hi-tech world!

Acknowledgments

I would like to express my sincere gratitude to the people and communities who supported and inspired me throughout the process of writing this book.

Firstly, I would like to thank my family once again—my wife Valeria and my daughters, Matilda and Bruna—for their constant encouragement, patience, and understanding during the long hours dedicated to writing, reviewing, and refining this work.

I am deeply grateful to the Microsoft MVP community, and especially to Enrique Dutra, for opening the doors for me to the program, and for the trust and support along the way. Being a part of this community has been a continuous source of learning, collaboration, and professional growth.

I would also like to thank the Microsoft Advocates community, with special appreciation to Bruno Capuano and Henk Boelman, for their generosity, guidance, and for including me in impactful initiatives that continuously push the boundaries of innovation and knowledge sharing.

My heartfelt thanks goes to the Microsoft Foundry (Azure AI) team, whose work and vision continue to shape the future of AI platforms and have strongly influenced the concepts and architectures presented in this book.

Finally, I want to express my gratitude to OZ Digital, particularly to Jason Milgram, for trusting in my work and leadership. I am thankful for the company's strong culture of innovation, its deep sense of community, and the freedom it provides to create, experiment, and grow professionally, while building meaningful AI solutions.

Preface

Artificial intelligence or AI is no longer an emerging technology–it is a foundational force transforming industries, business models, and everyday experiences. As organizations accelerate their adoption of AI, professionals are expected not only to understand individual tools, but also to design secure, scalable, and responsible solutions that deliver real business value. Keeping pace with this evolution requires continuous learning and, increasingly, recognized certifications that validate practical expertise.

This book was written to support that need by helping professionals prepare for the AI-102: Designing and Implementing an Azure AI Solution certification, while also providing a broader and practical understanding of how artificial intelligence is designed and implemented on Azure.

At its core, the book goes well beyond exam preparation. Its goal is to provide a comprehensive, practical, and up-to-date guide to the Azure AI ecosystem–bridging foundational concepts with real-world implementation patterns used in modern cloud environments.

Rather than treating services in isolation, this book focuses on how Azure AI components work together in production scenarios. You will find clear explanations of Azure AI services and tools, practical examples drawn from real enterprise use cases, and best practices for designing solutions that are secure, scalable, cost-aware, and aligned with responsible AI principles. Throughout the chapters, architectural decisions are explained not only in terms of how to implement them, but also why they matter in real-world deployments.

Who This Book is for:

This book is intended for a broad but well-defined audience. It is written for professionals preparing to validate their skills through the AI-102 certification, as well as for developers, AI engineers, and architects who want to design and implement robust AI solutions on Azure. It is equally relevant for technical leaders responsible for guiding the responsible adoption of artificial intelligence within their organizations, and for students or self-learners seeking a practical and current perspective on cloud-based AI.

As Satya Nadella, CEO of Microsoft, has observed:

"How do we make sure we think about every layer of the tech stack from a first principles perspective for the new AI workloads that are being built, and then really stitch it together so that it meets the real-world needs of customers?"

– Satya Nadella, 2025

This question sits at the heart of the book. The pages that follow are intended to help you become a professional capable of answering it–someone who can connect strategy, architecture, and implementation to create meaningful impact with Azure AI.

Structure and Progression:

This book is organized into nine chapters that build progressively toward a complete and practical understanding of how to design, implement, and prepare for the deployment of Azure AI solutions–while staying tightly aligned with the AI-102 certification objectives. The structure starts by framing the certification and the Azure AI Engineer role, then moves through planning and implementation across key AI workloads (generative AI, agents, vision, language/speech, and knowledge mining), and finally closes with targeted exam preparation and practice scenarios.

Chapter 1. Introduction to the AI-102 Certification and Azure AI

The book begins by establishing context: what the AI-102 certification validates, what an Azure AI Engineer is expected to do, and how Azure AI services have evolved–culminating in Microsoft's Foundry direction. This chapter clarifies professional responsibilities, success metrics, and the career value of the certification, setting a clear roadmap for the learning journey ahead.

Chapter 2. Planning and Managing Azure AI Solutions

This chapter lays the architectural and operational foundation for real-world implementations. You will learn how to select the right Azure AI Foundry services for specific scenarios, provision and manage resources, and apply the best practices for deployment (including containerization where applicable). It also addresses monitoring, cost control, authentication and access control, secret management recommendations, and Responsible AI principles–such as fairness, transparency, and content safety.

Chapter 3. Implementing Generative AI Solutions

Here, the focus shifts to building and scaling generative AI applications with Azure AI Foundry and Azure OpenAI Service. You will explore solution planning, hub/project organization, model lifecycle management, and the implementation of prompt flows and prompt templates. The chapter also covers data grounding and Retrieval-Augmented Generation (RAG), evaluation practices, SDK integration, and multimodal use cases—including image generation and broader model modality considerations.

Chapter 4. Implementing Agent-Based Solutions

This chapter provides hands-on guidance for building agent-based systems using the Azure AI Foundry Agent Service and Semantic Kernel. You will learn how to create and manage agents, handle tools and quotas, apply orchestration patterns, and design multi-agent workflows. The chapter emphasizes governance, security, observability, resilience, and best practices for evaluation, optimization, deployment, and continuous operations.

Chapter 5. Implementing Computer Vision Solutions

This chapter covers computer vision implementations using Azure AI Vision for image analysis and Azure AI Video Indexer for video insights. You will learn core image analysis capabilities, practical use cases, version comparisons, and best practices. It also introduces custom model development with Azure Custom Vision for classification and object detection, along with guidance for evaluation and enterprise integration via APIs.

Chapter 6. Implementing Natural Language Processing (NLP) Solutions

This chapter dives into language and speech workloads, including language detection, translation, sentiment analysis, and PII recognition. It also covers speech-to-text, speech translation, text-to-speech, and avatar-based solutions. Finally, it introduces conversational AI patterns using CLU and Custom Question Answering (CQA), including architecture, orchestration approaches, and operational considerations like observability and security.

Chapter 7. Implementing Knowledge Mining and Information Extraction Solutions

This chapter focuses on building intelligent search and extraction systems using Azure AI Search, Azure AI Document Intelligence, and Azure AI Content

Understanding. You will learn how to implement indexes, enrichment pipelines (skillsets), semantic and vector search, and knowledge store projections. The chapter also covers RAG patterns over enterprise content, document processing with prebuilt and custom models (including composed models and classification), production-ready patterns, and multimodal analysis scenarios.

Chapter 8. Exam Preparation Strategies

This chapter prepares you for the AI-102 exam with a structured breakdown of the exam format, timing, scoring, and question types. It also provides practical study strategies, recommended workflows, guidance on using Microsoft Learn and official documentation effectively, along with tactics for exam-day performance–time management, stress management, and how to navigate resources during the exam.

Chapter 9. Practice Test and Sample Questions

The final chapter consolidates learning through realistic practice questions and exam-style scenarios spanning all domains covered in the book. It includes scenario-based case studies (for example, vision automation, document intelligence and knowledge mining, generative AI and agents), standalone questions, knowledge checks, and an answer key with explanations to reinforce correct reasoning.

Rather than treating these chapters as isolated topics, the book emphasizes how real AI solutions come together end to end–linking planning, governance, security, evaluation, and operational practices to the implementation of Azure AI workloads and to AI-102 exam readiness.

How to Get the Most from This Book:

Each chapter includes hands-on code samples, architectural guidance, and practical examples that allow you to follow along as you explore Azure AI services. Source code is provided so you can experiment directly with the services, reinforce key concepts, and better understand how individual components behave in real implementations.

Special emphasis is placed on core concepts, design decisions, and trade-offs, helping you understand not only how to use Azure AI services, but also why specific architectural choices are made. This approach is designed to strengthen both your technical execution and your ability to reason about AI system design–skills that are essential for both the AI-102 certification and real-world projects.

Looking Ahead:

The journey toward mastering artificial intelligence on Azure–and toward earning the AI-102 certification–is both challenging and rewarding. It demands curiosity, discipline, and a commitment to continuous learning in a rapidly evolving field. More importantly, it offers a unique opportunity, that is to be among the professionals shaping how AI is responsibly designed, deployed, and governed.

Every concept you master, every architecture you design, and every solution you implement strengthens your role in this new technological era. Thus, AI is not just about models, codes, or cloud services–it is about solving real-world problems, enabling better decisions, and creating systems that amplify human potential.

This book is more than a certification guide. It is an investment in your professional growth, and an invitation to join a global community building the future of intelligent solutions on Azure. Hence, move forward with confidence–AI is already here to assist those who choose to lead the Tech world!

DID YOU KNOW

Did you know that Orange Education Pvt Ltd offers eBook versions of every book published, with PDF and ePub files available? You can upgrade to the eBook version at **www.orangeava.com** and as a print book customer, you are entitled to a discount on the eBook copy. Get in touch with us at: **info@orangeava.com** for more details.

At **www.orangeava.com**, you can also read a collection of free technical articles, sign up for a range of free newsletters, and receive exclusive discounts and offers on Print Books and eBooks.

PIRACY

If you come across any illegal copies of our works in any form on the internet, we would be grateful if you would provide us with the location address or website name. Please contact us at **info@orangeava.com** with a link to the material.

ARE YOU INTERESTED IN AUTHORING WITH US?

If there is a topic that you have expertise in, and you are interested in either writing or contributing to a book, please write to us at **business@orangeava.com**. We are on a journey to help developers and tech professionals to gain insights on the present technological advancements and innovations happening across the globe and build a community that believes Knowledge is best acquired by sharing and learning with others. Please reach out to us to learn what our audience demands and how you can be part of this educational reform. We also welcome ideas from tech experts and help them build learning and development content for their domains.

REVIEWS

Please leave a review. Once you have read and used this book, why not leave a review on the site that you purchased it from? Potential readers can then see and use your unbiased opinion to make purchase decisions. We at Orange Education would love to know what you think about our products, and our authors can learn from your feedback. Thank you!

For more information about Orange Education, please visit **www.orangeava.com**.

Table of Contents

CHAPTER 1
Introduction to the AI-102 Certification and Azure AI

Introduction

In this chapter, readers will be introduced to the core building blocks that define the Azure AI ecosystem and its evolution within Microsoft's cloud platform. The chapter explains the distinction between task-specific Azure AI Services and platform-level capabilities provided by Microsoft Foundry, clarifying how modular APIs, foundation models, Retrieval-Augmented Generation (RAG), and intelligent agents fit together in real-world enterprise architectures. These concepts form the technical and architectural foundation required to design scalable, secure, and production-ready AI solutions on Azure.

The chapter also establishes a clear understanding of the Azure AI Engineer role, outlining the professional responsibilities, required competencies, and success criteria associated with designing and operating AI solutions in cloud environments. Key themes such as responsible AI, governance, lifecycle management, and business impact are introduced early to frame the mindset expected of certified professionals. Finally, the chapter contextualizes the AI-102 certification as both a validation of technical expertise and a guide for navigating the tools, services, and architectural patterns that will be explored throughout the rest of the book.

Structure

In this chapter, we will cover the following topics:

- The Rise of AI and the Role of Microsoft Azure
- Professional roles and responsibilities of an Azure AI Engineer
- The Importance of Azure AI and Technological Democratization

- From Cognitive Services to Microsoft Foundry: The Evolution of AI in Microsoft Azure
  - The Birth of Cognitive Services
  - Unification: Azure AI Services (2020-2023)
  - The Generative AI Era: Azure AI Studio (2023)
  - Azure AI Foundry (Ignite 2024): Unifying Models and Agents
  - Microsoft Foundry (Ignite 2025): A broader, Enterprise AI Ecosystem
- Microsoft Foundry as the Core of AI Strategy
  - Azure AI Services and Microsoft Foundry
- The Professional Role of the Azure AI Engineer
  - A Multidisciplinary and Strategic Profile
  - Professional Expectations and Opportunities
  - Success Metrics, Challenges, and Opportunities
- The Value of the AI-102 Certification
  - International Recognition and Professional Differentiation
  - Continuous Learning and Alignment with Best Practices
  - Comprehensive Development: Beyond the Exam
  - Career Impact and Access to New Opportunities

The Rise of AI and the Role of Microsoft Azure

Artificial Intelligence has become one of the defining forces of modern digital transformation. In less than a decade, AI has evolved from a research concept into an indispensable component of business operations across industries such as banking, healthcare, retail, education, logistics, and the public sector. Organizations now rely on AI to automate tasks, improve decision-making, understand customers, enhance accessibility, and accelerate innovation at an unprecedented speed.

Microsoft Azure has played a central role in this global transition by democratizing access to artificial intelligence. Instead of requiring specialized infrastructure or deep machine learning expertise, Azure ensures advanced AI capabilities are available through scalable cloud services, foundation models, and Generative AI tools, and are fit for consumption as per the demands of the organization. This democratization has empowered millions of developers and businesses to rapidly unlock value and build intelligent solutions.

Today, Azure AI is able to automate document processing, detect fraud in real time, power regular conversational agents, integrate real-time translation and sentiment analysis, and create inclusive solutions using voice, vision, and natural language technologies. The strength of Azure AI lies in its modular, open, and ever-evolving ecosystem, which integrates seamlessly into existing applications and workflows.

One of the most transformative advancements in this ecosystem is **Retrieval-Augmented Generation (RAG)**. RAG combines **Large Language Models (LLMs)** with advanced search engines–such as Azure AI Search–to generate responses grounded in accurate, up-to-date organizational data. Instead of relying solely on model pre-training, the system retrieves relevant information at query time, offering higher accuracy, transparency, and explainability. RAG enables a variety of tasks, from context-aware enterprise bots and technical support systems to document automation and regulatory compliance, thereby increasing faith and functionality in mission-critical environments.

The Importance of Azure AI and Technological Democratization

The impact of artificial intelligence depends not only on model performance, but also on accessibility, governance, and responsible adoption. Microsoft Azure has been instrumental in turning AI into a global, inclusive technology used by organizations of all sizes.

Azure democratizes AI through several foundational principles. These are:

- **Simple and Flexible Access:** Any organization can leverage AI through APIs, pre-built services, and ready-to-use foundation models. Teams can begin with modular Azure AI Services and advance to powerful generative models and agents in Microsoft Foundry.
- **Global Scalability**: The worldwide infrastructure of Azure offers compliant, and high-availability environments that supports various projects from prototypes to large-scale enterprise deployments.
- **Multidisciplinary Collaboration**: Integrations with GitHub, Visual Studio, VS Code, Azure DevOps, and Microsoft 365 enables cross-functional collaboration between developers, data teams, and business stakeholders.
- **Responsible and Ethical AI**: Azure includes tools for transparency, fairness, privacy, and security–such as content safety, auditing, and evaluation–aligned with Microsoft's Responsible AI principles.
- **Continuous Innovation**: Azure consistently updates its ecosystem with frontier models, multimodal capabilities, RAG architectures, intelligent agents, and multi-provider model catalogs. Microsoft Foundry, in particular, provides rapid access to new model families (such as GPT-5.1, Claude, Grok, Phi-4, and others) as they become available.

With the help of these capabilities, AI is no longer solely reserved for advanced research teams or large enterprises. Any organization can analyze data in real time, automate processes, personalize customer experiences, and create more inclusive digital products, easily through the flexibility and power of Azure AI.

By combining **Azure AI Services** (task-specific, production-ready APIs) with **Microsoft Foundry** (a unified platform for models and agents), Azure provides a complete and scalable ecosystem that supports organizations at every stage of their AI adoption journey.

From Cognitive Services to Microsoft Foundry: The Evolution of AI in Microsoft Azure

This section traces the evolution of artificial intelligence within Microsoft Azure, from the early introduction of Cognitive Services to the emergence of Microsoft Foundry as a unified, enterprise-scale AI platform.

The Birth of Cognitive Services

The journey of Microsoft AI in Azure began with Project Oxford in 2015, a set of APIs designed to simplify vision, speech, language, and knowledge tasks. These quickly matured into Azure Cognitive Services, enabling developers to add intelligent features such as face detection, OCR, speech recognition, and text analytics without building or training models themselves.

As the needs of customers increased, Microsoft introduced more specialized services like:

- **Form Recognizer (2019)**: Later expanded as Azure AI Document Intelligence, focused on extracting structured information from documents.
- **Azure Video Analyzer (2020)**: Real-time video understanding for events, objects, and scenarios as part of Azure Media Services.

These services supported concrete, domain-specific cases across sectors including finance, healthcare, logistics, and retail.

Unification: Azure AI Services (2020–2023)

As the catalog expanded, Microsoft consolidated its AI APIs and domain-specific solutions under the Azure AI Services brand. This provided a unified structure for services covering vision, language, speech, search, translation, content understanding, safety, and decision-making. Azure AI Services gradually became the foundation for thousands of enterprise applications, particularly, those requiring predictable performance, low latency, and production-ready AI capabilities.

The Generative AI Era: Azure AI Studio (2023)

With the rise of Large Language Models and Generative AI, Microsoft launched Azure AI Studio in 2023. This platform offered:

- Integrated access to GPT-4 and other advanced models
- Tools for prompt engineering and orchestration
- Evaluation and safety testing capabilities
- End-to-end workflows for experimentation and deployment

Azure AI Studio marked the beginning of the unified Generative AI development at a large scale within Azure.

Azure AI Foundry (Ignite 2024): Unifying Models and Agents

During Microsoft Ignite 2024, Azure AI Studio was rebranded as Azure AI Foundry, emphasizing a more comprehensive and integrated approach to building AI applications and agents. Azure AI Foundry introduced:

- A unified SDK
- Prebuilt templates and deployment workflows
- Native support for agents and RAG architectures
- Enterprise knowledge systems (Bing, Fabric, SharePoint)
- A platform-wide experience for governance, evaluation, and observance

The name Azure AI Foundry highlighted the platform's tight integration with the Azure cloud, and was used from November 2024 through November 2025.

Microsoft Foundry (Ignite 2025): A Broader, Enterprise AI Ecosystem

At **Microsoft Ignite 2025**, the platform was officially renamed **Microsoft Foundry**. This change signaled a shift from an Azure-centric brand to a **Microsoft-wide AI ecosystem**, expanding its role across:

- Multi-provider and open model catalogs
- Intelligent agent orchestration

- Interoperability across clouds and systems
- Enhanced security, governance, and modularity for enterprise AI

Importance of the name change:

- **Azure AI Foundry (2024):** It emphasized the role of the workspace of Azure for generative AI and agents.
- **Microsoft Foundry (2025):** It reflects a broader strategic vision—an enterprise AI "*factory floor*" that spans models, agents, data, tools, and integrations across the entire Microsoft Cloud.

In summary, the name **Azure AI Foundry** was used from November 2024 until November 2025, when finally, it was consolidated as **Microsoft Foundry** to reflect a wider strategic focus on enterprise AI.

From Project Oxford to Microsoft Foundry, the evolution of the AI ecosystem of Azure demonstrates the commitment of Microsoft in simplifying access to AI, supporting generative and agent-based workloads, enabling multi-model and multi-provider environments, and providing a unified, governed platform for organizations to build and operate AI responsibly at scale.

Microsoft Foundry as the Core of AI Strategy

At Microsoft Ignite 2025, Microsoft announced the evolution of Azure AI Foundry into **Microsoft Foundry**, positioning it as the unified platform for building, operating, and governing AI solutions across the Microsoft Cloud. Microsoft Foundry centralizes models, agents, tools, observability, and governance into a single environment, allowing organizations to design, test, deploy, and scale AI applications with consistent security, compliance, and operational reliability.

Microsoft Foundry now hosts one of the largest and most diverse AI model catalogs in the industry. As of late 2025, the ecosystem includes more than 11,000 models from Microsoft, Azure OpenAI, Anthropic, Cohere, Mistral, DeepSeek, Meta, xAI, NVIDIA, Black Forest Labs, and others. This extensive collection enables enterprises to choose the most suitable model for any scenario—from frontier reasoning to lightweight multimodal inference—without leaving the unified Foundry environment.

Recent additions highlight the commitment of Microsoft in providing multi-provider, enterprise-ready AI. The Claude models of Anthropic are available as fully managed, production-ready endpoints within Foundry, bringing top-tier reasoning and safety capabilities to Azure. Likewise, Azure OpenAI now includes the **GPT-5.1 family**, designed for advanced reasoning, deep analytics, and long-context business workloads, as well as tightly integrated into the evaluation and safety tooling of Foundry. Azure remains one of the few clouds offering both Azure OpenAI models and the Claude family of Anthropic as first-class, governed services under a single platform.

The ecosystem also includes cutting-edge models such as **Grok 3** and **Grok 3 Mini** from xAI, optimized for tool-use and problem-solving; **FLUX.1.1 [pro]** and related models from Black Forest Labs for high-fidelity text-to-image workflows; and the own **Phi-4** family of Microsoft–mini, multimodal, and flash-reasoning variants–engineered for efficient, low-latency inference and on-device or edge scenarios. This breadth allows Azure AI Engineers to combine strengths from different model families to achieve the right balance of latency, accuracy, cost, and modality for each business requirement.

Across all these models, Microsoft Foundry provides a unified layer for security, governance, telemetry, evaluations, routing, and deployment. Capabilities such as **Model Router**, advanced fine-tuning (LoRA/QLoRA, supervised fine-tuning, and Direct Preference Optimization), and the fully managed **Foundry Agent Service** allow enterprises to orchestrate multi-agent workflows, integrate agents with corporate knowledge using Bing, Fabric, SharePoint, and Azure AI Search, and deploy solutions confidently at scale.

In essence, Microsoft Foundry represents the new strategic core of the AI platform of Microsoft: a unified, flexible, and extensible environment that empowers organizations to innovate faster, maximize model value, and deliver secure, reliable AI solutions across every business domain.

Azure AI Services and Microsoft Foundry

Digital transformation and the growing adoption of artificial intelligence have driven Microsoft to evolve its portfolio of cloud-based solutions. Today, two main pillars define the value proposition of Azure for AI: **Azure AI Services** and **Microsoft Foundry**.

Azure AI Services: Modularity and Specialization

Azure AI Services is a family of modular services designed to address specific AI needs for businesses of all sizes and industries. According to the official website of Microsoft, the updated catalog includes:

- **Azure AI Content Safety**: It monitors text and images to detect offensive or inappropriate content, ensuring safe digital environments.
- **Azure AI Content Understanding**: It accelerates the development of multimodal solutions by combining text, image, and other data analysis.
- **Azure AI Document Intelligence**: It extracts text, key-value pairs, tables, and document structures using advanced machine learning.

- **Azure AI Language**: It enables the development of conversational interfaces, document summarization, and text analysis using pre-trained AI functions.
- **Azure AI Search**: It provides relevant search capabilities using keyword, vector, and hybrid search methods to find the most accurate information.
- **Azure AI Speech**: It incorporates advanced features such as speech-to-text, text-to-speech, speech translation, and speaker recognition.
- **Azure AI Translator**: It translates documents and text in real-time into more than 100 languages, facilitating global communication.
- **Azure AI Video Indexer**: It analyzes and extracts relevant information from video content, such as automatic transcripts, object identification, face recognition, scene detection, and intelligent search in large audiovisual collections.
- **Azure AI Vision**: It analyzes images, detects faces, and reads text using OCR and machine learning.
- **Azure OpenAI**: It enables integration and deployment of advanced models for natural language generation and understanding, as well as models for analyzing and processing textual and visual information, supporting the development of custom intelligent solutions.

These services are designed for easy integration into new or existing applications, allowing organizations to leverage artificial intelligence without having to build models from scratch while ensuring flexibility, scalability, and rapid implementation.

Microsoft Foundry: Models, Agents, and Orchestration

While Azure AI Services provides specialized, task-focused APIs, **Microsoft Foundry** offers a unified environment for developing, customizing, and managing generative AI applications and agents. The primary differentiator however, lies in providing a centralized platform where teams can:

- Access an extensive catalog of language, vision, and intelligent agent models from Microsoft and multiple partners.
- Orchestrate and customize AI agents that can interact with each other and with enterprise systems, automating processes and improving operational efficiency.
- Integrate familiar tools such as GitHub, Visual Studio, VS Code, and Copilot Studio, accelerating collaboration and the development cycle.
- Ensure governance, security, and ethics with regulatory compliance controls, responsible AI practices, and built-in observability and evaluation tools.
- Implement generative AI solutions, RAG architectures, and multimodal workflows easily and at scale.

Together, Azure AI Services and Microsoft Foundry give organizations the flexibility to:

- Start quickly with ready-to-use APIs.
- Evolve toward advanced generative and agent-based solutions.
- Centralize governance, safety, monitoring, and model lifecycle management.

This dual ecosystem ensures that enterprises can adopt AI at their own pace, leveraging both pre-built capabilities and next-generation AI technologies under a single, coherent strategy.

The Professional Role of the Azure AI Engineer

As artificial intelligence becomes the driving force behind digital transformation in organizations of all sizes, there is an increasing need for professionals capable of designing, implementing, and operating AI solutions on robust, scalable platforms. In this context, the **Azure AI Engineer** has become a highly strategic and an in-demand role within the current technology ecosystem.

A Multidisciplinary and Strategic Profile

The Azure AI Engineer stands out for their ability to bridge cloud technical expertise with advanced skills in artificial intelligence and machine learning (Refer to *Figure 1.1*). This professional is not simply a developer or a traditional data scientist; they represent the intersection between engineering, advanced analytics, and a deep understanding of business needs.

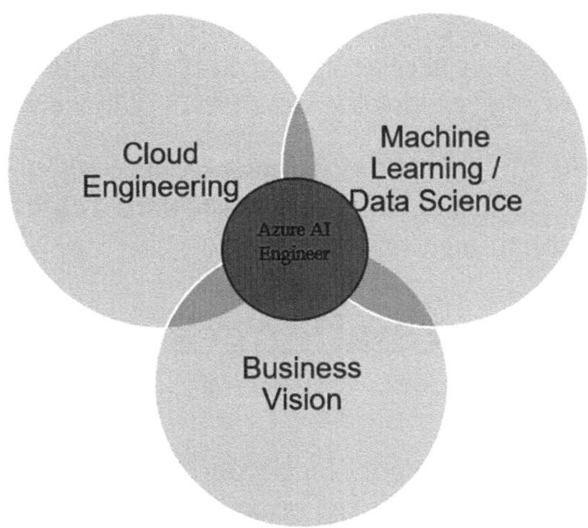

***Figure 1.1:** The Multidisciplinary Profile of the Azure AI Engineer: at the Intersection of Cloud Engineering, Machine Learning/Data Science, and Business Vision*

Key competencies of an Azure AI Engineer include:

- **Designing Intelligent Architectures**: The ability to select, integrate, and orchestrate the different Azure AI services–from vision and language to generative agents and advanced search systems–according to the requirements of each project.
- **Implementing and Customizing Models**: Proficiency in working with both pre-trained and custom models, adapting solutions to specific use cases, and maximizing thc value delivered to the organization.
- **AI Lifecycle Management**: Mastery of MLOps practices, monitoring, versioning, and model deployment, ensuring optimal performance and compliance with data governance and security policies.
- **Governance and Ethics**: Application of responsible AI principles, aligning solutions with standards of transparency, fairness, privacy, and regulatory compliance.
- **Communication and Leadership**: The ability to collaborate with multidisciplinary teams, translate business needs into technical requirements, and lead the adoption of new technologies in dynamic environments.

Professional Expectations and Opportunities

The Azure AI Engineer is the enabler of AI-driven digital transformation. Their work directly impacts operational efficiency, product and service innovation, personalized experiences, and the creation of sustainable competitive advantages. Additionally, the role requires constant learning, as the Azure AI ecosystem rapidly evolves with new tools, models, and methodologies.

Opportunities for this role are expanding: from leading automation projects and designing intelligent customer service agents to orchestrating multimodal solutions, and ensuring the ethical and responsible use of AI in global organizations.

Ultimately, the Azure AI Engineer is more than a technology implementer–they act as an architect of innovation, guiding organizations toward a digital future that is secure, efficient, and aligned with human values.

Success Metrics, Challenges, and Opportunities

The impact of an Azure AI Engineer goes far beyond the mere technical implementation of artificial intelligence solutions. Today, organizations are looking for professionals who can deliver measurable results, tackle technological and ethical challenges, and quickly adapt to a constantly evolving landscape.

Success Metrics: From the Lab to Real Value

The success of an AI project on Azure is evaluated not just by its technical deployment but by the value it brings to the business. Some key metrics include:

- **Reduction in Operational Time**: Did the AI solution automate processes that previously required manual intervention? How much time is saved?
- Model Accuracy and Reliability: How accurately does the solution fulfill its purpose (for example, document recognition, sentiment analysis, fraud detection)?
- **Cost Savings**: To what extent has adopting Azure AI optimized resources or reduced expenses related to manual processes, errors, or fraud?
- **Scalability and Adoption**: How easy is it to replicate the solution in other business areas or regions? How many internal users or clients are effectively adopting it?
- **Compliance and Security**: Does the solution adhere to privacy, ethical, and security regulations, and how is compliance audited?

Measuring these variables not only demonstrates Return on Investment (ROI) but also helps identify opportunities for continuous improvement and scaling up results.

Current Challenges of the Role

Despite the maturity of cloud-based AI platforms, Azure AI Engineers face significant challenges:

- **Constant Technological Updates**: Azure AI evolves rapidly, with frequent releases and improvements. This demands ongoing learning and adaptability to new tools and services.
- **Managing Complexity**: Integrating modular services, customizing models, and ensuring interoperability among systems can present challenges in architecture, data management, and performance.
- **Governance and Ethics**: The widespread adoption of AI raises questions on responsible data use, algorithm transparency, and bias mitigation. Professionals must ensure solutions are not only effective but also fair and aligned with organizational values.
- **Cybersecurity and Information Protection**: Implementing robust controls and ensuring regulatory compliance is crucial, especially when handling sensitive data or automating critical decisions.

Opportunities in the Era of Generative AI and Intelligent Agents

The rise of generative AI, architectures such as *Retrieval-Augmented Generation* (**RAG**), and more recently, **intelligent agents** (AI *Agents*), opens up new possibilities for Azure AI Engineers:

- **Automation of Complex Processes**: From advanced virtual assistants to the generation of reports, summaries, and personalized documents.
- **Orchestration and Deployment of Intelligent Agents**: Agents are autonomous applications capable of interacting with users, systems, and other agents, solving complex tasks, integrating different data sources, and adapting to various business contexts.
- **Large-Scale Personalization**: Creating unique, adaptive experiences for each user, client, or employee, based on intelligent analysis of data and context.
- **Innovation in Products and Services**: Developing new digital offerings, business models, and disruptive solutions that place organizations at the forefront of their sectors.

With these agents, it is now possible to build systems that go beyond providing point solutions—managing dialogues, performing automated actions, and proactively collaborating in business tasks.

In this environment, the Azure AI Engineer has the opportunity to be a true change agent, driving digital transformation from experimentation to sustainable value creation, and leading the adoption of technologies that will define the future of enterprise artificial intelligence.

The Value of the AI-102 Certification

In an environment where artificial intelligence is increasingly strategic for organizational competitiveness, the **AI-102: Designing and Implementing an Azure AI Solution** certification has become a mark of professional excellence and a gateway to new career opportunities.

International Recognition and Professional Differentiation

The AI-102 certification validates that a professional not only masters Azure AI services and tools, but is also capable of designing, implementing, and maintaining intelligent solutions aligned with industry standards. This recognition, awarded by Microsoft, is valued globally by employers, clients, and strategic partners alike. In highly competitive markets, holding the AI-102 certification makes a clear difference and can be the deciding factor when applying for leadership roles in AI projects.

Continuous Learning and Alignment with Best Practices

Preparing for the AI-102 certification requires staying up to date with the latest Azure AI technologies, including modular services, generative models, responsible AI practices, and new agent-based and Retrieval-Augmented Generation (RAG) architectures.

Since Microsoft certifications require annual renewal, maintaining the AI-102 credential also encourages ongoing learning and keeps professionals aligned with the continuous evolution of the platform.

This ensures that certified professionals are current with industry trends and best practices, positioning themselves as technical leaders within their organizations.

Comprehensive Development: Beyond the Exam

Obtaining the certification is not just about passing a technical exam. The journey toward AI-102 strengthens transversal skills such as the ability to translate business needs into technical solutions, communicate complex concepts to diverse audiences, and lead multidisciplinary teams in dynamic environments. In essence, the certification is a validation of the ability of the self, to create a real impact with AI, from project conception through production deployment.

Career Impact and Access to New Opportunities

Organizations value certified professionals to lead digital transformation projects, process automation, and the adoption of artificial intelligence across the enterprise. The AI-102 certification enables access to strategic roles such as Azure AI Engineer, solutions architect, AI consultant, or technology innovation leader.

Additionally, earning the certification increases professional visibility within the tech ecosystem and facilitates networking with AI experts through events, forums, and specialized communities where trends, best practices, and continuous learning opportunities are shared. This visibility also enhances the professional profile on platforms like LinkedIn, expanding connections and opening doors to new career opportunities in artificial intelligence and cloud services.

In summary, achieving the AI-102 certification accelerates professional growth, establishes a competitive edge, and provides access to high-impact projects in a constantly evolving technological environment.

Conclusion

Azure AI is at the center of modern digital transformation, having evolved from basic cognitive services into an advanced, modular platform that democratizes access to artificial intelligence for organizations of all sizes and industries. With ready-to-use solutions for vision, language, speech, search, translation, documents, content, and video—as well as a unified platform in **Microsoft Foundry** for models, agents, and orchestration—Azure enables centralized development, customization, and management of intelligent applications.

The Azure AI Engineer plays a strategic role, bridging business vision with technology, designing secure, ethical, and scalable solutions, and leading high-impact teams and projects where true success is measured by the real value delivered to the business beyond technology alone. Architectures such as RAG and the deployment of intelligent agents are opening new opportunities for autonomous, personalized, and highly useful solutions, shaping the immediate future of enterprise AI.

Earning the AI-102 certification is a global professional differentiator, validating mastery of Azure AI and the ability to lead AI projects, accelerating career growth and unlocking new opportunities. This book serves as your guide—combining theory, hands-on practice, and real-world cases—to mastering the technical, strategic, and ethical aspects of building and deploying artificial intelligence solutions with Azure.

Looking ahead, Chapter 2 transitions from concepts and roles into practical execution. It focuses on how to plan, provision, and manage Azure AI solutions in real-world environments, guiding readers through service selection, resource creation, deployment strategies, monitoring, cost management, authentication, access control, and Responsible AI practices. This next chapter establishes the operational foundations required to design secure, scalable, and governed AI solutions aligned with business objectives and the requirements of the AI-102 certification.

Points to Remember

- Azure AI drives digital transformation by democratizing access to advanced artificial intelligence for organizations of all sizes, enabling automation, innovation, and efficiency across industries.
- The Azure AI ecosystem has evolved from standalone Cognitive Services to an integrated platform, culminating in Microsoft Foundry, which provides modular, scalable, and responsible AI solutions.

- Azure AI Services and Microsoft Foundry offer ready-to-use modules and a unified environment for building, customizing, and managing intelligent applications and agents, ensuring security, governance, and ethical AI practices.
- Technologies like Retrieval-Augmented Generation (RAG) and intelligent agents are enabling the development of autonomous, personalized, and context-aware solutions that enhance business value and user experience.
- The Azure AI Engineer role is strategic and multidisciplinary, combining expertise in cloud engineering, machine learning, and business vision to design and implement impactful AI solutions.
- Measuring AI success goes beyond technology—key metrics include business impact, time and cost savings, scalability, adoption, compliance, and security.
- The AI-102 certification is globally recognized, validating professional skills in Azure AI, boosting career growth, and opening opportunities in the dynamic field of enterprise artificial intelligence.

References

- Satya Nadella, Chairman and CEO of Microsoft. "Quote: Satya Nadella." *Global Advisors*, May 29, 2025.

  Available at: https://globaladvisors.biz/2025/05/29/quote-satya-nadella-chairman-and-ceo-of-microsoft-2/
- Microsoft Azure. (May 2024). *The latest Azure AI Foundry innovations help you optimize AI investments and differentiate your business*. Available at: https://azure.microsoft.com/en-us/blog/the-latest-azure-ai-foundry-innovations-help-you-optimize-ai-investments-and-differentiate-your-business/
- Microsoft Azure. (2025). *Azure AI Services*. Available at: https://azure.microsoft.com/en-us/products/ai-services/

CHAPTER 2
Planning and Managing Azure AI Solutions

Introduction

In this chapter, we will delve into the planning and management phase of Artificial Intelligence solutions in Azure, which is a critical step to ensure efficient, secure implementations that are aligned with business objectives. We will learn how to identify the most appropriate Azure AI services for different scenarios, ranging from natural language processing and content generation to computer vision and knowledge mining, as well as how to provision and configure these services in a structured manner.

Additionally, we will explore how to deploy models to production using containers, establish robust monitoring, manage costs, and secure solutions through authentication and access control. We will conclude with a comprehensive overview of Responsible AI principles, covering governance, fairness, transparency, content moderation, and security, in order to implement reliable and ethical AI systems in real-world environments.

Structure

In this chapter, we will cover the following topics:

- Selection of Azure AI Foundry Services:
    - Generative AI: Azure Open AI and Azure AI Foundry
    - Computer Vision – Azure AI Vision
    - Natural Language Processing – Azure AI Language
    - Speech – Azure AI Speech

    - Information Extraction: Document Intelligence and Content Understanding
    - Knowledge Mining: Azure AI Search
- Creating and Managing Azure AI Resources
    - Provisioning Options for Azure AI Services
    - Practical Examples of Provisioning
    - Recommendation on Secret Management
- Deployment of AI Model and Containerization Strategies
    - Deployment Options in Azure AI Services
    - Azure AI Services Supporting Container Deployment
    - Deploying Azure AI Containers: Process and Best Practices
    - Limitations and Differences Compared to Cloud Consumption
- Monitoring, Cost Management, Authentication, and Access Control
    - Monitoring
    - Cost Management
    - Authentication
    - Access Control
- Responsible AI:
    - Azure AI Foundry Content Safety: Safeguarding Content Integrity and Ethics

Selection of Azure AI Foundry Services

While selecting Azure AI Foundry services, it is essential to understand the nature of the business challenge or objective and map that objective to the capabilities of the available AI services. Azure AI organizes its capabilities into specialized services that range from content generation to advanced interpretation of multimedia data and enterprise-scale knowledge extraction.

Choosing the appropriate services not only optimizes resources and streamlines development, but it can also make the difference between an innovative solution and an outcome that fails to meet business expectations. It is critical to analyze the type of data that will be handled—text, images, audio, video, or documents—as well as the expected outcomes: Is the goal to automate processes, discover patterns, create interactive experiences, or extract value from large volumes of information?

Azure AI offers a robust and continuously evolving portfolio designed to accommodate both highly specific needs and complex digital transformation challenges. As we explore each service category, we will see how alignment between business objectives and the technical capabilities of Azure AI accelerates innovation and enables organizations to achieve genuine competitive advantages in the market.

Generative AI: Azure OpenAI and Azure AI Foundry

Generative artificial intelligence enables the automated creation of original content such as text, code, images, and natural conversations. Within the Azure ecosystem, the primary service for addressing these scenarios is Azure OpenAI, which is included within the Azure AI Foundry platform.

Azure OpenAI provides access to a variety of state-of-the-art models, each optimized for specific scenarios and capabilities within generative artificial intelligence. Among the natural language models, GPT-4.1 and GPT-4o stand out for their versatility in tasks such as text generation and comprehension, automated writing, summarization, language translation, code analysis and generation, as well as the development of chatbots and conversational assistants. The O-Series family (including models such as o-3 and o-4) is specifically geared towards tasks that require advanced reasoning, complex problem-solving, and deep contextual analysis, making them an ideal choice for business applications that demand precise, well-reasoned responses.

In the multimodal domain, models such as DALL·E and gpt-image-1 enable the generation and analysis of images from textual descriptions, integrating generative AI capabilities in both text and image. For audio processing, GPT-4o audio models expand the possibilities for audio comprehension, synthesis, and transformation, facilitating the creation of voice applications and natural interaction.

Additionally, embedding models available in Azure OpenAI allows the generation of vector representations, which are fundamental for semantic search tasks, information retrieval, and similarity analysis between texts. This variety of models makes it easier to select the most appropriate solution for each use case, optimizing performance and efficiency in implementations on Azure AI Foundry.

A key advantage of Azure OpenAI is its native integration with Azure services and tools. This facilitates the implementation of virtual assistants, intelligent copilots, and conversational agents tailored to the security, compliance, and privacy requirements of enterprise environments.

However, Azure AI Foundry goes beyond Azure OpenAI, as it provides a unified environment for incorporating, managing, and deploying a variety of generative models. In addition to OpenAI proprietary models, it is possible to integrate open-source models—such as Llama or Mistral—models developed internally by organizations, and even models from other compatible providers. This allows organizations to select and combine the most suitable model for each need or use case, providing flexibility and reducing dependence on a single provider.

The flexibility of Azure AI Foundry is fundamental for scenarios that require specific capabilities, whether for reasons of performance, cost, governance, or regulatory compliance. In this way, organizations can design generative AI solutions tailored to their objectives, whether by automating administrative tasks, generating creative content, assisting with programming, personalizing user experiences, or performing advanced analysis of information in natural language.

Computer Vision - Azure AI Vision

When business challenges involve the interpretation and analysis of images or videos, Azure AI Vision is the specialized service designed to address these needs. This service enables the extraction of relevant information from visual files, facilitating tasks such as object detection and classification, scene analysis, text recognition in images (OCR), and real-time understanding of visual content.

Azure AI Vision leverages deep neural networks and state-of-the-art computer vision models to identify people, places, emotions, products, and visual patterns. It also offers the capability to generate automatic image descriptions, create tags, perform real-time video analysis, and conduct intelligent visual searches within large volumes of multimedia files.

An advanced feature of this service is its support for multimodal embeddings, which allows for the joint comparison and analysis of both visual and textual information. This enables use cases such as the semantic visual search, where images can be found based on natural language descriptions, or the combined analysis of scanned documents containing both text and images.

Azure AI Vision integrates easily with other Azure solutions, enabling the automation of document processing, intelligent monitoring through cameras, quality control on production lines, and visual identity verification, along with many other applications where in-depth understanding of visual content is key to operations and decision-making.

Natural Language Processing - Azure AI Language

When the objective is to work with large volumes of text or to understand the many nuances of human language, Azure AI Language is the reference service within the Azure ecosystem. This service brings together a set of advanced tools for natural language processing, allowing organizations to analyze, structure, and extract value from textual data from various sources.

Azure AI Language enables capabilities such as sentiment analysis, entity extraction and classification (people, organizations, locations, dates), intent recognition, automatic document summarization, topic and trend detection, translation between multiple languages, and content moderation. These features are essential for use cases such as automated customer service, social media management, reputation monitoring, the classification and organization of large documentation repositories, and the automatic generation of executive summaries.

One of its major advantages is the ability to integrate these analyses with other Azure solutions, such as conversational assistants powered by Azure OpenAI, intelligent search engines, or automated document processing workflows. In addition, Azure AI Language provides customizable models that can be tailored to the specific language and terminology of each industry, ensuring more accurate results aligned with business contexts. In this way, Azure AI Language transforms text into actionable data, facilitating informed decision-making and enhancing innovation in language-centric business processes.

Speech – Azure AI Speech

When the work involves audio processing or voice-based interaction, Azure AI Speech offers a comprehensive platform to enable advanced spoken communication experiences. This service covers everything from speech-to-text conversion to natural text-to-speech generation, including automatic translation of conversations and speaker recognition.

Azure AI Speech utilizes state-of-the-art neural models to accurately transcribe audio, generate realistic synthetic voices, and adapt models to the specific vocabulary, accents, or contexts of each organization. This enables the creation of voice-enabled virtual assistants, automation of contact centers, meeting transcription, call analysis, and much more.

A relevant functionality is support for the OpenAI Whisper model, which can be used within Azure AI Speech for batch transcriptions. Whisper is especially useful for processing large volumes of audio files, offering advanced features such as speaker diarization (identification of different speakers), word-level timestamps, and support for multiple languages. However, it is important to note that Whisper is intended for asynchronous transcription and is not optimized for real-time use cases, where the native Azure Speech models are recommended.

The integration of Azure AI Speech with other Azure ecosystem tools facilitates the creation of intelligent workflows where voice becomes an input and output channel as natural and secure as text or image. In this way, organizations across all sectors can design inclusive, accessible, and highly personalized user experiences, enhancing communication and operational efficiency.

Information Extraction: Document Intelligence and Content Understanding

In enterprise environments, a significant portion of information resides in unstructured data, such as scanned documents, PDFs, contracts, images, emails, audio or video recordings, and other scattered formats. The ability to extract and structure valuable information from this data is necessary for optimizing processes, automating tasks, and enabling decision-making based on concrete facts.

- **Azure AI Document Intelligence** is the specialized solution of Azure for automated information extraction from documents. Previously known as Form Recognizer, this service enables the conversion of documents into structured data ready for digital processing. Using pretrained models, it can identify and extract text, tables, key-value pairs, specific fields, and other elements from common documents such as invoices, receipts, forms, and contracts. For scenarios that require customized formats, Document Intelligence offers training capabilities using the organizational data, adapting to any document workflow. Its integration with other Azure services facilitates the automation of workflows, information validation, data preparation for search solutions, and the development of advanced AI applications such as enterprise digital assistants.
- **Azure AI Content Understanding,** currently in preview, represents a further step toward multimodal information comprehension. This service unifies the analysis of text, images, documents, audio, and video into a single workflow, allowing the definition of custom schemas and the validation of information according to business needs. Content Understanding not only extracts relevant entities and fields but can also classify, analyze conversations, and enrich information by integrating external models. This enables use cases such as call analysis, intelligent media management, extraction of insights from complex documents, and the preparation of data pipelines for solutions based on Retrieval-Augmented Generation (RAG) and advanced search engines.

Knowledge Mining: Azure AI Search

Once data has been extracted and structured, the next challenge is to make it accessible and searchable efficiently for users and business applications. This is where knowledge mining comes into play, through services such as Azure AI Search.

Azure AI Search is the central platform for semantic search and exploration in Azure. Its goal is to transform large volumes of information–whether structured or unstructured–into knowledge that is easily discoverable and usable. This service offers intelligent indexing capabilities, traditional text search, semantic and vector search, and native integration with language models for Retrieval-Augmented Generation (RAG) scenarios. These features, makes it possible to create conversational experiences where users can ask questions in natural language and receive precise answers without having to manually browse through extensive repositories.

The flexibility of Azure AI Search enables connections to multiple data sources, including files, databases, websites, and other enterprise systems. In addition, indexed data can be enriched using cognitive skills such as automatic translation, image analysis, or entity recognition, achieving a higher level of intelligence in information retrieval. Continuous index updates ensure that information is always available and up to date for queries.

Creating and Managing Azure AI Foundry Service

To enable any artificial intelligence service in Azure, the first step is to create an appropriate resource within your Azure subscription. This resource defines the endpoint for consuming APIs, provides authentication keys, and centralizes the management and billing of service usage. Proper provisioning and management of these resources are essential to ensure secure, efficient, and scalable access to Azure AI capabilities from any application or solution.

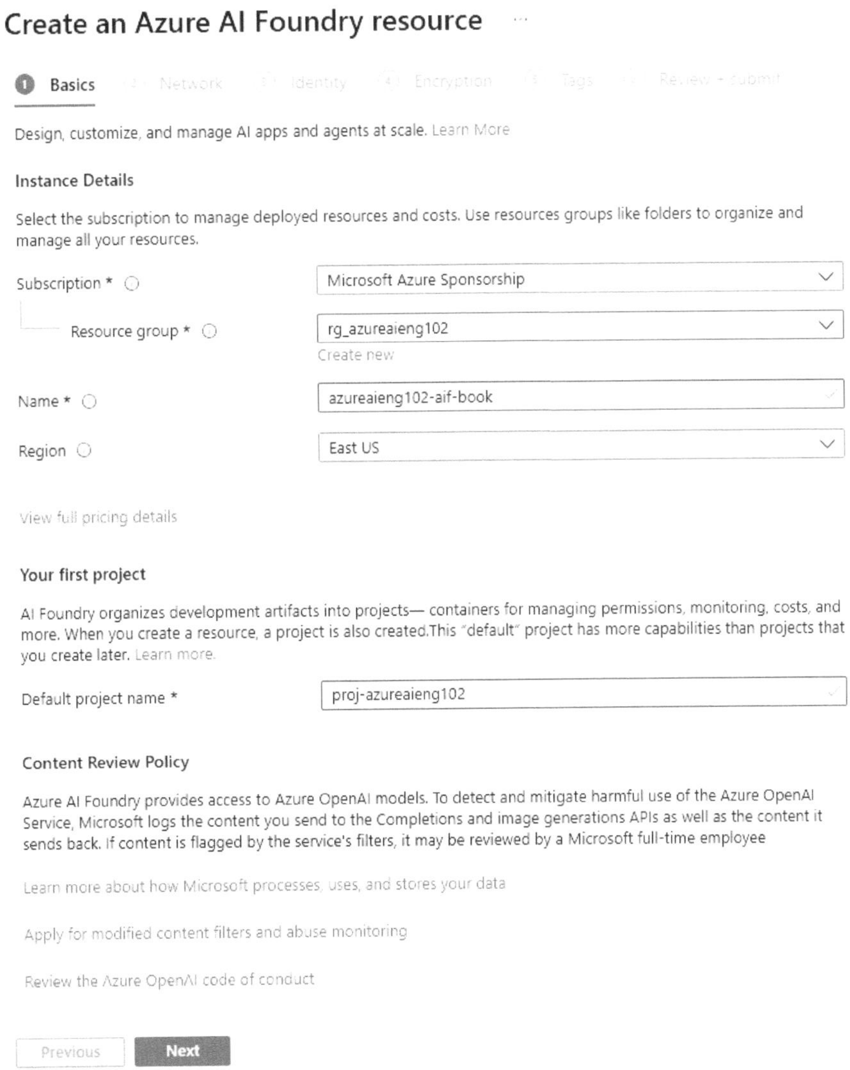

Figure 2.1: *Process of Creating an Azure AI Foundry Resource in the Azure Portal*

Provisioning Options for Azure AI Services

Azure AI Foundry offers various alternatives for provisioning services, adapting to diverse integration and operational control needs. There are two main approaches: multi-service resources and single-service resources.

Multi-Service Resources

This model integrates various artificial intelligence capabilities, such as AI Foundry, which provides access to project functions, including agents, evaluations, and language, vision, speech, and text analytics capabilities. It also enables access to Azure OpenAI services through a single resource.

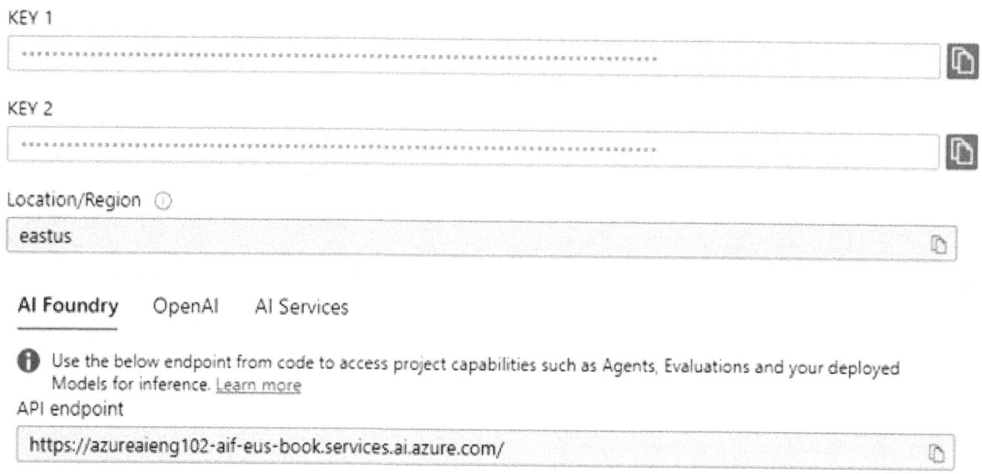

Figure 2.2: *Authentication Keys, Region, and Endpoint for Accessing Azure AI Foundry Services*

Thus, it is possible to use different services via one to three endpoints, depending on the category, with a single set of credentials. Additionally, consolidated billing simplifies cost monitoring and access management.

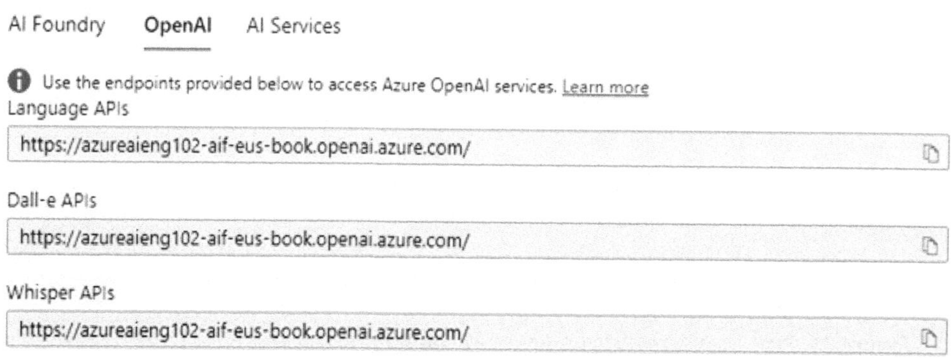

Figure 2.3: *Available Endpoints for Accessing Azure OpenAI Services*

Creating a multi-service resource is especially advantageous in scenarios where multiple AI capabilities need to be consumed from a single application, or when the goal is to reduce complexity in managing credentials and integration points.

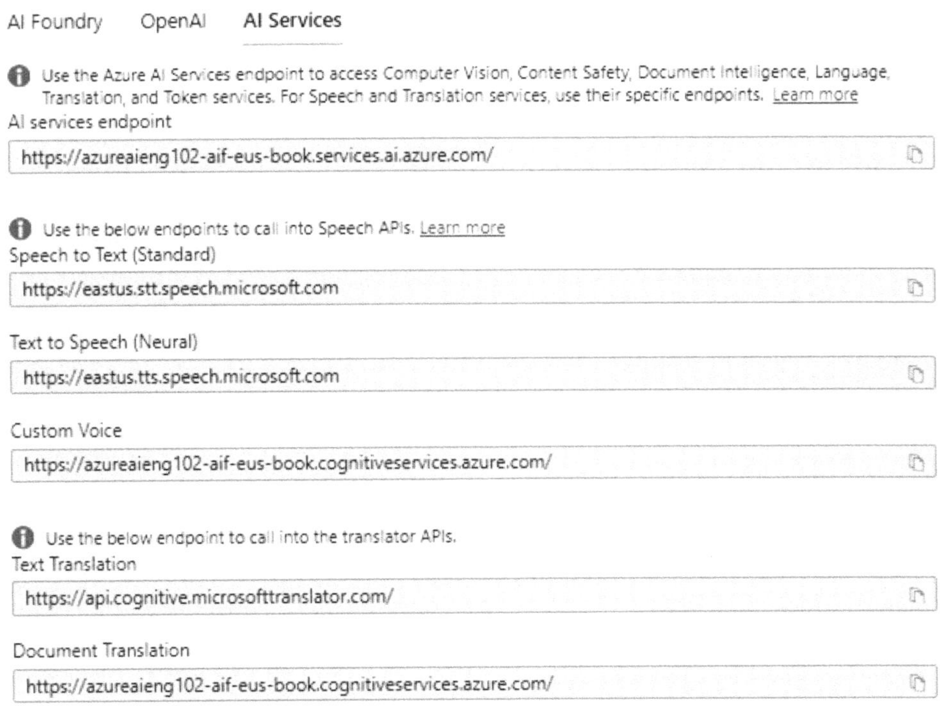

Figure 2.4: *Available Endpoints for Accessing Azure AI Services*

Single-Service Resources

Alternatively, it is possible to create independent resources for each AI service, such as Azure AI Language or Azure AI Vision, assigning them their own endpoints and credentials. This option is useful when greater control over management is needed, for example, by separating resources by geographic region, work teams, or projects. Furthermore, single-service resources often offer free tiers, which are ideal for development, testing, or early-stage exploration.

For solutions requiring isolation between services, granular access control, or differentiated billing management, the individual resource approach is typically the most appropriate.

Separation between Training and Prediction Resources

For some services, especially those that allow for training custom models, Azure distinguishes between resources dedicated to training, and those for prediction or inference. This approach enables separate management of costs and security for each stage of the model lifecycle. For example, the training resource can be restricted to advanced users, while the prediction resource is exposed to final applications that consume the trained model.

Considerations for Resource Provisioning

The choice between multi-service and single-service resources depends on the technical, security, and operational requirements of each project. It is advisable to plan your provisioning strategy by considering factors such as geographic proximity to users, regulatory requirements, identity management, and cost optimization.

After resource provisioning, Azure provides the necessary endpoints and keys to integrate AI services into applications. It is the best practice to manage these secrets using tools such as Azure Key Vault and to monitor usage and performance directly from the Azure portal.

Practical Example of Provisioning

Resources can be created either from the Azure graphical portal or through automated tools such as Azure CLI. For example, to provision a multi-service resource from the command line, the following command creates a resource with access to multiple cognitive services:

```
az cognitiveservices account create \
  --name my-ai-foundry \
  --resource-group my-resource-group \
  --kind AIServices \
  --sku S0 \
  --location eastus
```

Recommendation on Secret Management

A fundamental aspect of securely operating artificial intelligence solutions in Azure is the proper management of keys and endpoints that enable access to services. It is highly recommended to store these secrets in specialized services such as Azure Key Vault, rather than including them directly in source code or exposed configuration files. Azure Key Vault allows you to centralize, audit, and protect access to credentials, secrets, certificates, and other sensitive data, facilitating periodic key rotation and compliance with security regulations. Additionally, integration with Azure Managed Identities enables applications to access secrets securely, without the need to manage explicit credentials. Adopting these practices significantly reduces exposure risks and strengthens the security posture of any solution, based on Azure AI services.

Deployment of AI Models and Containerization Strategies

Deploying artificial intelligence models in enterprise environments requires flexibility, scalability, and compliance with various operational and regulatory requirements. Azure AI Services addresses these challenges by offering different options for consuming its capabilities, enabling access to pre-trained models through managed cloud endpoints as well as deployment of these same services via containers. The latter option supports advanced scenarios, such as execution on on-premises infrastructure, edge environments, or even on other cloud platforms, without sacrificing the advantages provided by Azure AI services.

The selection of the appropriate deployment strategy depends on factors such as latency, data control, regulatory constraints, the need to operate in disconnected environments, or integration with local systems. Understanding the available options and their implications is essential for designing robust, efficient solutions that adhere to the best practices of artificial intelligence implementation.

Deployment Options in Azure AI Services

Azure AI Services provides two main approaches for consuming AI models:

- **Consumption through Cloud Endpoints**: As previously discussed, this approach allows the use of the pre-trained Azure models directly through calls to endpoints exposed in the Azure cloud. It is the simplest option to implement, as the infrastructure, maintenance, and scalability are fully managed by the platform. You only need the credentials and the corresponding service endpoint to begin consuming capabilities such as vision, language, text analytics, speech, and others. This approach is ideal for applications with standard connectivity requirements, dynamic scalability, and no restrictions regarding data residency.
- **Deployment via Containers**: For scenarios requiring greater operational control, compliance with local regulations, reduced latency, or the ability to function in disconnected environments, Azure AI Services enables the execution of certain pre-trained models in Docker containers. In this way, cognitive capabilities can be deployed in on-premises data centers, at the edge, or in other clouds, maintaining the Azure experience and API, but with complete control over the execution environment.

Comparison of Approaches

In the following table, Cloud Endpoints and Container Deployment, managed by Azure and the Customer respectively, are distinguished on the basis of certain specific features:

Feature	**Cloud Endpoints (Managed by Azure)**	**Container Deployment (Customer Managed)**
Infrastructure Management	Azure (managed)	Customer (self-managed)
Flexibility and Portability	Limited to Azure	Multiplatform (on-premises, edge)
Scalability	Automatic	Manual
Latency	Depends on connectivity	Reduced/local
Compliance/Regulation	According to Azure region	Customizable
Updates	Automatic	Manual

Table 2.1: *Comparison between Cloud Endpoints and Container Deployment*

Azure AI Services Supporting Container Deployment

Azure AI Services allows execution of some pre-trained models via Docker containers, facilitating the integration of cognitive capabilities in on-premises, edge, or hybrid environments. This option is especially useful when sensitive data must be processed locally, when compliance with specific regulations is required, or to minimize response latency.

Currently, the main Azure AI services that support container deployment are:

- **Computer Vision**: It enables image analysis, Optical Character Recognition (OCR), object detection, and extraction of relevant visual information. Using containers for Computer Vision is common in industrial scenarios, edge devices, and applications where image privacy is a priority.
- **Text Analytics**: It provides natural language processing capabilities such as sentiment analysis, entity recognition, and confidential information detection. Running Text Analytics in a container is ideal for analyzing sensitive documents or textual data within a controlled infrastructure.
- **Speech Services**: It includes features such as speech recognition, text-to-speech conversion, and audio translation. Container execution allows for solutions that require real-time audio processing, enhanced privacy, or independence from cloud connectivity.

Reference: For more information on Azure AI services that support container deployment, visit: **https://learn.microsoft.com/es-es/azure/ai-services/cognitive-services-container-support**.

Advantages of Using Containers in AI

Deploying Azure AI services via Docker containers offers a series of technical and operational advantages, which are crucial for advanced enterprise scenarios and regulated environments. Key advantages include:

- **Portability and Flexibility**: Containers allow the execution of artificial intelligence services in any Docker-compatible environment, whether in on-premises data centers, edge devices, or other clouds. This portability facilitates integration of AI capabilities in hybrid or distributed architectures, adapting to the specific needs of each organization.
- **Regulatory Compliance and Data Residency**: Running models locally ensures that sensitive data remains within the controlled infrastructure of the organization, which is essential to comply with data privacy and protection regulations such as GDPR, HIPAA, or other industry frameworks.
- **Latency Reduction and Performance Improvement**: By processing information in the same environment where the data is generated, dependency on internet connectivity is eliminated and service response latency is minimized. This is especially relevant in industrial applications, IoT devices, or environments that require real-time processing.
- **Offline Operation Scenarios**: Containers allow AI services to run in environments with limited, intermittent, or no connectivity to the Azure cloud, while maintaining the full functionality of the pre-trained models.
- **Operational Control and Customization**: Deploying services in containers provides greater control over their configuration, updates, and monitoring. Organizations can adjust resources, manage the container lifecycle, and apply security and audit policies according to their own standards.

These advantages position containerization as a fundamental strategy for organizations seeking to integrate artificial intelligence into complex environments with high requirements for privacy, availability, and control.

Deploying Azure AI Containers: Process and Best Practices

Deploying Azure AI services in containers involves a series of technical steps that, combined with best security and operational practices, ensure robust solutions aligned with enterprise standards. The typical process and key recommendations for effective deployment are outlined as follows:

Obtaining the Container Image

- Container images for supported services (for example, Computer Vision, Text Analytics, and Speech Services) can be downloaded from the Azure portal, official documentation, or via automated tools.
- A valid subscription is required, as container use still requires authentication against Azure.

Prerequisites

- Docker must be installed and properly configured in the environment where the container will be deployed.
- Check hardware requirements, especially for services that may require GPU acceleration or intensive processing.
- Have the credentials and endpoints for the corresponding Azure AI resource available.

Configuration and Deployment

- Azure AI containers require configuration of certain environment variables, such as subscription keys and the resource endpoint, to authenticate service usage.
- A basic command to run a Computer Vision container might be:

```
docker run -it --rm -p 5000:5000 \
  -e EULA=accept \
  -e AZURE_API_KEY=<your_key> \
  -e AZURE_ENDPOINT=<your_endpoint> \
  mcr.microsoft.com/azure-cognitive-services/vision/computer
vision:latest
```

- Adjust the parameters according to the service, port, and required network configuration.

Best Practices for Deployment

- **Security**: It manages keys and endpoints using services like Azure Key Vault or secure secret injection mechanisms in the runtime environment. It avoids exposing credentials in public files or scripts.
- **Isolation and Network Control**: It runs containers on protected networks, limiting access only to authorized applications. Further, it uses firewalls and access rules to reinforce security.

- **Monitoring and Maintenance**: It monitors container usage and performance using logging and metric tools, and update images as new versions or security patches are released.
- **Scalability**: In high-demand environments, consider implementing multiple instances and using load balancers.
- **Updates and Lifecycle**: It plans for regular container image updates and document the deployment process to facilitate continuous and secure operation.

Thus, by following these technical steps and best practices, Azure AI services deployed in containers will be secure, efficient, and easy to maintain, maximizing the benefits of containerization in enterprise environments.

Limitations and Differences Compared to Cloud Consumption

Although deploying Azure AI services via containers provides flexibility and control over the execution environment, there are important differences compared to traditional consumption of these services in the cloud. One key difference is that not all features available in the managed Azure version are present in containers; some advanced functions, integrations, or specific models may be limited or unavailable. Therefore, it is critical to consult the official documentation to confirm that the functional requirements of the solution are met before implementing this approach.

Another key difference is the responsibility for maintenance and updates. While cloud services are automatically updated by Azure, container use requires the technical team to manually download and deploy new image versions to access improvements, fixes, or security updates. In addition, the scalability and high availability provided transparently by the cloud must be managed by the IT team in containerized environments, using appropriate tools and architectures according to project needs.

Finally, it is important to note that although processing is performed locally, containers require authentication and registration against Azure for licensing and billing. Some telemetry is sent to Azure to validate usage according to the terms of service. This requires appropriate planning for key management, monitoring consumption, and understanding the support schemes available for this type of deployment. These differences highlight the importance of carefully evaluating the solution requirements before choosing containerization as a deployment strategy.

Monitoring, Cost Management, Authentication, and Access Control

In production environments based on **Azure AI Services** and **Azure AI Foundry**, success depends not only on building intelligent models but also on managing them securely, efficiently, and cost-effectively. This section addresses four fundamental pillars that ensure operational excellence:

- **Monitoring**: It ensures that AI endpoints are always available and operate at the expected quality, proactively detecting errors or performance degradation.
- **Cost management**: It controls expenses through consumption-based pricing models (tokens, compute, storage), uses tools such as Azure Cost Management, and adoption of FinOps best practices.
- **Authentication**: It describes how to protect endpoints using keys or, preferably, Microsoft Entra ID managed identities, integrating Azure Key Vault and adopting secure credentials.
- **Access control**: It implements access control policies with **Azure RBAC**, auditability, and advanced measures such as policies, MFA, and network restrictions to adhere to AI governance and responsibility standards.

Together, these four elements form the foundation for deploying and operating AI solutions that are:

- Secure (protection of identities and resources)
- Reliable (active monitoring and resilience)
- Efficient (cost and performance optimization)
- Governed (access control and regulatory compliance)

All of these align with the objectives of the AI-102 exam, which requires designing secure, auditable, and sustainable Azure AI solutions, as well as with the **Responsible AI** principles that will be discussed in the next section.

Monitoring

Monitoring is a fundamental component in the management of solutions based on Azure AI Services and Azure AI Foundry. It enables control over the availability, performance, and health of artificial intelligence models and allows for the anticipation of potential incidents before it impacts users or critical processes. Proper monitoring facilitates informed decision-making, enables continuous improvement, and forms the basis for safe and efficient operation of AI in production.

Monitoring in Azure AI relies on the integration of tools such as Azure Monitor, Log

Analytics, and customizable dashboards, providing a centralized, real-time view of service operation. The recommended process for implementing and leveraging monitoring in this context is as follows:

Enabling Diagnostic Settings

The first essential step for effective monitoring is to enable **Diagnostic Settings** on the relevant Azure AI resource. This functionality allows you to define which data will be collected and where it will be sent for analysis and visualization. From the Azure portal, simply select the resource, go to the *Monitoring* section, and within it, open *Diagnostic Settings*.

On the configuration screen, it is recommended to select the following categories:

- **`AllMetrics`**: To capture all relevant platform metrics, such as latency, availability, and consumption.
- **`RequestResponse`**: To log details of each request made to the endpoint, including responses, processing times, and possible errors.
- **`Audit`**: To obtain traceability and evidence of administrative and access operations on the resource.

These logs and metrics can be directed to a **Log Analytics Workspace**, a **Storage Account**, or an **Event Hub**, depending on analysis or retention requirements.

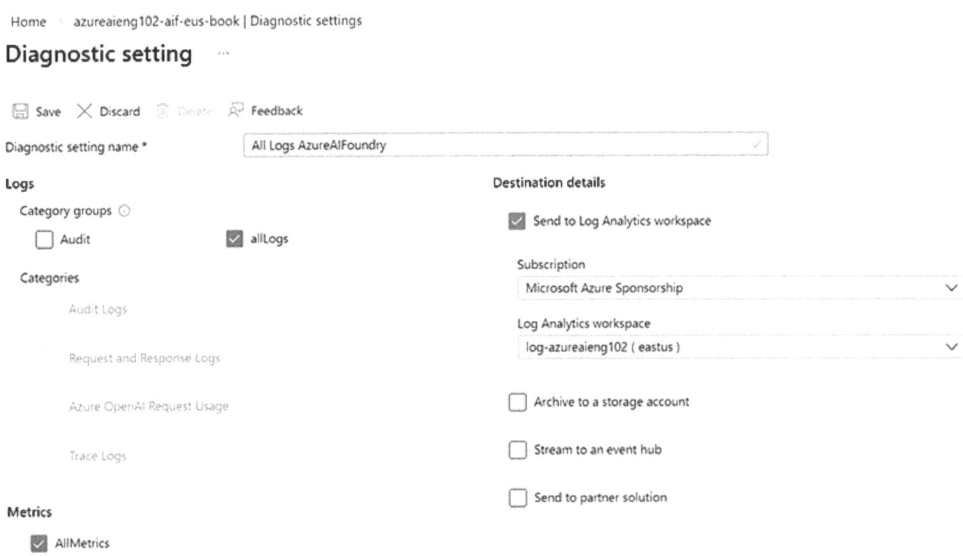

Figure 2.5: *Diagnostic Configuration in Azure AI Foundry*

Collection and Centralization of Metrics

Upon the activation of the Diagnostic Settings, Azure continuously collects and stores operational and usage data. The most relevant metrics for AI services include:

- **Response latency**: Enables identification of bottlenecks and optimization of user experience.
- **HTTP error rate**: Key for detecting integration failures or connectivity issues.
- **Tokens processed**: Fundamental in generative and language services, where cost and usage depend on token volume.
- **Endpoint availability**: Ensures that the model is accessible and online when needed.

All this information can be visualized and analyzed from the Azure portal using tools such as **Metrics Explorer**, which facilitates the creation of graphs and the comparison of metrics over time.

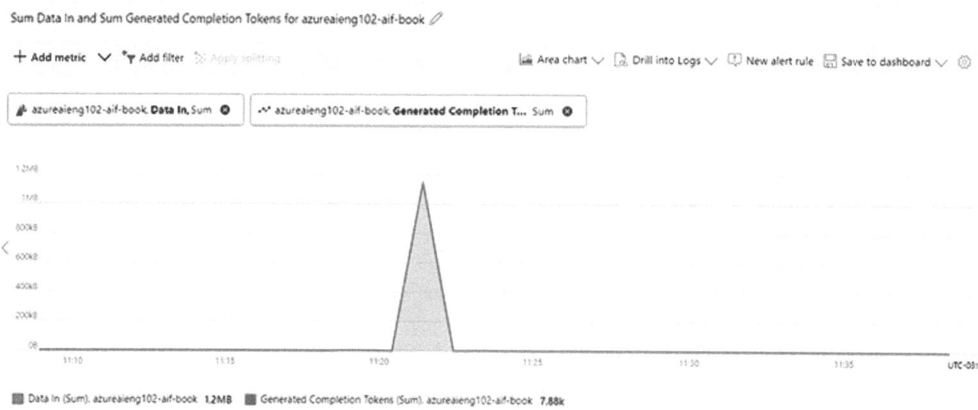

Figure 2.6: *Graph of Tokens Generated and Data Entered in Azure AI Foundry*

Proper monitoring instrumentation in Azure AI Services and Azure AI Foundry allows development and operations teams to anticipate incidents, maintain service stability, and make informed decisions about the health and performance of their artificial intelligence solutions. The combination of real-time metrics, dynamic dashboards, and configurable alerts enables a proactive stance against any operational deviation, ensuring business continuity and a consistent user experience.

This comprehensive monitoring approach not only provides visibility and control over the status of the platform but also lays the groundwork for optimizing resource usage and managing costs efficiently. Thus, monitoring becomes a key enabler for identifying optimization opportunities and connects naturally with the next critical operational dimension: efficient cost management in cloud solutions.

Cost Management

Cost management in solutions that utilize **Azure AI Services**, **Azure AI Foundry**, and **Azure OpenAI** requires a precise understanding of the billing model, as well as effective use of control tools and optimization best practices. This is especially relevant considering that, for most of these services, cost is directly linked to the amount of work performed or resource consumption.

Billing Models in Azure AI

For most Azure AI services, cost is usage-based. For example, in generative services such as Azure OpenAI, pricing is based on the number of tokens processed (input and output), while in **Azure AI Vision**, billing is per transaction (images analyzed), and in **Azure AI Speech**, per hour of audio processed or per million characters synthesized. A special case is **Azure AI Search**, which is billed according to the provisioned SKU and the number of scaling units, regardless of the volume of queries.

Azure provides dedicated pricing pages for all these services, where you can select the product, region, and currency to obtain up-to-date rate details for each relevant metric. However, for realistic planning, it is essential to know or estimate the expected workload (for instance, how many images will be processed per month, how many hours of audio will be transcribed, or how many tokens will be generated). For example:

- **Azure OpenAI**: The price may be around USD 5 per million input tokens for GPT-4o.
- **Azure AI Vision**: USD 1.50 per 1,000 images analyzed with the standard model.
- **Azure AI Speech**: Approximately USD 1 per hour of transcribed audio.

The accuracy of the estimate will depend on the quality of the input data–a poor projection may lead to significant budget deviations ("*garbage in, garbage out*").

Estimation and Analysis Tools

To plan and control expenses, Azure offers several integrated tools:

- **Pricing Page**: It allows to view price details by service, region, and commitment level, helping identify the unit cost of each operation.
- **Azure Pricing Calculator**: Ut enables simulation of usage scenarios, adding multiple services (for example, Vision and OpenAI), selecting region and plan, and specifying estimated volumes (transactions, tokens, hours). The result

displays the approximate monthly cost and allows comparison of options such as different commitment levels or model types.

- **Cost Analysis**: Within Azure Cost Management, allows you to visualize actual spending per day, resource, resource group, or subscription, and identify which services generate the most consumption.

At the operational level, it is possible to view daily spending graphs, identify which resources drive the highest cost (for example, an OpenAI instance, a Vision service, or a AI Search database), and break down spending by operation type (tokens, transactions, embeddings, and the like).

Proactive Expense Control

Azure makes it easy to create budgets at the subscription, resource group, or individual service level, enabling automatic alerts when a certain percentage of actual or projected spending is reached (for example, at 80% of the monthly budget). Budgets can be filtered to only include AI resources, and alert conditions can be set for both actual and forecasted spending at the current rate. Notifications may be sent by email, SMS, or can trigger automatic actions such as ticket creation or execution of flows in Logic Apps.

For **Azure OpenAI**, in addition to budget policies, there are specific quotas by model and resource type. The Azure OpenAI Studio or Azure AI Foundry portal displays current quota usage and allows users to request increases through support if required by the project.

Finally, **Azure Policy** can be used to restrict the creation of certain types of services or resources, helping prevent unauthorized deployments and, therefore, unnecessary costs.

Best Practices for Optimization and Cost Control

These are the following practices, best for optimization and cost control:

- Use the **Azure Pricing Calculator** before any deployment to anticipate financial impact and compare alternatives.
- Periodically review actual consumption via Cost Management dashboards and smart views, identifying resources or services with the highest spending.
- Configure budgets and alerts based on projected and actual usage to avoid end-of-month surprises.
- Optimize usage by selecting the most suitable models, plans, and configurations for each use case and dynamically adjusting resources according to demand.

- Remove or pause under-utilized resources and consolidate endpoints as and when possible.
- Review quotas and limits for each service, and only request increases when justified.

This systematic approach ensures that the growth and scalability of artificial intelligence solutions in Azure remain aligned with the financial capabilities of the organization and objectives.

Authentication

In operating artificial intelligence solutions on Azure, Authentication is the first layer of protection for resources, models, and data. Azure provides different mechanisms to ensure that only authorized users and applications can interact with AI services, thereby safeguarding integrity, traceability, and adherence to security best practices.

Authentication Approaches in Azure AI

Historically, authentication in Azure AI services was performed using **Access Keys (API Keys)**. While simple, this method poses security risks, especially when keys are shared or exposed in code repositories. Therefore, the current and recommended approach is to use **Microsoft Entra ID** (formerly Azure Active Directory), which enables centralized identity management without handling static secrets.

In most modern services, such as **Azure AI Foundry** and **Azure OpenAI**, fully "*keyless*" authentication is already possible, using managed identities or user accounts, thus limiting the exposure of sensitive credentials.

Entra ID-Based Authentication Configuration

To enable keyless authentication, the typical process is:

- **Assign the appropriate role**: From the Azure portal, in the **Access Control (IAM)** section of the AI resource, assign the *Cognitive Services User role* (or the specific role for the service) to the user, group, application, or managed identity that requires access.
- **Wait for permission propagation**: Changes usually take a few minutes to become effective.
- **Disable or rotate keys**: Once functionality with Entra ID is confirmed, it is recommended to disable or regenerate old access keys, minimizing leakage risks.

This approach facilitates centralized access control, integrates AI resources into the identity ecosystem of the organization, and allows the application of additional policies such as Multi-Factor Authentication or conditional access.

Application and SDK Usage

When implementing Entra ID authentication in code, it is recommended to use libraries such as **DefaultAzureCredential**, which automatically resolves the appropriate identity (user, service, managed identity) based on the execution environment.

Example in Python:

```
from azure.ai.inference import ChatCompletionsClient
from azure.identity import DefaultAzureCredential
client = ChatCompletionsClient(
    endpoint="https://<resource>.services.ai.azure.com/models",
    credential=DefaultAzureCredential(),
    credential_scopes=["https://cognitiveservices.azure.com/.
default"],
)
```

This pattern is valid for most Azure SDKs, as well as for calls to **Azure OpenAI** (adjusting the endpoint as needed).

Integration with Azure Key Vault

For scenarios that require storing and managing secrets (such as alternate endpoints, external credentials, or legacy keys), **Azure Key Vault** is the recommended repository. By combining managed identities and Key Vault access policies, applications can retrieve secrets dynamically, eliminating the need to store them in configuration files or environment variables.

Best Practices and Recommendations

Always prioritize the use of **Microsoft Entra ID** and **Managed Identities** over traditional keys.

- Review and minimize permissions assigned to each identity, applying the principle of least privilege.
- Deactivate or rotate API keys when they are not strictly necessary.
- Ensure that requested tokens use the correct scope and that endpoints match the resource type and SDK in use.
- Apply audit and access monitoring, integrating logs into Azure Monitor for traceability and early detection of unauthorized access attempts.

Hence, adopting a robust authentication strategy not only strengthens the security of the AI solution but also simplifies operation and regulatory compliance, preparing the environment for more granular access management aligned with modern identity standards.

Access Control

Access control in solutions based on **Azure AI Services**, **Azure AI Foundry**, and **Azure OpenAI** is essential to ensure security, governance, and the efficient operation of AI resources. A robust access control scheme not only defines who can perform actions on resources but also facilitates responsible collaboration, traceability, and compliance with corporate and regulatory standards.

Role-Based Access Control (RBAC)

Azure implements the **Role-Based Access Control (RBAC)** model, allowing granular permissions to be assigned to users, groups, managed identities, and applications, determining exactly what actions can be performed on specific resources.

Azure AI Foundry: Directly Managed Projects

In the current **Azure AI Foundry** experience, projects can be created directly from the Azure portal. If no hub exists, Azure automatically creates one associated with the new project, simplifying onboarding and management.

Access control is applied at both the project and hub levels, allowing pre-defined roles to be assigned according to responsibility:

- **Azure AI User**: Read-only access to the project and its data
- **Azure AI Project Manager**: Permissions to create and manage projects and assign roles to other users within the project
- **Azure AI Account Owner**: Full control of the hub and projects, permission management, and infrastructure administration

There are additional roles, such as *Azure AI Developer* or *Inference Deployment Operator*, which grant specific permissions for technical or deployment tasks. This granularity enables clear separation of administration, development, and operation roles, aligning permission assignment with the actual needs of each team.

Practical Recommendations:

- Assign the appropriate roles from project creation and periodically review assignments as teams or the scope of the solution evolve.
- Always prefer specific roles (for instance: *Project Manager*, *Developer*) to limit the scope of permissions and reduce the risk of unnecessary access.

Azure AI Services and Azure OpenAI: Custom Permissions

In services such as **Azure OpenAI**, **Speech**, or **Vision**, access is also controlled using RBAC. Some specific roles include:

- **Cognitive Services OpenAI User**: It allows consumption of existing models via Playground or APIs, but not deployment modifications.
- **Cognitive Services OpenAI Contributor**: It enables creation, modification, and management of deployments and fine-tuned models.
- **Cognitive Services Contributor**: It grants administrative permissions over the resource, ideal for technical management roles.

Services like **Speech** or **Vision** have their own dedicated roles, such as *Cognitive Services Speech User/Contributor* or *Computer Vision Contributor*, offering even more granular control over the functionalities exposed by each API.

For effective management:

- Always apply the principle of least privilege: grant only the permissions strictly necessary for the assigned role.
- Use **Managed Identities** so applications and services can access resources without managing static credentials, assigning appropriate roles directly to the identity of the application.
- Regularly review roles and access to maintain security and governance, removing obsolete or unnecessary permissions.

Private Communications Management

In addition to controlling who accesses services, it is crucial to control how that access is made. For scenarios requiring greater isolation, confidentiality, and compliance, Azure AI allows communication to be restricted exclusively to private networks using **Private Endpoint** and **Managed Virtual Network**.

Azure AI Foundry: Private Communications Configuration

When creating a project in Azure AI Foundry, it is possible to enable a **Private Endpoint** to ensure that access to the service is only through a private virtual network (VNet). From the portal, configure this in the **`Networking → Private endpoint connections`** section, where you select the VNet and subnet to which the service will be exposed.

Simultaneously, you can enable a **`Managed Virtual Network`**, which centralizes internal traffic between related resources (for example: Storage, Key Vault, AI Search) within the same network perimeter, applying outbound rules, access lists, and private domain (**`privatelink.*`**) DNS management.

Azure OpenAI and Other AI Services

Azure OpenAI resources and other Azure AI services also support private mode:

- From the Azure portal, the *Networking* configuration in the Resource, public access is disabled and a **`Private Endpoint`** is added, restricting service visibility to the selected VNet.
- Application traffic to the service travels entirely over the Azure backbone, with no exposure to the public Internet.
- Private DNS zones manage endpoint resolution, ensuring internal communications use secure, private routes.

Benefits and Recommended Workflow

This architecture enhances security by:

- Eliminating unnecessary exposure to the Internet, reducing the attack surface.
- Facilitating the integration of dependent services (such as Storage or Key Vault) within the same secure environment.
- Enabling hybrid architectures (on-premises + Azure) via VPN, ExpressRoute, or Azure Bastion, all under corporate security policies.

Recommended Workflow

1. When creating the resource or project, enable the **`Private Endpoint`** option and select the appropriate virtual network.
2. Configure a **`Managed Virtual Network`**, if necessary, to centralize security and internal routing.
3. Validate internal DNS resolution and access from authorized applications or services.
4. Periodically review and update network rules and private endpoint configuration as environment requirements evolve.

The combination of a solid access control model and private communications management ensures that your artificial intelligence solutions in Azure are not only powerful and flexible, but also secure, governed, and aligned with the highest industry standards.

Responsible AI

The adoption of responsible artificial intelligence is a guiding principle in Azure AI Foundry and forms the foundation upon which Microsoft builds its entire AI solutions ecosystem. Far from being optional, responsibility is a strategic and operational obligation that is embedded throughout every stage of the artificial intelligence lifecycle: from initial design to deployment, monitoring, and ongoing governance.

Microsoft enshrines this commitment in a framework structured around six essential principles, which are implemented across all its platforms and services:

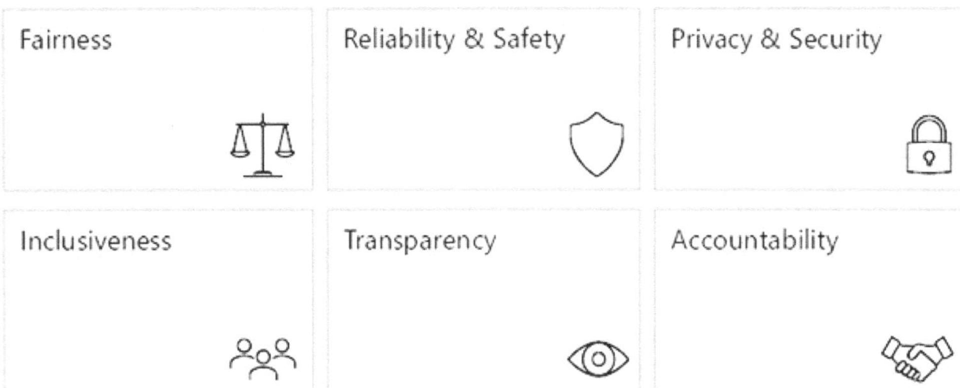

Figure 2.7: *Core Principles of Responsible AI*

- **Fairness:** The goal is to prevent AI systems from perpetuating or amplifying existing biases in data, ensuring that outcomes are fair and equitable for all users, regardless of their demographic group. Azure provides tools and metrics to audit model performance by subgroup and detect disparities, enabling adjustments to be made before models are put into production.
- **Reliability and Safety:** AI must behave predictably and robustly, even in unforeseen situations, and be resilient against malicious manipulation or unexpected failures. This involves validating models under different scenarios, continuously monitoring their behavior in production, and establishing operational boundaries to prevent potential harm to users or the organization.
- **Privacy and Security:** Protecting personal and sensitive data is an essential pillar. Azure AI Foundry incorporates advanced encryption mechanisms, granular access controls, and support for differential privacy techniques. Solutions also comply with major international data privacy and protection

regulations, such as GDPR, and facilitate auditability and traceability of information usage.

- **Inclusiveness:** A responsible AI system must be accessible and useful to the widest possible diversity of users. Microsoft promotes creation of solutions that take into account a range of abilities, cultural and linguistic contexts, including digital accessibility principles and the involvement of diverse communities throughout the development lifecycle.
- **Transparency:** Users and stakeholders must be able to understand how and why AI makes decisions. Azure facilitates this with explainability and analysis tools, enabling interpretation of models at both a global (overall behavior) and local (specific decisions) level, as well as identification of limitations, uncertainties, and potential areas for system improvement.
- **Accountability:** Accountability requires that processes, policies, and roles be clearly defined for the supervision, documentation, and auditing of AI systems. This includes mechanisms for human intervention, full traceability of automated decisions, and clear channels for handling incidents or failures, ensuring that AI operates in accordance with the organizational values and objectives.

Azure AI Foundry Content Safety: Safeguarding Content Integrity and Ethics

In the era of generative artificial intelligence, the risk of exposure to harmful content–whether generated by users or AI models–has become a central concern for any organization. **Azure AI Foundry Content Safety** emerges as the comprehensive solution of Microsoft to address these challenges, providing advanced and configurable defense against inappropriate and risky content.

Azure AI Foundry Content Safety is a managed moderation service that analyzes both text and images for potentially harmful content. Its state-of-the-art technology allows it to identify and categorize, with high accuracy, elements related to hate, violence, sexuality, and self-harm. The system automatically assigns severity levels, facilitating decision-making: block, flag for human review, or allow content according to the policies and regulations of the organization.

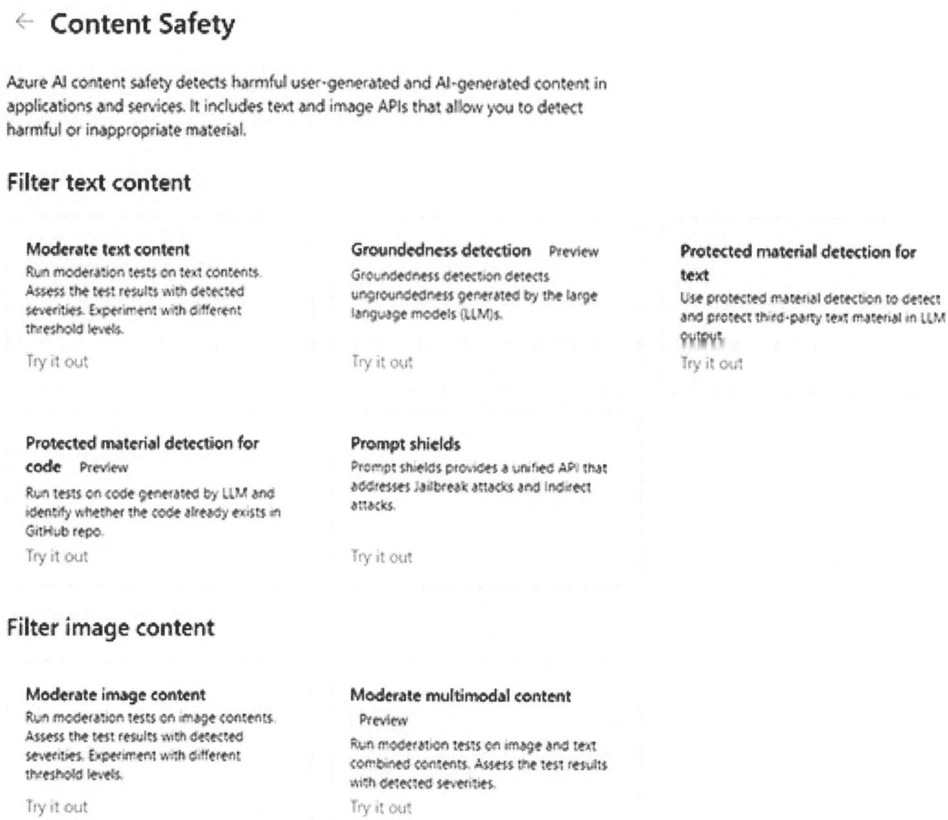

Figure 2.8: *Azure AI Foundry Content Safety*

Key Features

- **Multimodal Moderation**: It evaluates both text and images, providing comprehensive coverage for all input and output channels of AI systems.
- **Severity Analysis**: It classifies content by risk level, enabling automated responses tailored to the context and sensitivity of each use case.
- **Custom Blocklists and Filters**: It supports the integration of custom blocklists and the creation of custom categories to meet specific sectoral or corporate requirements.
- **Content Safety Studio**: It provides an interactive visual environment for testing, calibrating, and auditing filters, as well as analyzing key operational metrics, enabling continuous adjustment of security policies.
- **Comprehensive Protection**: It incorporates technologies such as prompt **shielding** to defend against manipulations in generative models and

groundedness detection to verify that responses are aligned with trustworthy and reliable sources.

Seamless Integration in Azure AI Foundry

The Content Safety functionality is fully integrated into the Azure AI Foundry experience, allowing filters and moderation rules to be applied directly from the portal in the **Guardrails + Controls** section. Filters can be configured to analyze both prompts and responses of generative models, with sensitivity levels adjusted according to the endpoint and operational context.

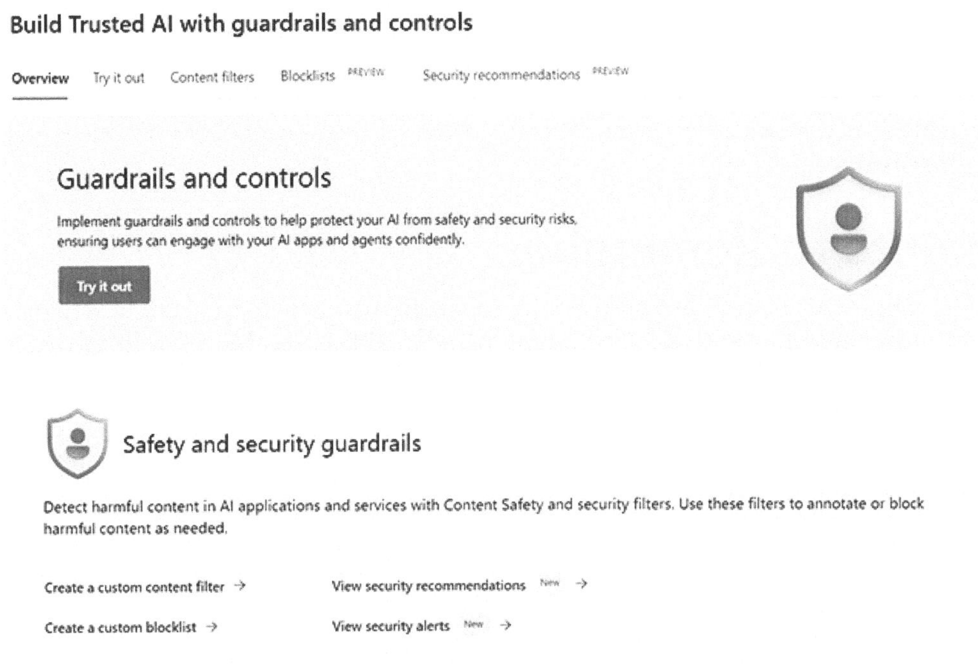

Figure 2.9: *Azure AI Foundry Guardrails + Controls*

Additionally, the solution is available via API and SDKs in several languages, facilitating its incorporation into modern development workflows and enterprise-scale applications.

Azure AI Foundry Content Safety forms the foundation upon which a safer, a more ethical, and a more trustworthy digital environment can be built. Its native integration, when combined with its flexibility and robustness, makes it an indispensable tool for organizations seeking to develop and deploy generative AI solutions that align with the highest standards of responsibility and governance.

Conclusion

This chapter explored the essential aspects of planning, deploying, and managing artificial intelligence solutions using Azure AI Foundry and Azure AI Services. It addressed the selection and provisioning of AI services, model deployment strategies–including cloud and container-based approaches–monitoring and cost management, secure authentication and access control, and the foundational principles of Responsible AI. Emphasis was placed on operational excellence, security, and ethical considerations, as well as the integration of advanced features such as multimodal content moderation and private networking.

The next chapter will build upon these foundations, focusing on practical implementation scenarios, advanced customization, and the integration of Azure AI solutions with broader enterprise architectures. Readers will learn how to apply these principles in real-world environments to drive innovation and deliver measurable business value.

Points to Remember

- Azure AI Foundry provides a comprehensive platform for designing, deploying, and managing AI solutions that meet business, technical, and regulatory requirements.
- Service provisioning in Azure can be done using multi-service or single-service resources, each offering distinct advantages in terms of flexibility, control, and cost.
- Model deployment options include managed cloud endpoints and Docker-based containers, supporting hybrid, edge, and disconnected scenarios.
- Effective monitoring, cost control, authentication, and granular access management are essential for maintaining secure, reliable, and compliant AI solutions.
- Responsible AI principles – fairness, reliability, safety, privacy, inclusiveness, transparency, and accountability – must guide every stage of the AI lifecycle.
- Azure AI Foundry Content Safety provides advanced tools for moderating and protecting content in generative AI applications, ensuring ethical and safe use.

CHAPTER 3
Implementing Generative AI Solutions

Introduction

Currently, generative artificial intelligence is transforming the way organizations approach innovation and problem-solving. This chapter is dedicated to exploring the process of implementing generative AI solutions using advanced platforms such as Azure AI Foundry and Azure OpenAI Service. It provides a comprehensive overview of planning, deployment, and resource management, enabling readers to understand how to enable and scale intelligent applications that leverage language models, image generation, and multimodal capabilities—all while adhering to enterprise security and governance standards.

Throughout the chapter, key topics will be examined, including the creation of prompt workflows and the use of data grounding (RAG) to maximize model effectiveness. Additionally, it will address model evaluation and monitoring, integration with the Azure AI Foundry SDK, and the provisioning and deployment of cloud resources. Finally, practical examples will be presented on how to generate natural language content, automated code, and images using DALL·E or GPT-image-1, as well as the integration possibilities for applications, with multimodal capabilities to drive innovative and scalable solutions across various industries.

Structure

In this chapter, we will cover the following topics:

- Introduction to Generative AI in Azure
    - Key Services in Azure: Azure AI Foundry and Azure Open AI Service

- Azure AI Foundry: Planning and Resource Management
  - Planning a Generative AI Solution
  - Environment Preparation: Hub, Projects, and Resources
  - Portal Evolution and Platform Direction after Microsoft Ignite 2025
  - Centralized Security and Connectivity
  - Resource Deployment with Azure AI Foundry
- Generative Models in Azure AI Foundry
  - Expansion of the Model Ecosystem Announced at Microsoft Ignite 2025
  - Model Lifecycle Management
- Implementation of Prompt Flows and Prompt Templates
- Data Grounding and Retrieval-Augmented Generation (RAG)
  - RAG Implementation from the Azure AI Foundry Chat Playground
- Model Evaluation and Integration with Azure AI Foundry SDK
- Provisioning and Implementation with Azure OpenAI Service
  - Model Deployment: Reasoning, Language, Audio, Embeddings, Image, and Video
  - Version and Availability Considerations
  - Costs and Scalability
  - Multimodal Capabilities and Applications Integration
  - Image Generation: From DALL-E to GPT-image-1 in Azure AI Foundry – Azure Open AI
  - Multimodal Capabilities of GPT-4o: Images, Audio, and Text
  - Best Practices and Recommendations

Introduction to Generative AI in Azure

Generative AI is transforming the way organizations create content, develop products, and automate processes. From generating natural language and code to creating images, these technologies drive operational efficiency, enhance customer experience, and enable new business opportunities.

In enterprise environments, generative AI is no longer limited to experimentation or isolated proof-of-concepts. Organizations are increasingly integrating these models into business-critical workflows such as customer support automation, intelligent document processing, software engineering assistance, and internal knowledge discovery. When combined with secure access to corporate data and integrated into existing applications, generative models can accelerate time-to-market, reduce operational friction, and scale expertise across teams.

However, adopting generative AI at scale introduces new technical and operational challenges. Beyond selecting a model, teams must address governance, security, cost control, latency, and compliance requirements from the start. This is why modern implementations require a unified platform that supports the full lifecycle–from planning and deployment to evaluation, monitoring, and continuous improvement–while enabling secure connectivity to enterprise systems and data sources.

Key Services in Azure: Azure AI Foundry and Azure OpenAI Service

Azure AI Foundry has become a primary platform for developing generative AI solutions in Azure. It provides a unified environment where data, development, and business teams can collaborate efficiently. Through its integrated catalog, Foundry allows users to explore, deploy, and manage models from OpenAI, Mistral, Meta, Hugging Face, DeepSeek, and others–while leveraging prompt workflows, RAG patterns, evaluations, governance, and security all in one place.

Azure OpenAI Service, which initially operated as a standalone service for consuming models such as GPT-4, Codex, and DALL·E, is now fully integrated within the Azure AI Foundry. This means that when you create a project in Foundry and access the model catalog, you can select OpenAI models–such as o4 mini, GPT-4.1, GPT-4o, or DALL·E–and deploy them without leaving the Foundry environment. As a result, there is no longer a need to use the Azure OpenAI portal separately: Azure AI Foundry now, acts as a central hub orchestrating all generative AI services within Azure.

The following table lists the advantages and challenges of implementing Generative Solutions:

Advantages	**Challenges**
Unified platform that facilitates collaboration between data, development, and business teams.	Variable costs linked to token consumption, compute, and storage; requires budget planning.
Access to state-of-the-art models and multiple providers, with integrated governance and monitoring.	Risks of bias, data security, compliance, and ethical responsibility in the use of generative models.
Orchestration of Prompt Flows, RAG, evaluation, security filters, and monitoring from a single interface.	Integrating RAG architectures, prompt flows, and security requires robust design for production environments.

Scalability from proof of concept to production with deployable APIs, endpoints, and agents.	Requires strong configuration of roles, networks, costs, and continuous oversight.

Table 3.1: *Advantages and Challenges of Implementing Generative Solutions*

The Azure AI Foundry platform represents a paradigm shift: moving from isolated tools in separate portals or studios to a cohesive, scalable environment that covers the entire lifecycle–including ideation, prototyping, production, monitoring, and continuous improvement.

Azure AI Foundry: Planning and Resource Management

Azure AI Foundry provides the tools and governance foundation required to plan generative AI projects in a structured and scalable way. Before deploying models or integrating advanced workflows such as RAG (Retrieval Augmented Generation) and prompt flows, it is essential to define the use case, environments, access controls, and data connectivity strategy to ensure security, compliance, and operational readiness.

Planning a Generative AI Solution

A structured planning approach ensures that the solution is aligned with business objectives, technical requirements, and governance constraints. The following steps provide a practical framework for defining the scope, environments, roles, and data connectivity of a generative AI project.

Step 1: Identifying the Use Case

- **Precise objective definition**: Before choosing any technology, one must determine whether the project requires language generation (for example, chatbots), image generation (DALL·E), code assistance, or agents capable of taking actions. This decision guides both the model selection and the deployment approach–for example, whether you will use RAG, fine-tuning, or simply prompts.
- **Assessment of Functional Requirements:** The solution must be defined by its operational needs–whether it involves real-time inference, batch processing, or autonomous services. Multichannel capabilities, including text, voice, and vision, should also be considered. Prior to architectural design, it is essential to conduct a thorough analysis of latency, scalability, operational costs, and regulatory compliance related to data handling.

Step 2: Separation of Environments (Dev/Test/Prod)

- **Isolated spaces by lifecycle stage**: Use separate resources (subscriptions or *resource groups*) for development, testing, and production. Azure AI Foundry supports multiple instances (accounts) to deploy isolated environments, making it easier to control and manage progressive transitions from POC to production.
- **Progressive scalability**: Start with minimal resources for rapid validation, and expand in phases as complexity or adoption increases.

Step 3: Roles and Access Control

- **RBAC Model in Azure AI Foundry:** Define roles based on responsibilities. The *Azure AI Account Owner* manages global configurations; the *Azure AI Project Manager* builds and manages projects; the *Azure AI User* has read-only or usage access.
- **Application of the Principle of Least Privilege:** Grant granular access according to roles. Use account-, project-, or resource-level roles depending on the context.

Step 4: Data Strategy and Connectivity

- **Secure connections**: Configure connections to access data storage, databases, Key Vault, or external services. These are available at both the hub (shared) and project (isolated) levels.
- **Authentication with managed identities**: Use Managed Identity or Entra ID pass through tokenization to ensure secure and auditable access to external resources.

Environment Preparation: Hub, Projects, and Resources

At **Microsoft Build 2025**, Microsoft announced a new way to manage projects in Azure AI Foundry. Now, instead of configuring multiple resources across different portals, you can create a single resource called Azure AI Foundry (formerly known as AI Services). This resource serves as a central hub for storing models, agents, flows, connections, and policies—all under one roof. This represents an evolution toward a cohesive platform, making governance, traceability, and access control easier with a unified RBAC model, defined networks, and regulatory compliance, all managed from a single instance.

Distinction between Project Types

Azure AI Foundry offers two types of projects, reflecting different levels of integration and maturity:

- **Foundry project**: Recommended for most generative AI scenarios, as it allows direct access to models (OpenAI, Mistral, Meta, and the like.), agents in GA, evaluations, playgrounds, and native prompt flows–all within the integrated catalog.
- **Hub-based project**: Maintains compatibility with legacy architectures, advanced isolation, and connectivity to external resources such as Azure Machine Learning. It operates through connections and provides preview access to agents, Prompt Flow, and additional tools.

The difference is visible in the portal: the "`Foundry project`" displays "`(AI Foundry)`" in the navigation, while the "`hub-based project`" appears as "`(Hub)`."

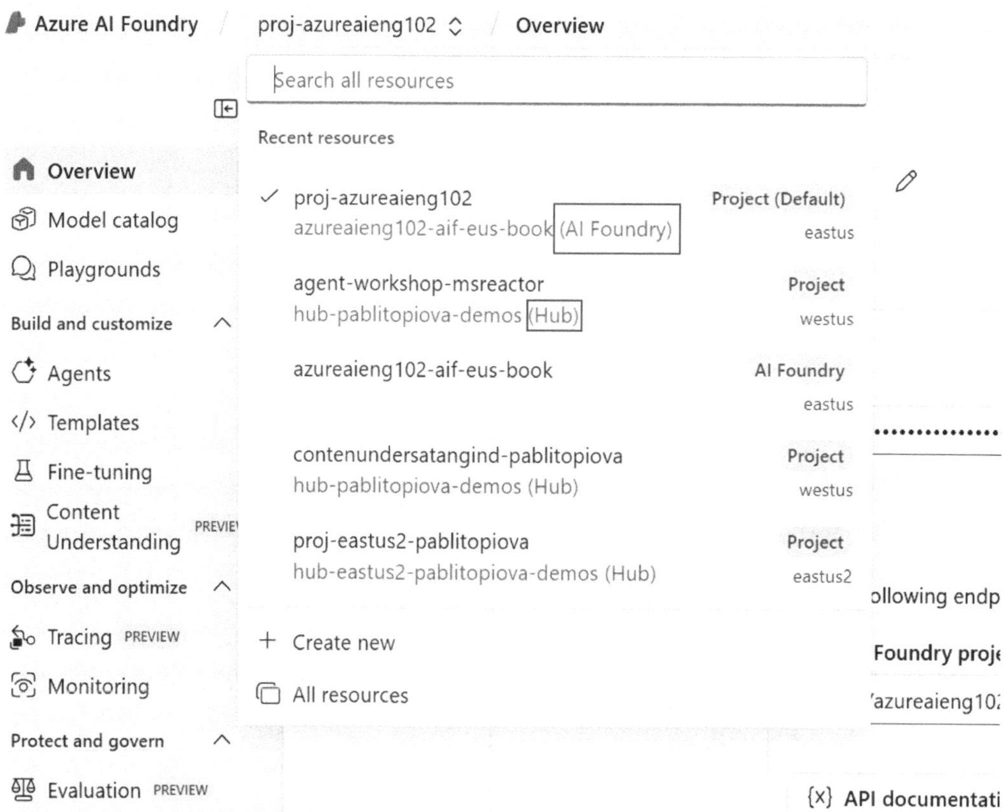

Figure 3.1: Azure AI Foundry with Recent Resources and Options for AI Foundry and Hub-Based Projects

Based on this foundation, Microsoft presented a comparative table on Microsoft Learn that clearly summarizes the unique capabilities of each project type:

Capability	Foundry project	Hub-based project
Agents	✓(GA)	✓ (Preview only)
AI Foundry API for working with agents and models	(Native support)	Available via connections
Models sold directly by Azure (OpenAI, DeepSeek, xAI, and the like	✓	Available via connections
Partner or community models (Stability, Bria, Cohere, and the like	✓	Available via connections
Open source models (e.g., Hugging Face)	✓	✓
Evaluations	✓	✓
Playground	✓	✓
Prompt Flow		✓
Content understanding	✓	✓
File upload to project for experimentation	✓	✗
Isolation of files and outputs per project	✓	✓
Required Azure dependencies	-	Storage account and Key Vault

Table 3.2: *Comparison of Capabilities of Foundry and Hub-based Projects in Azure*

To access this updated table, visit Microsoft Learn: ***https://learn.microsoft.com/en-us/azure/ai-foundry/what-is-azure-ai-foundry***.

This summary shows that the Foundry project is the most modern, comprehensive, and recommended option for most generative AI development. The hub-based project, while more traditional, remains useful when strong isolation or integration with Azure ML components is required.

The Core Experience of the Azure AI Foundry Resource

Previously, when creating an Azure AI Foundry **Hub** (the legacy model), the platform would automatically provision critical resources: an AI Services account (including Azure OpenAI), a **Storage Account** to store artifacts and results, a **Key Vault** for secure key management, a **Container Registry** (ACR) for container-based workflows, as well as **Application Insights**, **Log Analytics**, and a **Managed VNet** to ensure network isolation and private endpoints. This hub environment brought together shared resources and centralized security, all necessary to support multiple projects.

With the updates announced at **Microsoft Build 2025**, this approach has evolved. Now, a **centralized Azure AI Foundry resource** (AI Foundry type) is used, allowing you to create multiple **Foundry projects** directly within it. Each project inherits enterprise configuration (governance, networks, roles, policies) from the main resource but maintains complete isolation for files, connections, and endpoints. This enables teams to collaborate independently, without duplicating infrastructure or compromising overall security.

In addition, native **APIs and SDKs** (.NET, Python, Java, JavaScript/TypeScript) are available, designed to manage models, agents, and environments declaratively–fully integrated into CI/CD pipelines, Visual Studio Code, or command-line interfaces. This empowers advanced LLMOps or GenAIOps practices, with environments that are reproducible, auditable, and aligned with industrial DevOps standards.

Portal Evolution and Platform Direction after Microsoft Ignite 2025

In November 2025, during **Microsoft Ignite**, Microsoft introduced a major evolution in the Foundry experience–one that redefines how developers and organizations interact with the platform. While the foundational changes were first revealed at Build 2025, Ignite served as the formal announcement of the new **Microsoft Foundry portal**, which now becomes the recommended entry point for all new generative AI projects.

This announcement marks a strategic shift: Microsoft is guiding customers away from the legacy, hub-based architecture and toward the modern, unified **Foundry project model**, supported by a simplified and more powerful portal experience.

Two Co-Existing Portals: Foundry Classic and Foundry New

Following the Ignite 2025 announcement, Microsoft confirmed that two portals will continue to coexist, but each serves a distinct purpose:

- **Microsoft Foundry (classic):** This is used for legacy resources such as Azure OpenAI deployments, hub-based projects, and older Foundry projects.
- **Microsoft Foundry (new):** This is the modern interface where *only* Foundry projects created with the new architecture appear.

This dual experience ensures backward compatibility while enabling organizations to gradually transition toward the new model.

Microsoft summarized the following in an updated Microsoft Learn table:

Portal	Banner display	When to use
Microsoft Foundry (classic)	"`New Foundry`" toggle OFF 	Use when working with Azure OpenAI legacy deployments, hub-based projects, or mixed-resource environments.
Microsoft Foundry (new)	"`New Foundry`" toggle ON 	Recommended portal for all modern Foundry projects, offering a streamlined, unified experience with integrated agent tools, evaluations, flows, and multi-model catalogs.

Table 3.3: *Comparison of Microsoft Foundry Portal Versions*

Why Microsoft Recommends the New Portal

During Microsoft Ignite 2025, Microsoft provided a clear explanation of why the new Microsoft Foundry portal has become the recommended environment for all future generative AI development. The central message revolves around unification, modernization, and the need for an operational foundation that supports enterprise-grade AI workloads at scale.

One of the primary reasons behind this shift is the move towards a **unified experience**. In legacy model, developers had to navigate, and configure multiple Azure services individually linking resources across distinct portals and relying on a combination of external dependencies. The new portal changes this paradigm entirely: Microsoft Foundry now consolidates models, agents, flows, connections, governance policies, and file storage into a single resource and a single visual interface. This significantly reduces operational friction while ensuring that every component of a generative AI solution is governed under the same compliance and RBAC configuration.

A second motivation is the **modern architecture** introduced with the centralized Foundry resource. Each Foundry project created within this resource automatically inherits enterprise-level networks, roles, and security policies. At the same time, every project maintains full isolation of its files, flows, outputs, and endpoints. This duality—shared enterprise governance combined with strong project-level isolation—creates an ideal environment for organizations that needs to scale multiple AI initiatives, while ensuring separation of responsibilities, auditing, and regulatory compliance.

Microsoft also emphasized that the new portal is the only environment that offers native tools for multi-agent AI systems. Capabilities such as agents in General Availability, evaluations, Prompt Flow, content understanding tools, and the integrated model catalog (which includes OpenAI, xAI, DeepSeek, Mistral, Meta, OSS, and community models) are built directly into the platform. Unlike hub-based architectures, these tools no longer require external connections or additional manual configuration. The result is a smoother, more predictable workflow from prototyping to production.

Additionally, the new portal is **optimized for LLMOps and GenAIOps**, allowing organizations to adopt mature operational practices around large-scale AI development. It integrates natively with GitHub Actions, Azure DevOps, Visual Studio Code extensions, and CI/CD pipelines, providing versioned, auditable, and reproducible workflows for both models and agents. This alignment with modern DevOps practices reflects the intention of Microsoft to make Foundry a platform not just for experimentation, but also for robust enterprise operations.

Impact of the Ignite 2025 Announcement

The announcement at Ignite 2025 was direct and unambiguous: all new projects should be created using the new Microsoft Foundry portal and the modern Foundry project type. Microsoft made it clear that this is not a temporary recommendation but the strategic direction of the platform moving forward.

Despite this shift, **Foundry Classic** remains available and is, fully supported for existing customers who rely on the older architecture, particularly those using hub-based projects or Azure OpenAI legacy deployments. These environments will continue to function as expected; however, Microsoft also confirmed that they will no longer receive new feature investments. All future innovation—including enhancements to agents, evaluations, content tools, model integrations, governance capabilities, and operational workflows—will be delivered exclusively through the new portal.

To support this transition, Microsoft updated its official documentation, introducing a dedicated **Foundry Classic** view that helps organizations identify which version of the platform their projects belong to. This documentation,(available at **https://learn.microsoft.com/en-us/azure/ai-foundry/what-is-azure-ai-foundry?view=foundry-classic**)clarifies the distinctions between the classic and modern experiences and provides transparency for enterprises assessing the future of their workloads.

In precise terms, the Ignite 2025 announcement establishes a clear direction: while Foundry Classic continues to serve legacy and specialized scenarios, the modern Foundry portal is the definitive platform for innovation, scalability, and long-term development in the AI ecosystem of Microsoft.

Centralized Security and Connectivity

Security and connectivity have reached a new level of sophistication in Azure AI Foundry following the latest announcements at Microsoft Build 2025. One of the pillars of this environment is authentication based on **Managed Identities**, both for the central Foundry resource and for each individual project. This approach allows full access to critical services–such as Azure OpenAI, AI Search, Cosmos DB, and Storage–to occur without the need to store or manage secrets. Managed Identities are fully integrated with **Microsoft Entra ID**, ensuring traceability, centralized control, and compliance with corporate access policies. Through RBAC, it is possible to limit the privileges of each identity to the minimum necessary, thereby strengthening operational security posture, and preventing accidental exposures.

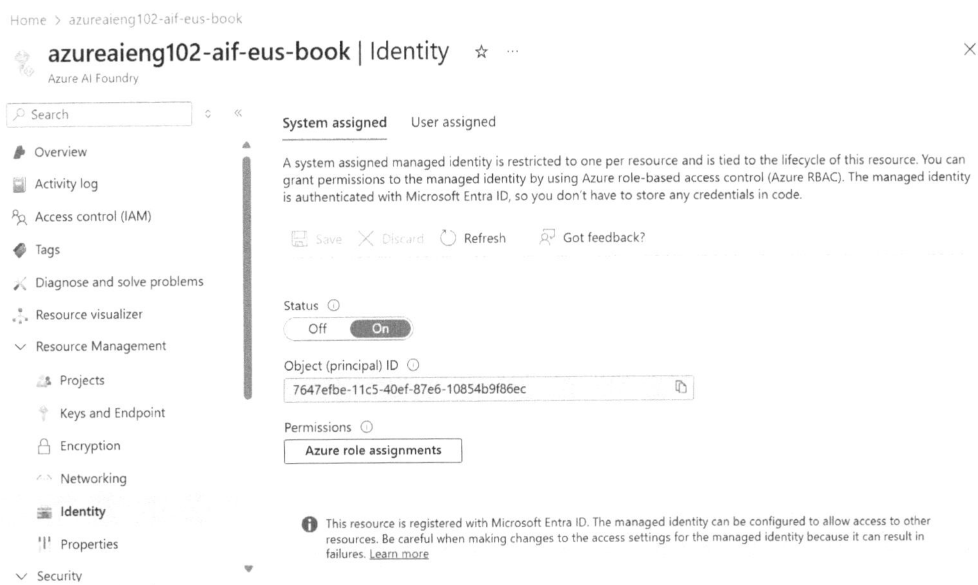

Figure 3.2: *Managed Identity Configuration in Azure AI Foundry*

Another key advancement is the ability to deploy environments on managed or custom virtual networks (BYO-VNet). This enables the definition of dedicated subnets for services such as agents, as well as the ability to establish private endpoints for critical resources like Storage, Key Vault, and Container Registry. Azure AI Foundry also allows granular control over outbound traffic: teams can choose to allow full internet access, restrict it to approved domains only, or even block all outbound connections entirely. This flexibility is essential for meeting the regulatory and security requirements of the most demanding enterprise environments, and provides effective isolation between different projects or deployed solutions.

Connections to external services–whether global (shared across projects) or project-specific–are always managed using managed identities and RBAC, eliminating credential exposure and ensuring that each workflow or agent can only access the resources it needs. This architecture makes multi-team and multi-environment collaboration possible without losing control over security or access management.

Observability and compliance have also been strengthened. Azure AI Foundry integrates advanced monitoring and traceability capabilities, allowing teams to visualize performance, security, and quality metrics centrally and in real time. Logs and traces for models, agents, and connections can be audited and analyzed to detect anomalies, optimize performance, and ensure compliance with current regulations. Additionally, integration with enterprise tools such as Defender for Cloud and Purview Compliance Manager enables proactive risk management and regulatory control at every stage of the generative AI solution lifecycle.

Together, these security and connectivity mechanisms provide technical teams with a reliable foundation for deploying, operating, and scaling generative AI solutions in Azure—meeting both current technological standards and the governance, and compliance requirements of the current enterprise environment.

Resource Deployment with Azure AI Foundry

Azure AI Foundry offers several deployment options for generative AI models and solutions, allowing organizations to tailor their architecture to different business, performance, and operational control requirements.

The most widely used and recommended option is the standard deployment on the Foundry resource. This model allows models to be exposed as API endpoints, configurable by region, data zone, or globally, with throughput options based on the expected usage volume. Costs are primarily based on token consumption and the contracted performance tier. This mode provides native integration and high availability, making it suitable for both testing and production environments, and enabling direct use of catalog models within Foundry projects.

For scenarios requiring elasticity or the absence of dedicated infrastructure, Foundry also provides the option of serverless API endpoints. In this case, the platform automatically handles the provisioning and management of resources, and users pay only for the actual usage of the model—ideal for prototypes or solutions with variable workloads. However, availability may be limited to certain models or regions, and sometimes, a specific Marketplace subscription for models is required.

On the other hand, for organizations working with open source models, deep customizations, or specialized APIs, there is the **Managed Compute** option. This involves provisioning dedicated instances within Azure AI Foundry (such as virtual machines or managed clusters), where organizations can deploy their own or third-party models. While this offers greater control and customization, it also requires active resource management and involves compute related costs, as well as potential charges for Marketplace model usage.

Regarding the exposure of prompt flows as services, it is important to note that, so far the current state of the platform is considered, **Prompt Flow deployments** – that is, publishing a prompt flow as an online endpoint for real-time API interaction–are only available in hub-based projects. AI Foundry projects, for now, do not support the creation or management of Prompt Flow endpoints. This distinction is significant when planning architectures that require orchestrated interactive flows as web services.

Another key consideration is the location of data processing. Azure AI Foundry allows you to choose, in standard deployments, whether processing is kept within a specific region, a data zone (to meet geographic regulations), or is at a global level. This flexibility is essential for meeting both latency requirements and data residency or sovereignty regulations.

All deployment modes support the use of **managed private networks**, allowing inference and data traffic to remain within the Virtual Network associated with the Foundry resource. This is especially important in regulated contexts or where information confidentiality and traffic security are priorities.

In summary, Azure AI Foundry provides a wide range of technical options for deploying generative models and solutions, enabling teams to adapt architecture according to the objectives and constraints of each use case. It is critical to consider, from the outset, both the appropriate project type (AI Foundry or hub-based), the deployment mode, and network and security configurations, to ensure that the solution can scale, integrate, and operate reliably within the enterprise environment.

Generative Models in Azure AI Foundry

Selecting the Right Generative Model for Your Use Case:

Azure AI Foundry provides access to over 1,900 models through its catalog. This includes a wide variety of official models–from Microsoft, OpenAI, DeepSeek, xAI, Mistral, Meta, and others–as well as community options like Hugging Face, Stability AI, and Cohere. To not further, open-source versions are also available for deployment in *managed compute* environments or as `serverlessAPIs`.

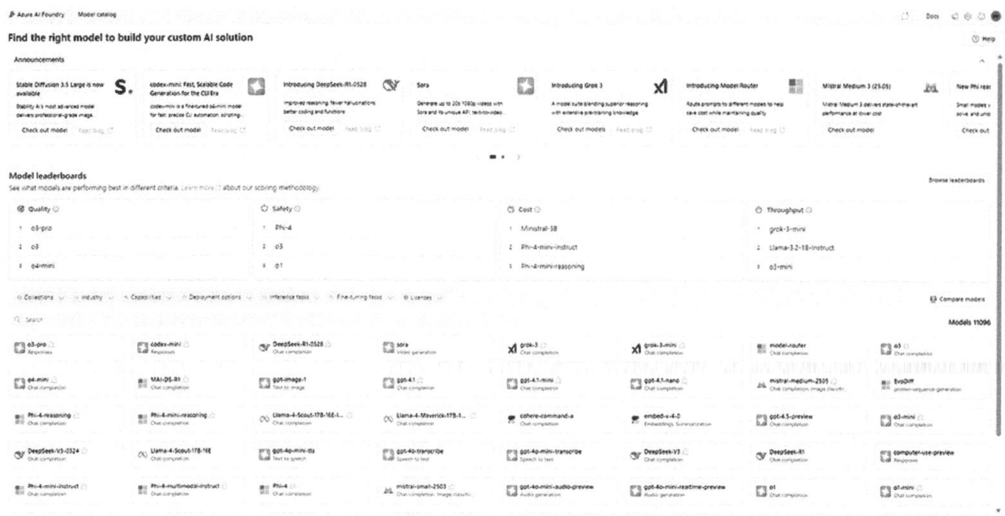

Figure 3.3: *Azure AI Foundry Model Catalog*

To select the most appropriate model for a given use case, it is important to consider criteria such as:

- **Task Type**: This includes text generation, code generation, images, multimodality, or embeddings.
- **Performance and Latency**: OME models are optimized with *provisioned throughput* (PTU) capabilities for intensive and consistent workloads.
- **Data Residency**: Deployment can be global, regional, or data-zone specific, depending on latency or residency regulations.
- **Support and Service-Level Agreements (SLAs)**: Official Microsoft models typically include robust SLAs and guaranteed support.
- **Cost**: Here, you must consider the billing scheme (tokens + throughput, token-based, or compute hours).

Azure AI Foundry provides three deployment modes:

1. **Standard (Foundry resources):** Models are deployed directly on Foundry resources, with global, regional, or data-zone options and scalable performance configurations (Standard/PTU). This is the most comprehensive mode, offering private networks and Content Filtering capability.
2. **Serverless API:** Ideal for variable workloads, the platform manages the infrastructure and charges only for token usage. Compatible with catalog models and allows for network restrictions using private endpoints.

3. **Managed Compute:** Designed for open-source, custom, or specialized models. Requires a user-managed compute quota and allows deep control over the execution environment.

All these three modes offer private networking via VNet, traffic control, and optional content filtering. While the standard deployment is the most convenient, the other options provide flexibility depending on the scenario.

Expansion of the Model Ecosystem Announced at Microsoft Ignite 2025

During **Microsoft Ignite in November 2025**, Microsoft revealed a major evolution of the model ecosystem within Azure AI Foundry, positioning the platform as one of the most comprehensive and unified environments for enterprise-grade generative AI. While the catalog had already provided access to more than 1,900 models earlier in the year, Ignite marked a turning point: Microsoft officially expanded the Foundry catalog to include over 11,000 models, sourced from a wide and diverse set of providers. This includes advanced models from **Microsoft, OpenAI, xAI, Anthropic, DeepSeek, Mistral, Meta, Cohere, Stability AI, Hugging Face**, and others, as well as highly specialized open-source architectures and emerging community-driven innovations.

This expansion reflects a broader strategic shift: Foundry is no longer just a model catalog, but rather, a unified AI platform integrating agents, models, flows, governance, orchestration, and deployment under a single experience. Microsoft emphasized that future innovation–including new model families, enterprise-tuned variants, and multi-agent intelligence frameworks–will be delivered exclusively through the modern Foundry portal, now considered the authoritative entry point for AI development in the Microsoft ecosystem.

Another key highlight from the Ignite announcements was the incorporation of new classes of models designed for domain-specialized reasoning, advanced code generation, multimodal processing, and compact high-efficiency inference. These additions provide organizations with a flexible spectrum of capabilities, ranging from high-performance Large Language Models to lightweight, cost-optimized architectures suited for real-time scenarios or edge-based workloads.

With this broadened model ecosystem, Foundry enables a new level of granularity when selecting the right architecture for each use case. Developers can now differentiate models not only by performance, cost, and modality, but also by deployment region, compliance constraints, tuning capabilities, inference patterns, and multi-agent compatibility. This positions Azure AI Foundry as a leading platform for constructing robust, scalable, and secure generative AI solutions across industries such as finance, healthcare, manufacturing, retail, and public sector environments.

Ultimately, the Ignite 2025 updates reinforce the long-term vision of Microsoft: a unified, extensible, and enterprise-ready platform where organizations can adopt, govern, optimize, and deploy AI at scale with unprecedented flexibility. The dramatic expansion of the model catalog, combined with the architectural modernization announced throughout 2025, marks an inflection point in the evolution of Microsoft Foundry and sets a new standard for generative AI ecosystems worldwide.

Model Lifecycle Management

Azure AI Foundry delivers a comprehensive approach to generative model lifecycle management, covering everything from pre-deployment evaluation to production monitoring. Before a model goes live, teams can use the **Evaluation SDK** to conduct rigorous evaluations within the Foundry environment. These evaluations analyze metrics such as accuracy, consistency, safety, and responsibility, ensuring that the model meets the standards of the project and requirements before deployment.

Versioning and model retirement are handled in a structured manner. Models can go through various states–such *as Legacy*, *Deprecated*, and eventually *Retired*–throughout their lifecycle. Azure AI Foundry proactively notifies users when a model is approaching retirement, enabling teams to plan migration to newer versions and minimize disruption to production systems.

When performing a model update, it is essential to review and adjust not only the model itself but also all dependent components, such as prompt configurations, flow logic, and grounding sources. This approach helps prevent regressions and ensures operational continuity.

After deployment, the platform enables post-production monitoring through native dashboards and telemetry. Teams can track model usage, analyze response quality, detect drift, and monitor for potential bias, following best practices in MLOps and ModelOps. Continuous monitoring maintains high quality standards, identifies areas for improvement, and enables proactive response to incidents or data changes.

Overall, lifecycle management in Azure AI Foundry is designed to provide transparency, control, and reliability, supporting the ongoing maintenance and evolution of generative AI solutions over time.

Implementation of Prompt Flows and Prompt Templates

Azure AI Foundry includes the Prompt Flow tool, designed to make building prompt flows both visually and efficiently. This tool allows you to construct, test, refine, and deploy complex AI flows within a unified environment–ideal for experimental development and continuous production.

Developing a prompt flow follows a structured cycle:

1. **Initialization**: Define the use case and load sample data; create the visual flow using a DAG-style canvas, which includes tools such as LLMs, prompts, Python code, index searches, and security filters.

2. **Iteration and Refinement**: Run test flows, compare prompt variants, and adjust conditional logic and tools (for example, selecting document ranges or adding security features). The environment allows you to compare versions and measure performance before deployment.

3. **Evaluation**: Use dedicated evaluation flows to measure metrics such as coherence, accuracy, safety, and efficiency–ensuring quality before publishing the flow to production.

4. **Deployment**: Only **hub-based** projects support deployment as an online endpoint, turning the prompt flow into a real-time REST service. The deployment option is enabled in the portal with a wizard that lets you select endpoint parameters, authentication mode, and network configuration–including telemetry for post-deployment monitoring.

5. To execute a prompt flow, it is essential to start a **`computesession`**: A managed environment with a Python runtime, integrated LLM tools, defined dependencies (requirements.txt), and support for custom code. These sessions can be serverless or instance-based, and must be configured with managed identities that have permissions to access resources such as Storage or ACR.

6. It is also important to document the use of **prompt templates** with Jinja, which enables conditional logic and reuse of enriched variables (for example, dynamic system messages). This greatly simplifies maintenance, customization, and adaptability to different interaction contexts.

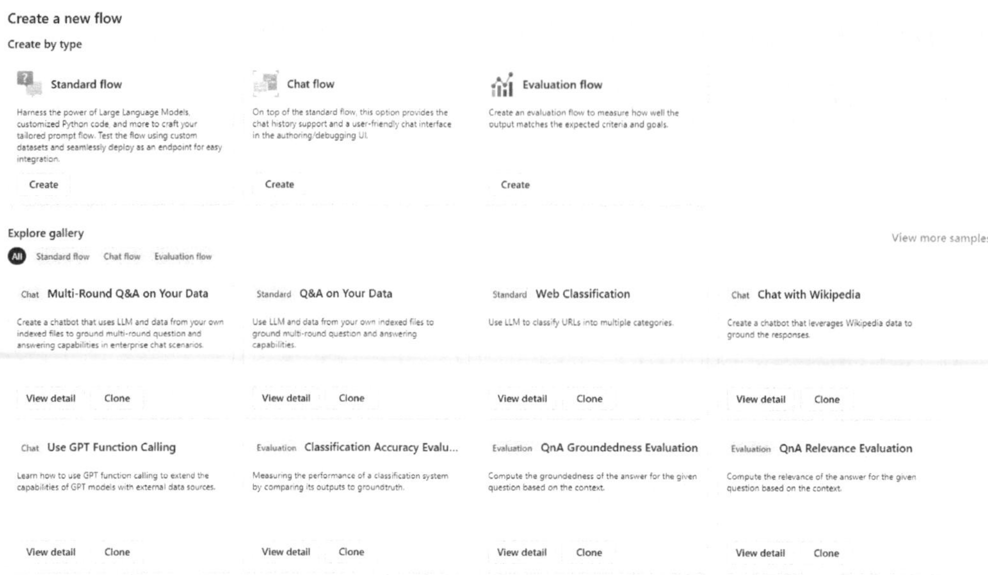

Figure 3.4: *Azure AI Foundry Prompt Flow – Flow Types*

The Prompt Flow functionality in Azure AI Foundry—including the creation, execution, and deployment of prompt - flows as online endpoints is only available in **hub-based** projects. Currently, Foundry projects do not support the execution or publishing of Prompt Flow as services.

Data Grounding and Retrieval-Augmented Generation (RAG)

The **Retrieval Augmented Generation (RAG)** technique is a modern approach that increases the accuracy and relevance of generative models by allowing them to ground their responses in up-to-date, domain-specific corporate information. Unlike simply extending the internal context of the model (known as a *large context window*), RAG dynamically connects the model to a live knowledge base, thereby surpassing the limits of pre-training and improving the auditability of responses.

RAG works through four phases: ingestion, retrieval, augmentation, and generation. First, documents or databases relevant to the organization are split into fragments ("chunking"), and each fragment is transformed into a semantic vector using embedding models. These vectors are stored in a **vector database**—a technology specialized for large-scale semantic searches—that enables highly efficient retrieval of the most relevant fragments for any given query.

The typical workflow is as follows: when a user asks a question, the system searches the vector database for the most semantically similar fragments, inserts them into the prompt, and the generative model uses this context to produce a response that is precise and aligned with the organizational data. This architecture minimizes misinformation errors (hallucinations) and enables the construction of auditable, secure solutions with document-level traceability.

While modern models allow expanded *context windows* of multiple tokens, the RAG approach remains essential: using efficient, relevant context–tailored to the specific query–reduces computational costs and improves accuracy, even for the latest generation models.

RAG Implementation from the Azure AI Foundry Chat Playground

Azure AI Foundry makes it easy to adopt RAG through a guided, visual experience directly within the **Chat Playground**.

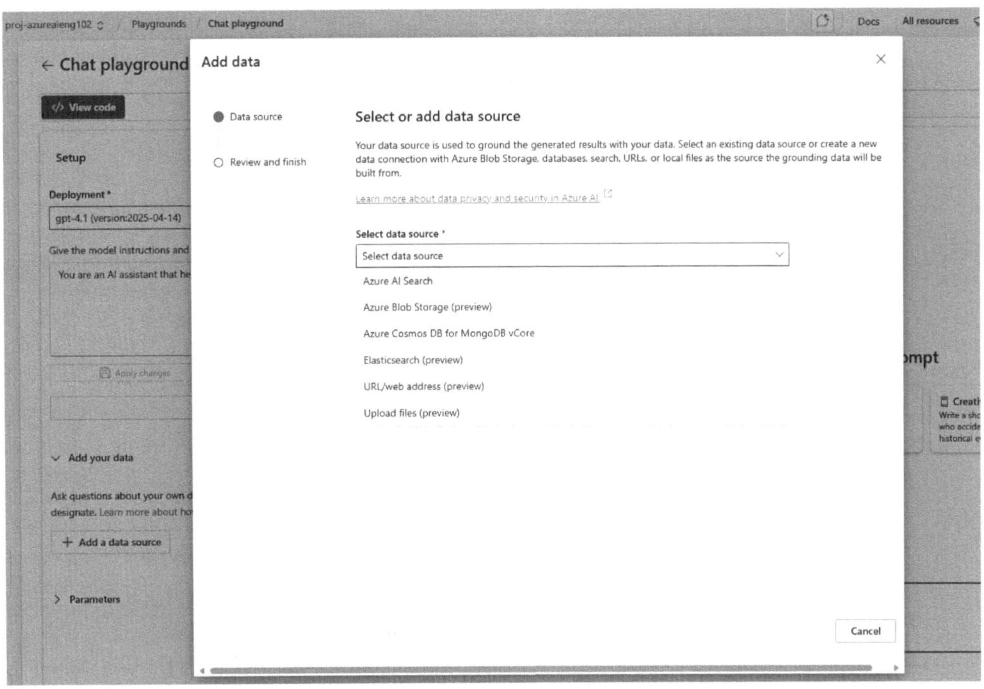

***Figure 3.5**: Add a "New Data Source" Button in the Chat Playground*

1. **Data Indexing**: From the Chat Playground, users can select "**`+ Add a new data source`**" to upload files, folders, or connect to data sources such as Azure Blob Storage. The system automatically performs *chunking* on the content, applies semantic embeddings (for example, text-embedding-3-large), and creates a

vector index in Azure AI Search—all fully integrated and without the need for coding.

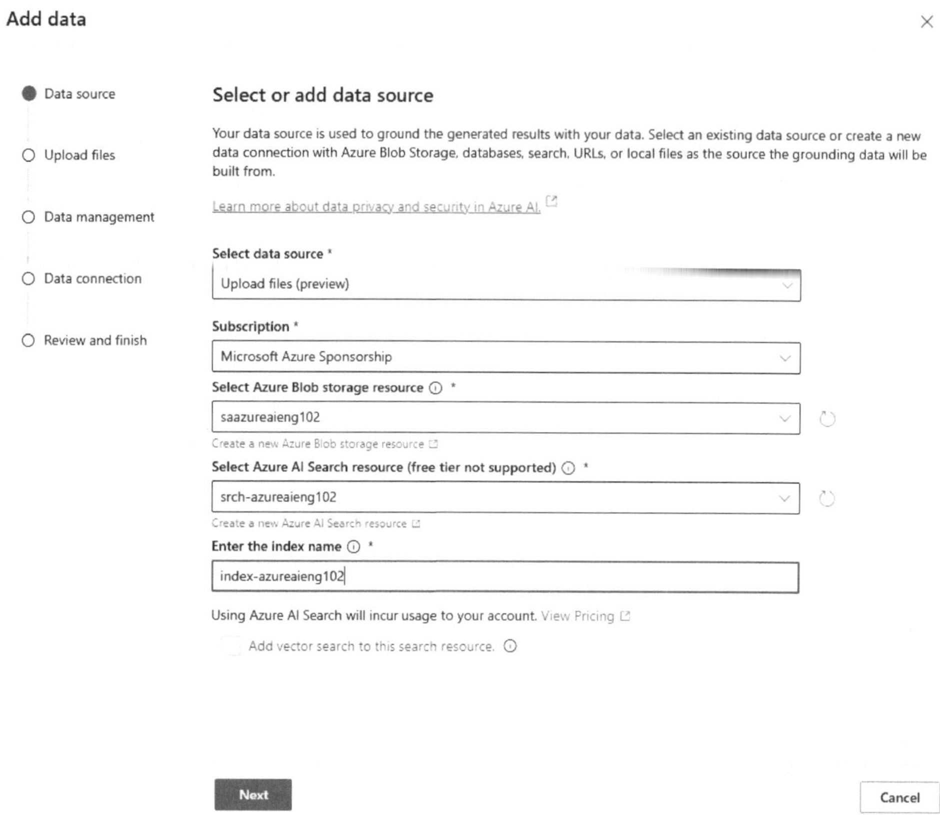

Figure 3.6: *Playground – Add a New Data Source– Create Index*

2. **Configuration and Testing**: Once the index is created, it is configured as the data source for the conversational session. Users can ask questions and observe how the model grounds its responses by displaying the retrieved fragments. This transparency allows for validation of the relevance and quality of the grounding before deploying the solution to production.

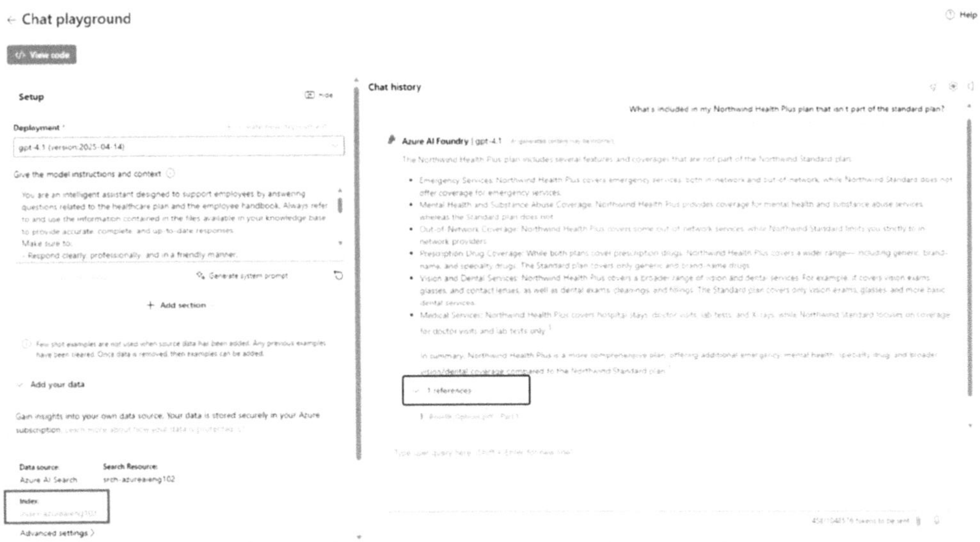

Figure 3.7: *Index Creation and Data Grounding in Azure AI Foundry - Chat Playground*

3. **Maintenance and Updation**: The portal allows for manual re-indexing when there are changes in the data, or scheduling automatic updates using Azure AI Search indexers. This ensures that generated responses are always based on the most up-to-date information.

Best Practices for RAG in Azure AI Foundry

- Adjust the chunk size (256, 512, 1024, or 1536) according to the complexity of your documents and the allowed prompt length.
- Prefer hybrid searches (vector and semantic) to achieve better results for complex queries.
- Conduct frequent tests in the Chat Playground and use the Evaluation SDK to measure grounding and coherence before deploying the solution.
- Maintain a periodic index update strategy to reflect any changes in the source data.

Model Evaluation and Integration with Azure AI Foundry SDK

In the context of enterprise generative solutions, evaluation is not a one-time process but rather, a continuous cycle of measurement, comparison, correction, and improvement. A generative model may perform well initially, but data, usage patterns, and business needs are constantly evolving. For this reason, Azure AI Foundry provides comprehensive mechanisms to ensure models remain aligned with quality, reliability, and compliance objectives throughout their entire lifecycle.

Pre-Deployment Evaluation: Importance and Execution Approach

Before deploying a generative model into production, it is crucial to verify that it meets both technical and business requirements. In Azure AI Foundry, this process can be performed directly from the portal, which is designed to guide users—even those without a data science background.

The **Evaluation Wizard** allows you to select the model you want to test, upload a test dataset in CSV or JSONL format, and choose from a range of evaluation metrics. These metrics cover key aspects:

- **Relevance**: Is the generated response pertinent to the question or context?
- **Groundedness**: Is the response actually based on the information provided, or is the model simply "*hallucinating*" an answer?
- **Coherence and fluency**: Is the generated text logical, clear, and natural for a user?
- **Safety and compliance**: Does the model avoid inappropriate language, bias, or the exposure of sensitive information?
- **Traditional automated metrics: `BLEU`, `ROUGE`, `F1`, `METEOR`**—useful for tasks like translation, summarization, or classification.

This process can be further customized by adding manual evaluations: team members or business experts can review and score each response, and can provide qualitative feedback. This is especially useful when human understanding of context exceeds the capability of automated metrics or when a subjective criterion is required (for example, tone, creativity, cultural appropriateness, and the like).

Upon completion, the portal provides clear, visual dashboards: score histograms, success rates, outliers, and a history of all evaluations. This material is highly valuable for presenting results to non-technical stakeholders and for informing business decisions regarding model deployment or retraining.

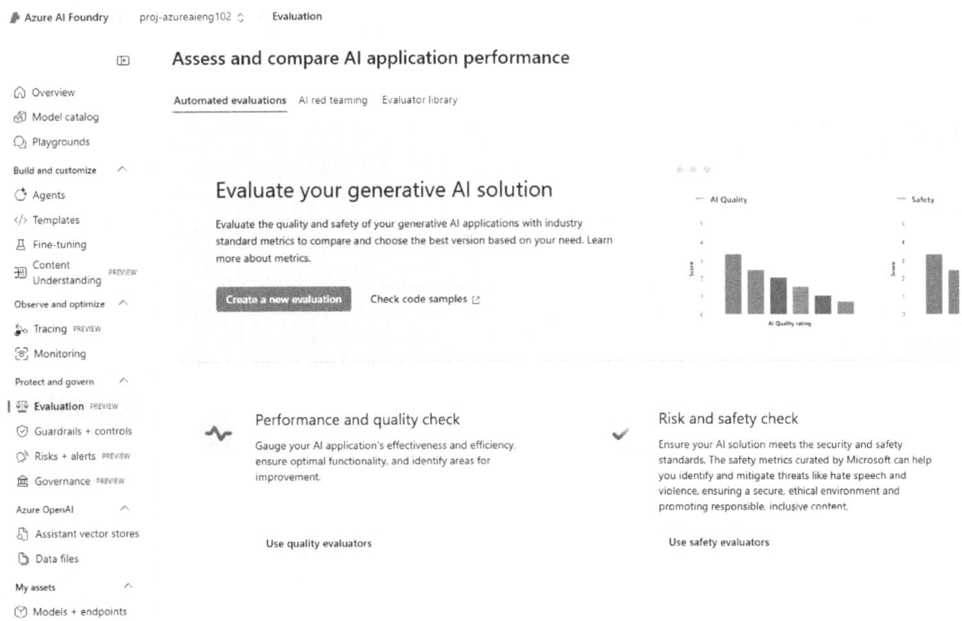

Figure 3.8: *Evaluation in Azure AI Foundry*

Automated and Continuous Evaluation: Ensuring Quality at Scale

As projects grow and data volumes increase, performing manual evaluations for every change becomes impractical. This is where the **Azure AI Evaluation SDK** comes into play, enabling automated evaluation with Python scripts integrated into CI/CD pipelines.

With the SDK, you can:

- Run batch evaluations on hundreds or thousands of examples.
- Define evaluators for different aspects (relevance, groundedness, safety, and the like).
- Schedule adversarial simulations and robustness tests to identify potential failure points before deployment.
- Export detailed results (for example, in CSV, JSON, or directly to the portal), making it easy to perform historical comparisons or external audits.

This is crucial for organizations that require traceability and reproducibility in their AI processes, or that must comply with governance regulations and controls over automated decision models.

For example, local evaluation can be performed as follows:

```
from azure.ai.evaluation import RelevanceEvaluator
# Model configuration (e.g., Azure OpenAI endpoint and deployment)
model_config = {...}
evaluator = RelevanceEvaluator(model_config)
# Evaluate relevance for a simple query-response pair
score = evaluator(query="What is the capital of Argentina?",
response="Buenos Aires.")
print(score)
```

For large-scale evaluations, integration with pipelines and cloud services enables full automation of the process from uploading datasets to publishing results and triggering automatic alerts in case of anomalies.

Interpreting and Analyzing Results: Beyond the Score

Evaluating a model is not just about obtaining a numeric "*score*." The real value lies in analyzing patterns, identifying trends, and discovering areas for improvement. The Azure AI Foundry portal allows you to:

- **Compare versions**: Did a prompt change improve relevance but affect fluency? Did a model update reduce grounding errors but introduce more vague responses?
- **Identify outliers**: Examples with very low scores can indicate comprehension failures, biases in the dataset, or gaps not covered during training.
- **Audit and compliance**: In regulated environments, being able to show the complete history of evaluations, along with comments and analyses, is essential for passing audits and defending decisions to regulators or customers.

The dashboards in the portal offer visualizations that allow non-technical users to get involved and contribute to the improvement cycle.

Observability, Monitoring, and Continuous Improvement in Production

The quality cycle does not end at deployment. Azure AI Foundry integrates advanced observability so that teams can continuously monitor model behavior in real-world usage. This includes:

- **Real-time metrics**: Token consumption, latency, grounding rate, content safety, and more.

- **Automatic alerts**: Configurable to detect anomalies, performance drops, or generation of sensitive content.
- **Continuous evaluation**: You can schedule recurring evaluations that scan the performance and safety of the model in production, applying both automated metrics and selected samples for manual review. This enables the detection and correction of regressions, model drift, or the emergence of new risks without waiting for serious incidents.

This approach ensures that models are not only strong at deployment but also maintain performance and alignment with business objectives throughout their entire lifecycle.

Recommendations and Best Practices

- **Representative dataset design**: Evaluation quality depends on data representativeness. Create datasets that reflect real use cases, include multi-turn conversations, and account for variations in language and tone. Include **ground truth** where possible to assess similarity and accuracy metrics.
- **Appropriate metric selection**: Use evaluators aligned with business objectives. For RAG applications, prioritize relevance and groundedness metrics. For customer support chatbots, fluency and coherence are essential. For sensitive applications, integrate safety evaluators.
- **Result interpretation**: Do not rely solely on numeric scores. Review the reason fields and explanations generated by evaluators; these provide insights on how to improve the model or prompt.
- **Iteration and improvement**: If evaluations reveal a gap between expected and actual quality, adjust the prompt, context, or the evaluator itself. Metrics are guides for iteration; the goal is not a perfect score, but achieving the required level of quality and safety.
- **Documentation and transparency**: It records all the steps, metrics, and decisions within the project. Transparency facilitates audits, reproducibility, and compliance with ethical and responsibility standards.

Following is an example of a Complete Evaluation Pipeline in Python:

```
import os
from azure.identity import DefaultAzureCredential
from azure.ai.projects import AIProjectClient
from azure.ai.projects.models import Evaluation, InputDataset
# Create the project client using the project endpoint and
default credentials
project_client = AIProjectClient(
    endpoint=os.environ["PROJECT_ENDPOINT"],
    credential=DefaultAzureCredential(),
```

```
)
# Upload dataset
dataset_id = project_client.datasets.upload_file(
    file_path="testset.jsonl",
    display_name="TestSet July",
    version="v1"
)
# Define evaluators configuration (example for relevance and safety)
evaluators = [
    {
        "evaluator_id": "RelevanceEvaluator",
        "input_mapping": {"query": "query", "response": "response"}
    },
    {
        "evaluator_id": "SafetyEvaluator",
        "input_mapping": {"response": "response"}
    }
]
evaluation = Evaluation(
    display_name="Cloud Evaluation",
    description="Relevance and safety test",
    data=InputDataset(id=dataset_id),
    evaluators=evaluators,
)
response = project_client.evaluations.create(
    evaluation,
    headers={
        "model-endpoint": os.environ["MODEL_ENDPOINT"],
        "api-key": os.environ["MODEL_API_KEY"],
    },
)
print("Evaluation submitted:", response.name, "Status:",
response.status)
```

In summary, evaluation in Azure AI Foundry is a comprehensive process that supports the model from the lab to production—and beyond. Through the combination of automated tools, manual evaluations, visual dashboards, and observability features, organizations can build and maintain generative AI systems that are aligned with their quality and business objectives, and are prepared to respond to the dynamic challenges of current enterprise environment.

Provisioning and Implementation with Azure OpenAI Service

Resource Setup: Options for Using Azure OpenAI Models in Azure AI Foundry

There are three ways to access Azure OpenAI models within Azure AI Foundry, each with different configuration and control implications:

1. **Create a Standalone Azure OpenAI Service Resource**

   From the Azure portal, CLI, or ARM templates, you can create an independent Azure OpenAI resource. Here, you configure the subscription, resource group, region, Standard (S0) plan, and network connections (public access, selected subnets, or private endpoints) to ensure secure enterprise environments. Once the resource is created, you obtain the required endpoint and keys from the *Keys and Endpoint* section.

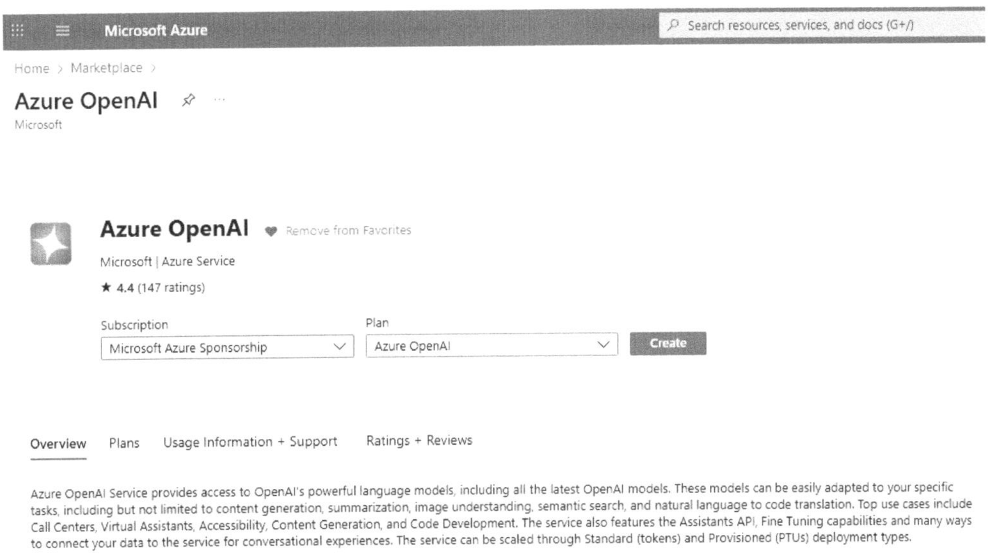

Figure 3.9: *Create Azure OpenAI Resource – Azure Marketplace*

2. **Directly Use a Multi-Service AI Foundry Resource**

   When you create an Azure AI Foundry resource (API Kind: AIServices), you are also creating a multi-service environment that provides immediate access to Azure OpenAI models–without the need to deploy an additional resource. This multi-service resource already includes the endpoint for inference with models such as GPT-4o or GPT-4.1, all managed from within the same Foundry container. This is the recommended option for generative projects that need to be integrated with other capabilities, such as agents, evaluations, and unified governance.

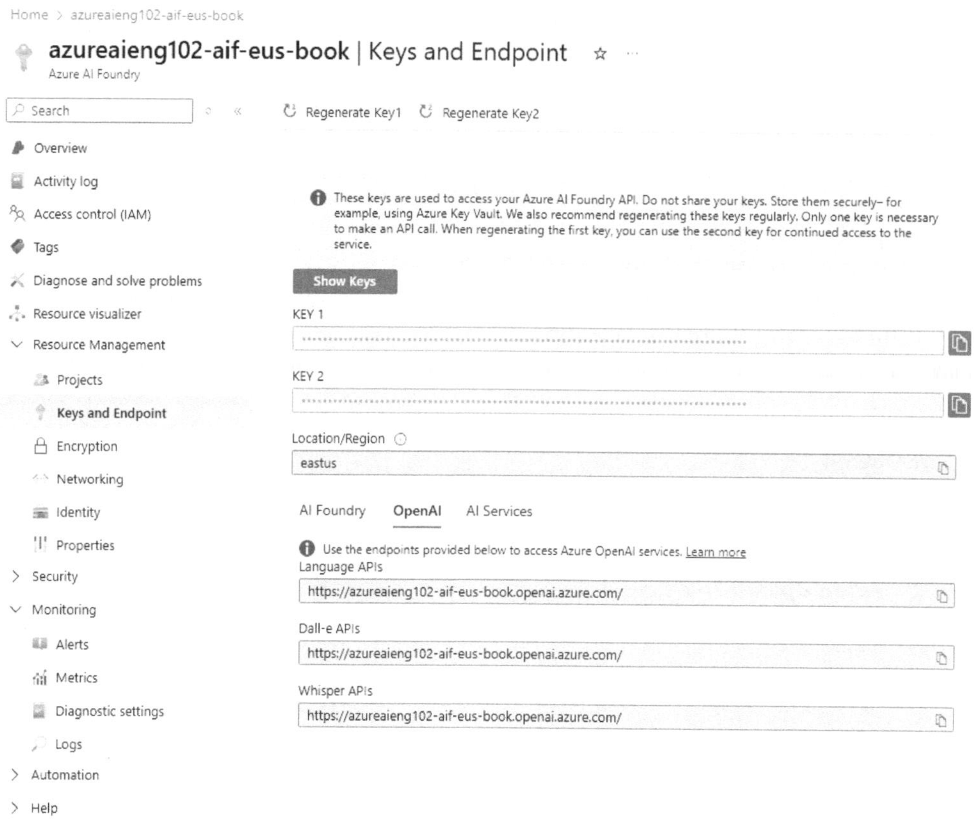

Figure 3.10: *Azure AI Foundry Service - Type AIServices - Multi-Service - OpenAI*

3. **Connect an Existing Azure OpenAI Resource**

   If you already have a previously created Azure OpenAI resource, you can link it from the Foundry portal. Within **`Management Center`** → **`Connected resources`** (New connection), select the connection type "**`Azure OpenAI`**" and add the resource. This way, the external resource is integrated into the model catalog of your project, allowing you to deploy and consume its models directly from the Foundry interface.

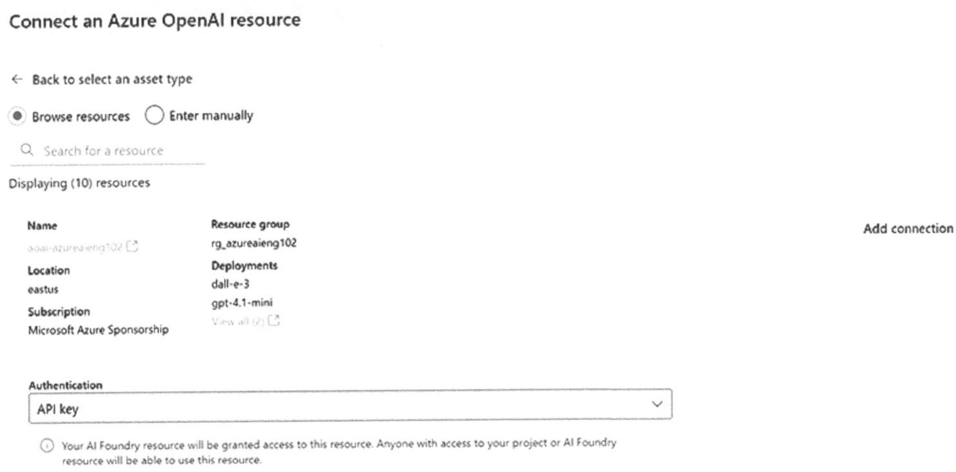

Figure 3.11: *Azure AI Foundry – Connect an Azure OpenAI Resource*

Model Deployment: Reasoning, Language, Audio, Embeddings, Image, and Video

Once your Azure OpenAI resource is available—whether as a standalone resource, multi-service Foundry, or a connected resource—you can deploy an increasingly wide range of models from the Azure AI Foundry Model Catalog. The following are the main model families, recent versions, and their recommended applications.

Reasoning Models (o-series)

The o-series models are specifically designed for deep reasoning tasks and cognitive complexity. These models have been trained to excel in mathematical analysis, technical problem-solving, structured logic, and advanced code generation.

- **o1-preview, o1-mini, o1:** The early versions focused on step-by-step reasoning, performing well on STEM exams, logic, and technical analysis.
- **o3-mini, o3, o3-pro:** These are the successors that improve accuracy, efficiency, and visual capabilities. o3-mini provides an optimal balance of cost and latency; o3 adds visual reasoning for tasks requiring diagram or image interpretation; and, o3-pro is intended for critical applications where accuracy is the top priority.
- **o4-mini:** This is the fourth-generation model designed for productive efficiency, external tool usage, and integrated visual and textual reasoning. It

is used in advanced enterprise workflows, scientific research, and educational applications.

- **codex-mini:** It is an o-series variant optimized for code generation, ideal for development flows, scripting, and automation of technical tasks with extended context.

These models enable, for example, the automation of complex mathematical problem solving, the creation of expert programming or data analysis assistants, the drafting of technically rigorous reports, and the design of advanced support systems in fields such as law, engineering, or consulting.

GPT-4o Language and Multimodal Models

The GPT-4o (Omni) series represents the multimodal evolution of the generative models of OpenAI. These models accept text, image, and audio inputs, and can generate equally rich responses in both format and content.

- **GPT-4o:** It is available in successive versions (for example, 2024-05-13, 2024-08-06, 2024-11-20), each introducing improvements in reasoning capability, multimodal quality, structured outputs, and handling of long contexts (up to 128K tokens).
- **GPT-4o-mini:** It is a lighter, more cost-effective alternative, maintaining multimodal capability and speed. It is recommended for high-traffic conversational agents or tasks where efficiency is critical.

These models are the ideal foundation for complex virtual assistants, multimedia chatbots, multichannel technical support solutions, and creative applications that require integration of text, voice, and image.

GPT-4.1 y GPT-4.5 Models

- **GPT-4.1, GPT-4.1-mini and GPT-4.1-nano:** Released in April 2025, these models offer context windows of up to one million tokens, significantly improving the performance on coding tasks (up to 21% better than GPT-4o), and cost reductions that are up to 80% per query.
- **GPT-4.5 (Orion):** It is a general-purpose model released in February 2025 as a preview, with enhanced writing abilities, expanded knowledge, and a lower hallucination rate compared to GPT-4o. Although initially only available in preview—and soon to be deprecated (retired July 2025)—it remains relevant as a bridge between GPT-4o and the o4 line.

These models are ideal for writing tasks, practical problem-solving, agent workflows, and environments where a deep understanding of context with high efficiency is required.

Audio and Real-Time Conversation Models

Advancements in audio models enable Azure OpenAI to offer next-generation conversational solutions:

- **gpt-4o-audio-preview:** It processes voice input and output, and performs automatic translation. It can further be integrated into voice assistants, transcription tools, or real-time translation systems.
- **Gpt-4o-realtime-preview and gpt-4o-mini-realtime-preview:** Specifically optimized for low-latency scenarios, these ideal for interactive kiosks, automated call centers, or embedded assistants in devices that require immediate voice responses.
- **gpt-4o-mini-tts and gpt-4o-transcribe:** These are models dedicated to text-to-speech and speech-to-text conversion, and are capable of operating with high accuracy in noisy environments and across multiplc languages.

These capabilities pave the way for voice-based customer service systems, intelligent personal assistants, accessibility applications, and immersive educational platforms.

Embedding Models

Azure OpenAI offers models such as text-embedding-ada-002, text-embedding-3-small, and text-embedding-3-large, which transform text into high-quality semantic vectors. These vectors are essential for:

- Building semantic search engines that find relevant information even when it does not literally matches the query of the user.
- Recommendation and personalization systems.
- Implementing RAG (Retrieval-Augmented Generation) architectures, where embeddings feed vector indexes used by generative models for grounding and contextualization.

Typical applications include corporate chatbots based on internal documentation, automatic analysis and clustering of large volumes of text, and search engines with deep semantic understanding.

Model-Router

The **model-router** is a specialized model that acts as an intelligent controller, selecting the most appropriate model for each prompt according to criteria such as cost, complexity, and task type. It is packaged as a single deployment endpoint, without the need to manually manage the underlying models.

Its initial version includes **GPT 4.1**, **GPT 4.1-mini**, **GPT 4.1-nano**, and **o4-mini** as underlying models. Selecting "*auto-update*" allows the underlying set to update automatically as new versions become available.

This approach is especially useful in enterprise environments where the goal is to optimize performance and costs without the need to code selection logic between models.

Image and Video Models

- **GPT-image-1**: This is the reference model for image generation and editing in Azure OpenAI, progressively replacing DALL·E 3. It enables image creation from textual descriptions, editing specific parts (inpainting), rendering text within images, and performing advanced transformations. It is ideal for creative workflows, automatic generation of visual assets, and enhancement of digital content.
- **Sora**: In preview, Sora enables the generation of short video clips from natural language descriptions. It supports different aspect ratios and resolutions, and is particularly useful for digital marketing, content creation for social media, rapid animation of ideas, and audiovisual prototyping.

Version and Availability Considerations

Each model described may have multiple versions (usually identified by dates or suffixes such as preview, mini, pro, and the like.), which vary in performance, features, and level of access (GA or Preview). Additionally, the availability of each model and version may vary depending on the selected Azure region, with support expanding progressively as the service evolves. It is always recommended to review the current catalog in Azure AI Foundry and consult release notes and official documentation to confirm compatibility, restrictions, and deployment of best practices at the implementation time.

Costs and Scalability

Deploying generative solutions with Azure OpenAI Service requires not only a clear understanding of models and technical resources, but also a solid cost control and scalability strategy. The platform offers various billing schemes and tools to ensure that both performance and budget are aligned with business objectives.

Pricing Models in Azure OpenAI Service

There are three main billing approaches for model consumption in Azure OpenAI:

- **Standard (On Demand)**: The charges are based on the number of tokens processed (input + output). This model is especially flexible, allowing you to scale up or down according to actual demand, making it ideal for prototypes, testing, or applications with unpredictable usage patterns.

- **Provisioned Throughput Units (PTUs)**: It allows you to reserve dedicated processing capacity through PTUs. This guarantees consistent availability and latency, which is essential for mission-critical or enterprise applications. Costs can be optimized by purchasing monthly or annual reservations, which offer significant discounts compared to hourly rates.
- **Batch**: It enables large-scale tasks to be executed asynchronously, with significantly reduced pricing compared to real-time processing. Responses may take up to 24 hours, making this option ideal for massive jobs that do not require immediacy, such as analyzing large volumes of text, generating reports, or training auxiliary models.

Optimal Selection by Scenario

Scenario	**Recommended Pricing Model**	**Main Benefit**
Prototypes or unpredictable loads	Standard (On Demand)	Flexibility and pay-as-you-go
Stable, mission-critical production	Provisioned Throughput (PTU)	Predictable performance and costs
Large-scale, non-urgent processing	Batch	Cost savings on extensive workloads

Table 3.4: *Consumption of Models in Azure OpenAI – Azure AI Foundry*

Scalability Considerations and Best Practices

- **PTU Management and Reservation**: PTUs (Provisioned Throughput Units) define your reserved processing capacity. You can reserve them hourly, monthly, or annually. For consistent workloads, it is recommended to use monthly or annual reservations to take advantage of significant discounts and ensure the necessary capacity for your key applications.
- **Usage Monitoring and Adjustment**: Azure dashboards are used to monitor actual token consumption, PTU utilization, and latency. If you notice that your typical PTU reservation exceeds your actual needs, reduce capacity to optimize costs.
- **Access Control and Cost Segmentation**: Service management is centralized in a single subscription and tools like Azure API Management or Azure Gateway GenAI are used to define quotas, control access, and assign costs by team or application. Apply tagging policies and RBAC to segment and accurately report costs.

- **Proactive Quota Management**: Set Token-Per-Minute (TPM) and Requests-Per-Minute (RPM) limits for each deployment. This helps prevent misuse or unexpected usage spikes and facilitates quota increase planning as new demands arise.
- **Regular Resource Review**: Regular audits of your deployments and active resources are conducted. Remove any that are not in use to avoid unnecessary costs and keep your environment optimized.
- **Strategic Use of the Batch Model**: Use this mode for intensive generation, analysis, or offline processing jobs. Discounts can reach up to 50% compared to Standard mode, allowing you to leverage resources outside of peak hours.

Recommendations for Efficient Scaling

Regularly evaluate your usage profile and adjust pricing models as workloads and business requirements change. Consider combining Standard and PTU to balance flexibility and savings; for example, you might use PTU for base demand and Standard to cover occasional peaks. Make use of alerts and automated reports to detect consumption anomalies or budget deviations. Stay up to date with new pricing updates, model availability, and supported regions, as the Azure OpenAI ecosystem evolves rapidly.

Azure OpenAI Service enables you to optimize cost-effectiveness based on your use case, adapting resources and pricing as your solution scales from prototype to large-scale production. Active and strategic management of reservations, quotas, and monitoring ensures you control spending, maximize efficiency, and maintain operational quality in any enterprise environment.

Multimodal Capabilities and Application Integration

Multimodal models expand the capabilities of generative AI beyond text, enabling scenarios that combine language, images, and audio in a single workflow. In Azure AI Foundry, these capabilities can be explored directly in the Playground and then integrated into real-world applications through the SDK or REST API. To ensure reliable and consistent results, it is important to understand the main configuration options, prompt design practices, and integration patterns that support both experimentation and production readiness.

Parameters and Initial Configuration in the Azure AI Foundry – Azure OpenAI Playground

Before you start sending prompts to generate text, code, or images, it is essential to understand the main parameters and controls available in the Azure OpenAI Playground. This will not only help you make the most of the capabilities of the model, but also allow you to tailor its behavior and responses to your specific needs.

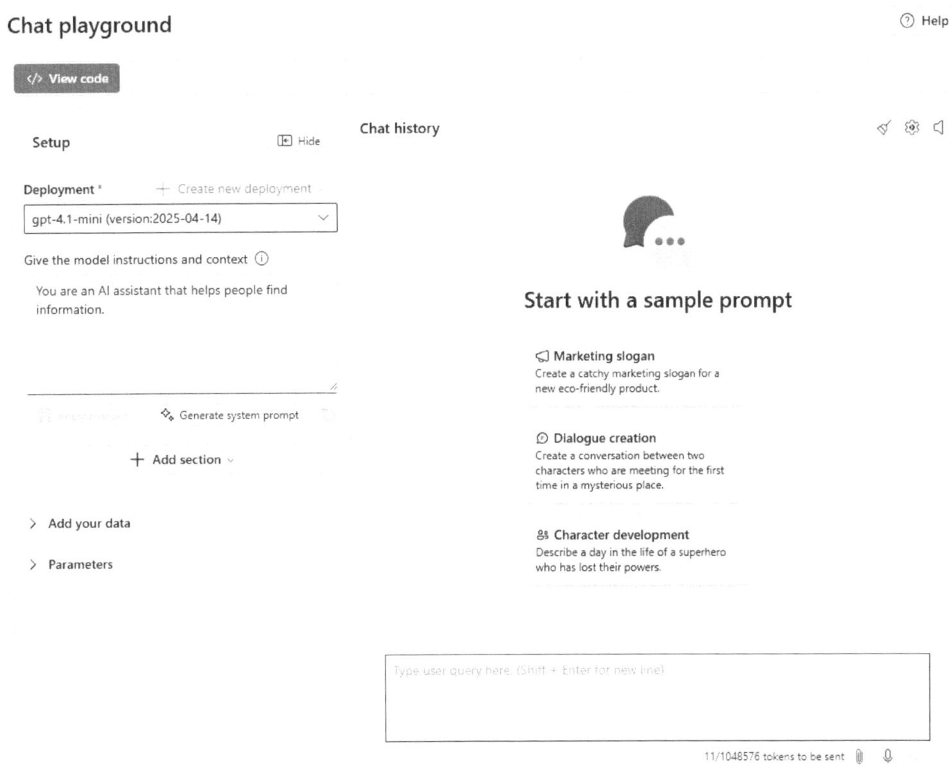

Figure 3.12: *Azure AI Foundry – Chat Playground Azure OpenAI*

System Instructions and Context

The first important section in the Playground is "**Give the model instructions and context**." Here you define how you want the model to behave throughout the session:

- **System message:** Allows you to set the role, tone, and general rules. For example: "*You are an AI assistant that helps people find information.*" If this field is left empty, the model will still respond, but without explicit context. It is recommended to use it to get results aligned with your specific use case.

Practical tip: The Playground includes a "**Generate system prompt**" option. By clicking this button, the AI can help you draft an appropriate system message based on your context or task type. This is very useful if you are not sure how to express instructions to the model, as you can use the automatic suggestions as a starting point and then customize them as needed.

- **Message roles:**
    - `system`: Provides initial context and rules
    - `user`: User input (your prompt)
    - `assistant`: The response generated by the model

This is especially important when working with the API, since you must manually construct the message array and clearly define the initial context using the system role.

Main Parameters

Just below the instructions and context section, you'll find controls that let you adjust the behavior of the model. The most relevant parameters are:

- **Past Messages Included**: It controls how many previous chat messages are included as context in each request. Higher value helps maintain longer, more coherent conversations, though it may consume more tokens.
- **Max Completion Tokens (Maximum Length)**: It sets the maximum number of tokens (words or fragments) the model can generate in its response, making it useful for limiting the length of answers.
- **Temperature**: It adjusts levels of creativity and randomness in the response: lower values (such as 0.1) produce more deterministic, precise answers–ideal for technical tasks, while higher values (such as 0.8 to 1) lead to more varied and creative outputs, which are great for brainstorming or creative writing.
- **Top-p (Nucleus sampling)**: It restricts the set of possible words to those with a cumulative probability equal to or greater than the top-p value; lower values yield conservative responses, while higher values allow for more diversity.
- **Stop sequences**: It lets you define specific text strings that, when generated, automatically stop the response, making them useful for delimiting output format or preventing the model from generating beyond what is required.
- **Frequency penalty**: It discourages repetition to reduce redundancy.
- **Presence penalty**: It penalizes the already mentioned words to encourage greater variety in the responses.

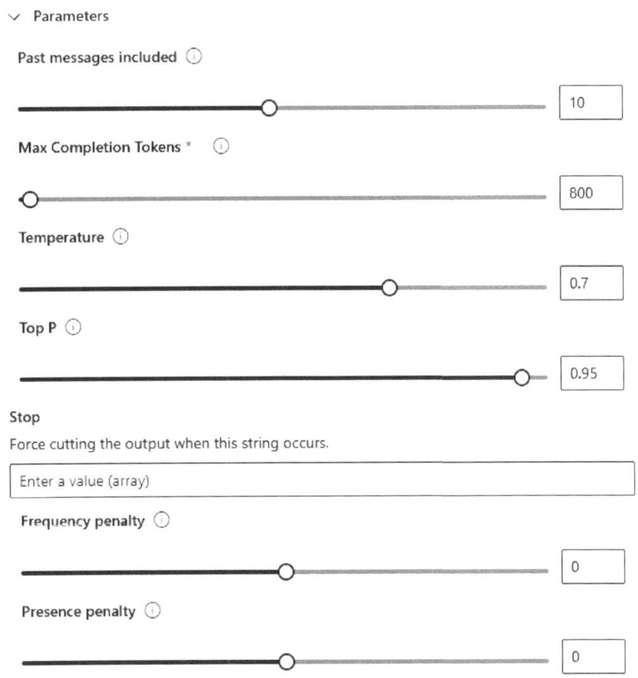

Figure 3.13: *Azure AI Foundry – Chat Playground Azure OpenAI – Parameters*

Sending Prompts for Code Generation and Natural Language Tasks

Once you have configured the context, parameters, and project type, you're ready to send prompts and leverage the models from Azure AI Foundry. These actions can be performed either from the **Playground** or from your own application using the **SDK** or **REST API**.

Important: Make sure you are working within a **Foundry Project**, not a hub-based project. Foundry Projects offer direct access to native models, the integrated Playground, and the latest APIs, while hub-based projects (designed for corporate environments with shared hubs) lack some advanced features and native access to new models.

The Playground is the most intuitive environment for experimenting with AI. First, select the deployed model (for example, GPT-4o-mini). Then, enter your prompt or query in the main input field. Adjust parameters such as temperature, top-p, and maximum length as previously explained. Click "`Generate`" to receive the response from the model. If you're not satisfied, you can click "Regenerate" for a different variation. If desired, use the "View code" feature to see integration examples in various programming languages.

Integration into Applications (SDK or REST API)

For automated or production solutions, you can send prompts from your own application using the Azure SDK or directly with the REST API.

Example in Python Using the Azure AI Foundry SDK

```
from azure.ai.projects import AIProjectClient
from azure.identity import DefaultAzureCredential
project = AIProjectClient.from_connection_string(conn_str="…",
credential=DefaultAzureCredential())
chat = project.inference.get_chat_completions_client()
response = chat.complete(
    model="gpt-4o-mini",
    messages=[
        {"role": "system", "content": "You are an expert AI
assistant for coding."},
        {"role": "user", "content": "Generate a JavaScript
function to fetch data from an API and handle errors."},
    ],
)
print(response.choices[0].message.content)
```

This snippet demonstrates how to structure the context (system) and the user prompt (user), and how to retrieve the response generated by the model.

Best Practices for Sending Prompts

- **Be specific and clear**: Clearly explain what you want, the expected language or response format, and any constraints.
- **Use examples**: If you need a specific format, include examples in your prompt to guide the model.
- **Adjust parameters**: Use a low temperature for technical tasks, or increase it if you are looking for more creativity.
- **Control length**: Limit the number of tokens to avoid overly long responses.
- **Iterate**: If the result is not what you expected, modify the prompt or parameters and try again.

Image Generation: From DALL·E to GPT-image-1 in Azure AI Foundry – Azure OpenAI

The Azure AI Foundry ecosystem not only enables text and code generation, but also provides access to advanced models for **generating images** from textual descriptions. Traditionally, this task has been dominated by the DALL·E model;

however, starting in April 2025, **Azure AI Foundry officially incorporates the GPT-image-1 model**, marking a significant leap in visual generation capabilities within the Azure OpenAI **DALL·E 3** platform.

For the past several years, **DALL·E** has been the benchmark for creating realistic, artistic, or stylized images from natural language descriptions. It offers a user-friendly interface in the Foundry Playground and a robust API for programmatic integrations.

Key Features of DALL·E 3 in Azure AI Foundry

- Generates one image per request (n: 1).
- Two available styles: "`natural`" and "`vivid`."
- Output is provided as a URL for easy viewing or download.
- Automatic content moderation to ensure responsible use policy compliance.
- Supports resolutions up to 1792×1024 pixels.

GPT-image-1: The New Standard for Image Generation in Azure (Launched April 2025)

In April 2025, Azure AI Foundry officially launched the **GPT-image-1** model as part of Azure OpenAI services, marking a major step forward in multimodal visual generation. Initially available in public preview, this model offers substantial improvements over DALL·E in terms of accuracy, versatility, and creative control.

Advantages and Capabilities of GPT-image-1

- Better understanding of complex prompts and higher visual fidelity.
- Supports multiple modes: It supports multiple modes, including **text-to-image** (generating images from textual descriptions), **image-to-image** (transforming or editing existing images), and **inpainting**, which enables localized editing of an image using a mask.
- High-resolution image generation (up to 1536×1024 pixels).
- Advanced text rendering within images (better than DALL·E).
- Output in base64 format, making direct integration into workflows or applications easier.
- Automatic content moderation and digital provenance marks (C2PA).
- Advanced controls over quality and creative variety.

The release of GPT-image-1 in April 2025 by Azure OpenAI within Azure AI Foundry marks the introduction of this model to the platform, and it is expected to gradually replace DALL·E for most professional and enterprise use cases.

Generating Images in Azure AI Foundry

From the Playground:

1. Select the desired model ("**dalle3**" or "**gpt-image-1**") in your Foundry project.
2. Enter the image description ("**prompt**") in the corresponding panel.
3. Adjust resolution, style, and quality parameters if available.
4. Click **Generate** to create the image. The result will be displayed in the interface, and you can download it or copy the code for API integration.

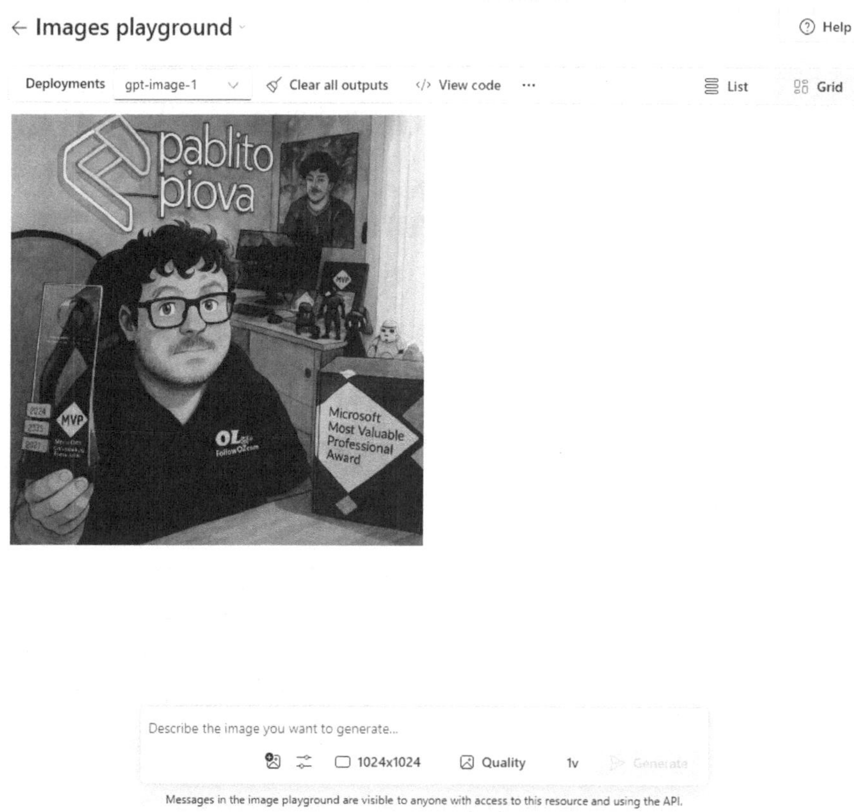

Figure 3.14: *Azure AI Foundry - Images Playground with GPT-Image-1, Ghibli-Style Edition*

From Code (Example Using REST API for GPT-image-1) - Python Example - Generate Image:

```
# Basic Image Generation with Azure OpenAI
# Requirements: pip install requests pillow azure-identity
import os, base64, requests
from io import BytesIO
```

```
from PIL import Image
from azure.identity import DefaultAzureCredential
# -- Minimal configuration ---------------------------------------
------------
ENDPOINT   = os.environ["AZURE_OPENAI_ENDPOINT"].rstrip("/") +
"/"
DEPLOYMENT = os.environ["DEPLOYMENT_NAME"]
API_VER    = "2025-04-01-preview"
# -- Get an access token via Microsoft Entra ID ----------------
-------------
token = DefaultAzureCredential().get_token(
    "https://cognitiveservices.azure.com/.default"
).token
# -- Call /images/generations ----------------------------------
--------------
url  = f"{ENDPOINT}openai/deployments/{DEPLOYMENT}/images/
generations?api-version={API_VER}"
body = {
    "prompt": "A tranquil seaside town at dawn, warm pastel
palette",
    "n": 1,
    "size": "1024x1024",
    "output_format": "png"
}
b64_png = requests.post(url,
    headers={"Authorization": f"Bearer {token}"},
    json=body, timeout=60
).json()["data"][0]["b64_json"]

# -- Preview the result ----------------------------------------
-------------
Image.open(BytesIO(base64.b64decode(b64_png))).show()
```

Edit that image in Ghibli style

```
# Basic Image Editing with Azure OpenAI (Ghibli style)
# Requirements: pip install requests pillow azure-identity
import os, base64, requests
from io import BytesIO
from PIL import Image
from azure.identity import DefaultAzureCredential
ENDPOINT   = os.environ["AZURE_OPENAI_ENDPOINT"].rstrip("/") +
"/"
DEPLOYMENT = os.environ["DEPLOYMENT_NAME"]
API_VER    = "2025-04-01-preview"
token = DefaultAzureCredential().get_token(
    "https://cognitiveservices.azure.com/.default"
).token
```

```
# -- Call /images/edits with multipart/form-data ----------------
-------------
url = f"{ENDPOINT}openai/deployments/{DEPLOYMENT}/images/edits?
api-version={API_VER}"
with open("input.png", "rb") as img_file:          # ≤ 20 MB, PNG/
JPG
    resp = requests.post(
        url,
        headers={"Authorization": f"Bearer {token}"},
        files={
            "image": ("input.png", img_file, "image/png"),
            # Optional mask example:
            # "mask": ("mask.png", open("mask.png", "rb"),
"image/png"),
        },
        data={
            "prompt": "Add a whimsical flying cat hovering above
the rooftops, Ghibli style",
            "model": "gpt-image-1",             # DALL·E 3
supports generation only
            "size": "1024x1024",
            "n": 1,
            "quality": "high",
        },
        timeout=60,
    )
b64_edit = resp.json()["data"][0]["b64_json"]
Image.open(BytesIO(base64.b64decode(b64_edit))).show()
```

Recommendations and Best Practices for Visual Prompts

- **Be specific**: Clearly describe key elements, desired style, colors, and composition.
- **Take advantage of the capabilities of GPT-image-1**: Use complex prompts and experiment with editing or transforming existing images, especially if you need precision or advanced manipulation.
- **Control resolution**: Choose the appropriate resolution and quality for your use case (presentation, prototyping, production).
- **Prototype in the Playground**: Experiment visually before automating the workflow using the SDK or API.
- **Validate output**: Use moderation tools and integrate review workflows when using images in enterprise or public environments.

- **Document prompts and results**: Save examples for reproducibility and iterative optimization.

Multimodal Capabilities of GPT-4o: Images, Audio, and Text

The evolution of language models toward multimodal capabilities has enabled platforms like Azure OpenAI Service to offer much more powerful and versatile solutions. With the introduction of **GPT-4o** (OpenAI Omni), users can interact through text, images, and audio, greatly expanding the range of possible applications both in the Playground and via the API. The following are the main features and best practices for leveraging these capabilities in real-world scenarios:

Multimodal Processing with GPT-4o: Images and Text in the Playground

The **GPT-4o** model in Azure AI Foundry allows you to analyze images, understand them, and use them as additional context alongside written instructions. This feature is especially useful for tasks such as interpreting graphs, visually analyzing documents, diagnosing issues in technical images, and much more.

How to Provide Visual Context in the Playground

1. **Model Selection:** In the Playground, select the GPT-4o model or the latest variant deployed in your project.
2. **Context and Instruction Setup:** In the instructions section ("Give the model instructions and context"), it is recommended to explicitly define how you want the model to process the image. For example: "*You are a visual assistant. I will provide an image and a question. Use the image to answer accurately and in detail.*"
3. **Uploading the Image and Entering Your Query:** Attach the relevant image and write your question or prompt in the corresponding field.
4. **Receiving the Response:** The model will process both the image and the text, generating a contextualized response enriched with visual content.

Practical Tip: *Use the message system (system, user, assistant roles) to control the conversation and ensure the model behaves consistently throughout the session.*

Real-Time Audio: GPT-4o-Realtime in Azure AI Foundry

One of the key differentiators of GPT-4o in Azure is **real-time audio interaction**. This capability enables the creation of conversational assistants that can listen, process, and respond with voice output, offering low latency and highly natural interactions.

Using the Audio Playground with GPT-4o-Realtime

1. **Deployment and Selection**: Make sure you have the gpt-4o-mini-realtime-preview model deployed in your Foundry project.
2. **Defining the Context**: You can use system messages to set the tone of and role of the assistant. For example: "You are a helpful assistant. Please respond with concise and friendly explanations.".
3. **Voice Interaction**: Use the Audio Playground, click "`Start listening`," and engage in real-time conversation. The model will recognize your voice and generate spoken responses within milliseconds.
4. **Typical Applications**: Typical applications include voice assistants for technical support or customer service, conversational educational tools, and solutions for real-time translation and accessibility.

The integration allows you to set preferences such as language, voice used, silence timeout for detecting pauses, and other advanced options. Additionally, you can combine voice conversation with **function calling** to trigger automated actions within an application.

Application Integration: Examples and Best Practices

The true potential of multimodal models is realized when they are integrated into workflows and custom applications, either through the Azure SDK or direct REST API calls. The `azure.ai.projects` SDK brings image integration with GPT-4o into a professional, robust environment that is fully aligned with MLOps, security, and governance standards of Azure. It enables unified authentication, versioning, deployment, and management of advanced AI models, simplifying both, rapid prototyping and the transition to production in demanding enterprise scenarios.

Key Principles for Image Integration with GPT-4o

- **Multimodal Messages**: Each message can combine text and image objects in the messages array, following the Python dictionary structure expected by the API. The model processes visual and textual content in parallel, enriching analysis and response quality.

- **Universal Image Support**: You can work with both locally encoded images as Data URIs, and public HTTPS links to images in the cloud. Converting images locally to Data URI is the safest and most compatible option, as it avoids reliance on external connectivity and additional permissions.
- **Configurable Level of Detail**: The detail parameter allows you to optimize between visual analysis quality, cost, and latency. The low setting keeps token usage constant and is sufficient for general tasks, while high delivers much greater accuracy for demanding use cases.
- **Automatic Resource and Authentication Management**: By Using **`AIProjectClient`** and the associated chat, the client eliminates the need to manually manage credentials, resources, and deployments, thereby allowing you to focus on business logic and use cases.
- **Cost and Efficiency Control**: It is essential to monitor token consumption and set the **`max_tokens`** parameter in responses, as multimodal processing adds the cost of both text and images, impacting both user experience and the assigned budget.

Example of Integration in Python (`azure.ai.projects` SDK)

```
# prerequisites: pip install azure-ai-projects azure-ai-inference
azure-identity
from azure.ai.projects import AIProjectClient
from azure.identity import DefaultAzureCredential
import base64
import mimetypes
from pathlib import Path
# ---------- 1. Helper: convert local image to Data URI --------
--
def to_data_uri(image_path: str) -> str:
    mime_type, _ = mimetypes.guess_type(image_path)
    encoded = base64.b64encode(Path(image_path).read_bytes()).
decode()
    return f"data:{mime_type};base64,{encoded}"
# ---------- 2. Create the project client ----------
project = AIProjectClient.from_connection_string(
    conn_str="PASTE_YOUR_CONNECTION_STRING_HERE",
    credential=DefaultAzureCredential(),  # or AzureKey
Credential("YOUR_KEY")
)
# ---------- 3. Get a ready-to-use ChatCompletionsClient --------
--
chat_client = project.inference.get_chat_completions_client()
# Optionally specify a connection name:
# chat_client = project.inference.get_chat_completions_client(-
connection_name="my-connection")
```

```
# ---------- 4. Build the multimodal request ----------
response = chat_client.complete(
    model="gpt-4o",                   # must match your deployment
name
    messages=[
        {
            "role": "system",
            "content": "You are an expert image analyst."
        },
        {
            "role": "user",
            "content": [
                { "type": "text", "text": "What is shown in this
picture?" },
                {
                    "type": "image_url",
                    "image_url": {
                        "url": to_data_uri("sample.jpg"),  #
could also be a public HTTPS URL
                        "detail": "high"                   # low
| high | auto
                    }
                }
            ]
        }
    ],
    max_tokens=256  # prevent overly long responses
)
print(response.choices[0].message.content)
```

Best Practices and Recommendations

When integrating images into your workflows with GPT-4o, it is essential to group all relevant information for each task into a single message—especially when the model needs to compare images, detect patterns, or extract complex relationships. Providing these images with contextual text instructions significantly improves the accuracy and usefulness of the generated responses. To optimize resources and processing time, it is recommended to reduce image resolution to 2 MP or less before encoding, except in cases where the highest level of visual dctail is required. Likewise, you should adjust the detail level parameter, starting with detail: "*low*" and only switching to high when your application requires greater analytical precision, since this directly impacts both cost and latency.

Operational management should include continuous monitoring of limits and quotas, checking Token-Per-Minute (TPM) and Requests-Per-Minute (RPM) usage in the Azure portal. As the project grows, it will be necessary to adjust workflows or request quota increases to avoid interruptions. It is also a good practice to keep versioning under control by declaring the deployment name and API version as external or environment variables, making updates easier without changing the source code. Finally, instrumenting your application to log usage metrics, latency, and errors is the key for anticipating scaling needs and optimizing both performance and cost of the solution.

Conclusion

Azure AI Foundry is positioned as the central hub for developing and managing generative artificial intelligence solutions in the cloud, providing a unified environment where projects can be planned, deployed, scaled, and monitored efficiently and securely. Building on this foundation, Azure OpenAI models further expand the capabilities of the ecosystem by integrating advanced technologies for language, image, and audio, making it easier to create intelligent applications that address real business needs.

In the next chapter, we will explore how to implement solutions based on intelligent agents using Azure AI Agent Service and open-source frameworks like Semantic Kernel and Autogen, with a deep dive into orchestration, multi-agent interaction, and best deployment strategies for real-world use cases.

Points to Remember

- Generative AI is revolutionizing content creation, product development, and process automation within organizations, enabling new business opportunities and improving operational efficiency across multiple sectors.
- Azure AI Foundry is the central platform for generative AI solutions in Azure, integrating access to models from OpenAI, Mistral, Meta, Hugging Face, DeepSeek, and others, in a unified environment that prioritizes governance, security, and multi-team collaboration.
- In Azure AI Foundry, there are two types of projects: Foundry projects, which are recommended for most scenarios as they provide direct access to the full catalog of generative AI models and agents; and hub-based projects, which are ideal for cases requiring greater isolation or advanced integration with services like Azure Machine Learning, offering increased flexibility and compatibility with legacy architectures.
- Azure AI Foundry supports various deployment modes (standard, serverless, managed compute) and allows models to be exposed as APIs, with control over performance, region, and costs, adapting to different business needs.

- RAG (Retrieval-Augmented Generation) architectures enable models to ground their responses in specific and up-to-date data, enhancing the accuracy and auditability of generative solutions.
- Model evaluation and monitoring in Azure AI Foundry is a continuous and automatable process, including metrics for relevance, groundedness, safety, and performance, which can be integrated into CI/CD pipelines and audited for regulatory compliance.
- Multimodal integration (text, image, audio) through models like GPT-4o and GPT-image-1 expands the reach of intelligent applications, enabling the creation of conversational assistants, image generation systems, visual analysis solutions, and real-time interactive experiences.

CHAPTER 4
Implementing Agent-Based Solutions

Introduction

Agent-based architecture in Azure AI Foundry enables the creation of intelligent, modular, and highly coordinated systems built upon large language models. These agents integrate pre-defined instructions, domain-specific tools, and governance controls within a managed runtime, allowing them to operate securely and at scale.

By combining Azure AI Foundry with **Semantic Kernel (SK)**, organizations can extend capabilities to multi-agent orchestration, structured workflows, and hybrid deployments that bridge local and cloud-hosted environments. This unified operational framework centralizes execution, observability, and governance, providing the foundation for enterprise-grade AI systems that are resilient, auditable, and adaptable to evolving business needs.

Structure

In this chapter, we will cover the following topics:

- Creating Custom Agents Using Azure AI Foundry Agent Service
    - Quotas and Limits in Azure AI Foundry Agent Service
    - Tool Management in Azure AI Foundry Agent Service
    - Observability
    - Security and Governance

- Implementing Agent-Based Solutions with Azure AI Foundry and Semantic Kernel
  - Orchestration Patterns
  - Process Framework
  - Resilience, Governance, and Observability
- Managing Multi-Agent Workflows and Interactions
  - Hybrid Composition of Agents
  - Interaction Patterns and Dynamic Delegation
  - Governance and Monitoring Considerations
- Evaluation, Optimization, and Deployment of Agent-Based Solutions
  - Comprehensive Evaluation
  - Optimization Strategies
  - Deployment Practices
  - Continuous Operations

Creating Custom Agents Using Azure AI Foundry Agent Service

Azure AI Foundry Agent Service is a managed runtime that combines Large Language Models, specific instructions, tools, and governance mechanisms into a single service. This design enables the development and deployment of agents with identity control, network isolation, and advanced observability capabilities, thereby, eliminating the need to build custom orchestration infrastructure.

The architecture is based on the interaction between clearly defined components:

- `Agent`: It encapsulates the instructions, model, and tools.
- `Thread`: It retains the interaction history and context.
- `Messages`: The units of communication are exchanged between the agent and the user.
- `Run`: It is an execution of the agent over the current state of the thread, with **Run Steps** representing individual actions within that execution.

The following image highlights the Azure AI Foundry Agents experience, where agents can be created, configured, and debugged within a single workspace. It provides a visual reference for how agent definitions, model deployments, and runtime settings are managed during development.

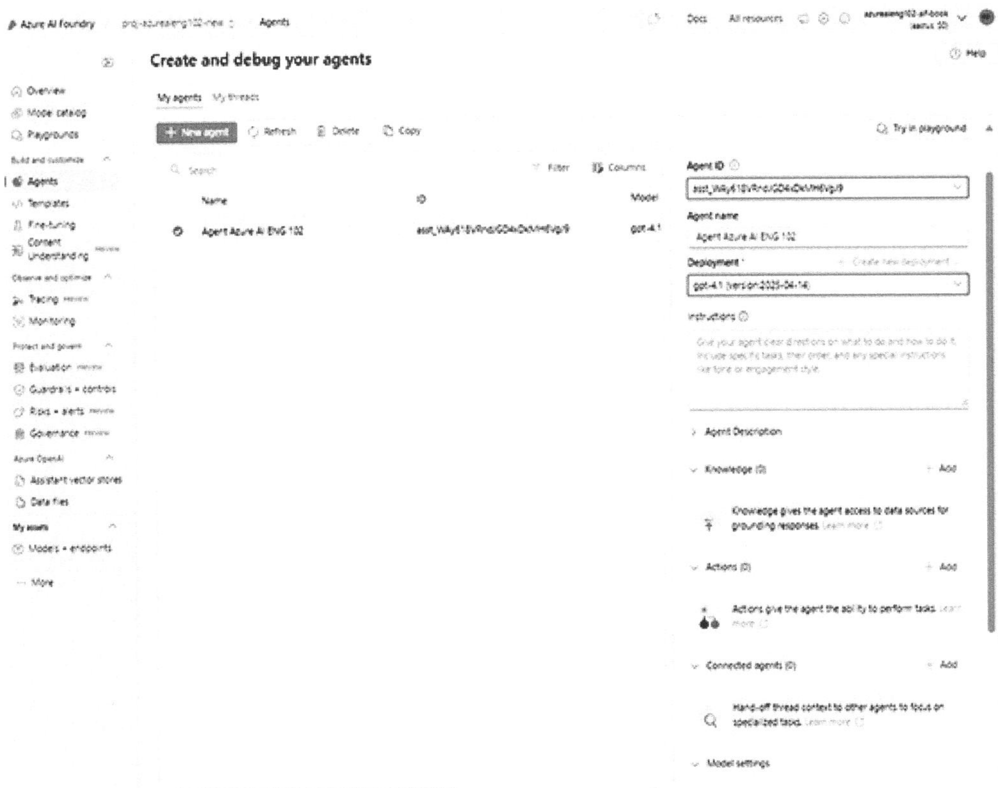

Figure 4.1: *Azure AI Foundry Agents - Create and Debug Your Agents*

Each execution is recorded with granular detail, making it possible to analyze decision-making and trace every step. These elements can be managed from the Azure AI Foundry portal or programmatically through the official Python, C# and JavaScript/TypeScriptSDKs.

The following image highlights the Azure AI Foundry Agents Playground, where developers can interact with an agent in real time, submit prompts, and observe responses, runs, as well as execution details. It provides a practical view of how agents are tested and validated before deployment.

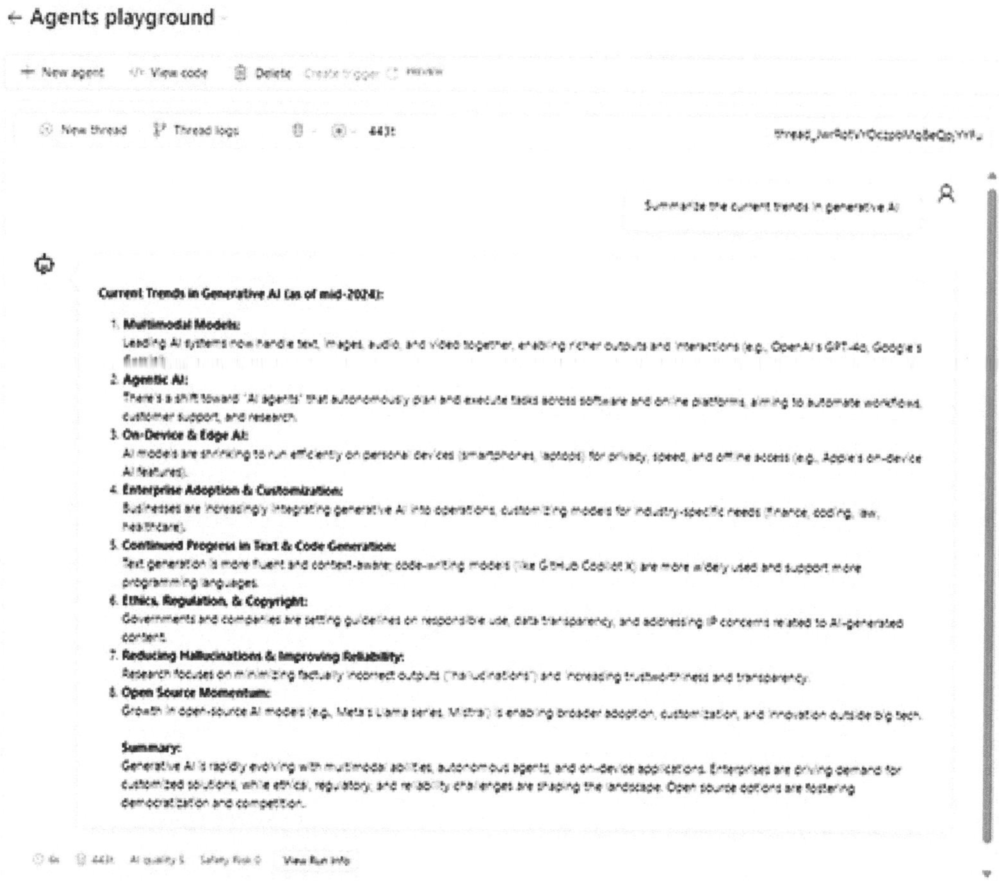

Figure 4.2: *Playground Azure AI Foundry Agents*

Before deploying an agent, the project must have a model deployed in its catalog, proper permissions assigned through Microsoft Entra ID with RBAC, and valid credentials to access the project endpoint. The agent configuration process involves defining precise instructions, selecting the appropriate model, and linking the tools required for the intended function.

Quotas and Limits in Azure AI Foundry Agent Service

Azure AI Foundry Agent Service enforces certain quotas and limits to ensure reliability, security, and predictable performance across tenants. Understanding these limits is essential when designing large-scale or resource-intensive agent-based solutions.

Limit Name	Limit Value
Maximum number of files per agent/thread collaboration between data, development, and business teams.	10,000
Maximum file size for agents and fine-tuning	512 MB
Maximum size for all uploaded files for agents	300 GB
Maximum file size in tokens for attaching to a vector store	2,000,000 tokens
Maximum number of messages per thread	100,000
Maximum size of *text* content per message	1,500,000 characters
Maximum number of tools registered per agent	128

Table 4.1: *Quotas and Limits in Azure AI Foundry Agent Service*

These limits are applied by default across all Azure regions. If your solution requires higher thresholds, you may need to contact Microsoft Azure Support to request an increase. In most production scenarios, these limits are sufficient, but workflows that involve very large datasets, high-frequency message streams, or a large number of registered tools, should be designed with these constraints in mind.

Thus, by planning ahead for these quotas, developers can avoid unexpected interruptions, optimize resource usage, and ensure smooth scalability in production environments.

Tool Management in Azure AI Foundry Agent Service

For an agent to access relevant data or perform specific actions, **Azure AI Foundry Agent** Service provides a wide range of built-in tools, organized into two main categories: **Knowledge Tools**, which enrich the agent's context by grounding responses in external and enterprise data sources, and **Action Tools**, which enable the agent to perform operations, invoke external systems, and execute tasks beyond pure language generation.

Knowledge Tools

It enriches the context of the agent with accurate, up-to-date, and relevant information:

- **Grounding with Bing Search**: Retrieves public information from the web
- **Azure AI Search and File Search**: Search private data or corporate documents
- **Microsoft Fabric**: Advanced connectivity to structured enterprise data and analytics
- **TripAdvisor and Morningstar**: Licensed data sources useful in sectors such as travel and finance

The following image highlights the Add Knowledge experience in Azure AI Foundry Agents, where data sources can be connected to ground agent responses. It provides a visual overview of the available knowledge connectors, including file-based sources, enterprise search, web grounding, and licensed third-party data.

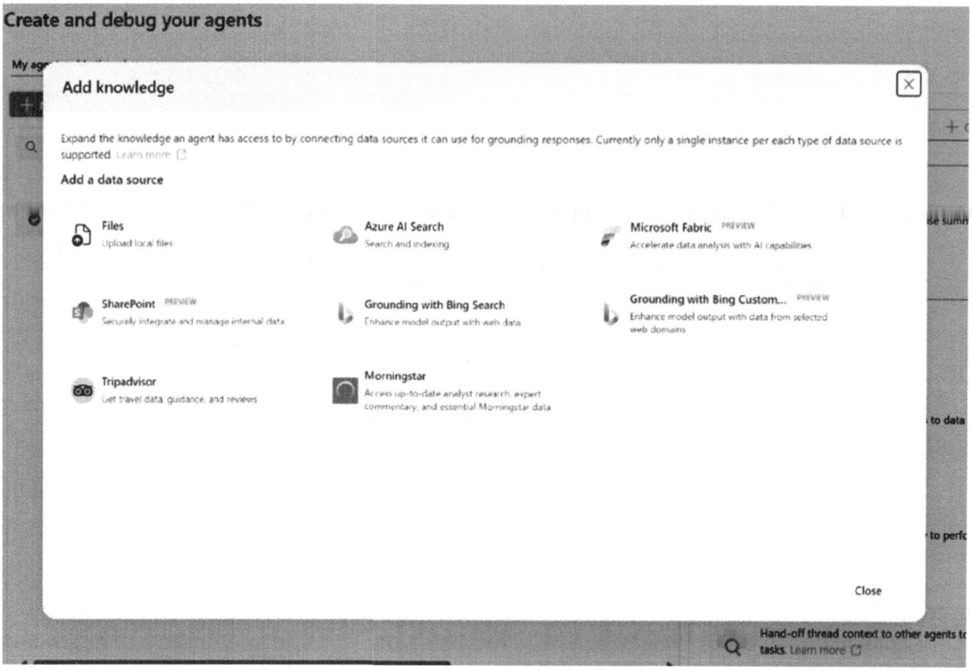

***Figure 4.3**: Playground Azure AI Foundry Agents – Add Knowledge*

Action Tools

It allows the agent to perform tasks beyond pure language output:

- **Deep Research (preview)**: It orchestrates in-depth research using the o3-deep-research model which is combined with Bing grounding for complex analysis.
- **Azure Logic Apps**: It enables low-code/no-code integration to trigger external workflows.
- **OpenAPI Spec Tool**: It directly integrates the existing APIs via standardized specifications.
- **Model Context Protocol (MCP)**: It connects to remote endpoints to extend tool capabilities.
- **Function Calling**: It defines specific stateless functions that can be invoked by the agent, based on context.
- **Azure Functions**: It handles more complex logic and state persistence.

- **Browser Automation**: It allows the agent to perform actions in a controlled browser session using natural language prompts.

How These Tools Work in an Agent

When a user sends a request, the language model of the agent evaluates the intent and, if needed, decides which tools to invoke. For example, if asked about the current weather in a city, the agent might automatically choose **Grounding with Bing Search** instead of relying solely on its pre-trained knowledge. If a specific priority is required, the **`tool_choice`** parameter can be used to force the use of a particular tool.

Tools can be configured at different levels – within the agent, within the thread, or for the current run, thereby, allowing for fine-grained control over their usage and behavior.

Example: Creating and Running an Agent Service agent (Python)

```
import os
from azure.identity import DefaultAzureCredential
from azure.ai.projects import AIProjectClient
from azure.ai.agents._models import MessageRole  # Adjust import
based on SDK version
PROJECT_ENDPOINT = os.environ["PROJECT_ENDPOINT"]
MODEL_DEPLOYMENT = os.environ["MODEL_DEPLOYMENT_NAME"]
credential = DefaultAzureCredential()
client = AIProjectClient(endpoint=PROJECT_ENDPOINT, credential
=credential)
# Create the agent
agent = client.agents.create_agent(
    model=MODEL_DEPLOYMENT,
    name="analyst-agent",
    instructions=(
        "Analyze data and produce concise, factual summaries."
        "Use tools when they add verifiable evidence."
    )
)
# Create a thread and send a message
thread = client.agents.threads.create()
client.agents.messages.create(
thread_id=thread.id,
    role=MessageRole.USER,
    content="Summarize the current trends in generative AI."
)
# Execute the run and wait for completion
run = client.agents.runs.create_and_process(thread_id=thread.id,
agent_id=agent.id)
if run.last_error:
```

```
        raise RuntimeError(f"Run failed: {run.last_error}")
    # Read the last assistant message
    last = client.agents.messages.get_last_message_by_role(thread_
    id=thread.id, role=MessageRole.ASSISTANT)
    if last and last.text_messages:
        print(last.text_messages[-1].text.value)
```

Observability

Azure AI Foundry integrates seamlessly with Azure Monitor to provide comprehensive observability through platform metrics. Azure Monitor delivers lightweight, near real-time platform metrics for most Azure services, with each metric individually defined per namespace and stored in a dedicated time-series database. These metrics enable users to track resource performance over time and support prompt alerting scenarios. Importantly, Azure Monitor automatically collects these platform metrics – no additional configuration is necessary.

For Azure AI Foundry Agent Service, a range of detailed metrics is surfaced in Azure Monitor, aligning with the monitoring standards across Azure AI services. Currently available metrics include:

- **`Agents`**: It tracks the total count of agents, aggregated as average, maximum, minimum, and sum, with dimensions such as **`EventType`**. Data is available in one-minute time grains.
- **`IndexedFiles`**: It counts indexed files, with dimensions such as **`ErrorCode`**, **`Status`**, and **`VectorStoreId`**, supporting multiple aggregation types.
- **`Messages`**: It monitors the number of messages, segmented by **`EventType`** and **`ThreadId`**, enabling granular message flow analysis.
- **`Runs`**: It captures run counts, categorized by **`AgentId`**, **`RunStatus`**, **`StatusCode`**, and **`StreamType`**, useful for execution tracking.
- **`Threads`**: It measures thread events with aggregation by **`EventType`**.
- **`Tokens`**: It tracks token usage, distinguished by **`AgentId`** and **`TokenType`**, supporting detailed cost and usage analysis.
- **`ToolCalls`**: It monitors tool invocation counts, with breakdowns by **`AgentId`** and **`ToolName`**.

All these metrics can be reviewed in the Azure Monitor metrics database and are designed for integration with observability dashboards, such as those built with OpenTelemetry and Azure Application Insights, that enable centralized analytics, usage monitoring, and alerting for Azure AI Foundry workloads.

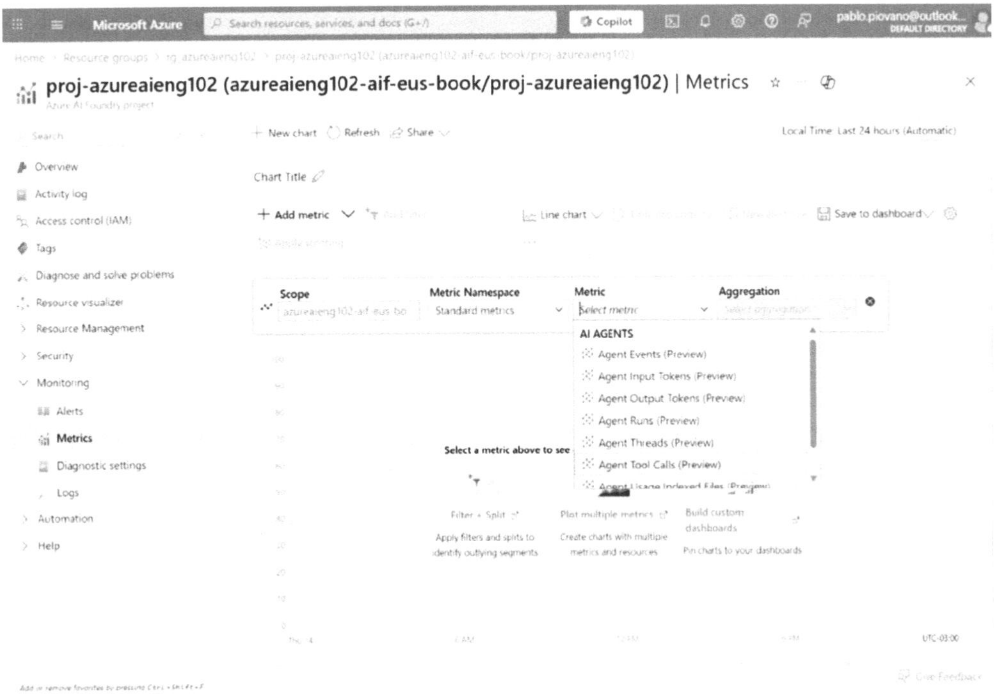

Figure 4.4: *Azure AI Foundry – Metrics View for AI Agents Showing Metric Selection Options*

Security and Governance

The service includes Microsoft Entra ID authentication and RBAC, network isolation via Private Link, encryption of data in transit and at rest, and configurable content safety filters for input and output moderation.

Implementing Agent-Based Solutions with Azure AI Foundry and Semantic Kernel

Semantic Kernel (SK) has evolved into a primary multi-agent orchestration framework within the Microsoft AI ecosystem, absorbing the majority of multi-agent capabilities that were previously associated with AutoGen. The current recommendation is to adopt SK for all production-grade agent applications, leveraging its orchestration and process frameworks, while maintaining interoperability with Azure AI Foundry Agent Service. This convergence allows solutions to run locally during development which then can be deployed into managed Foundry environments without changes in logic or structure.

Orchestration Patterns

SK provides pre-defined orchestration patterns optimized for common multi-agent collaboration scenarios:

- **Sequential**: It executes agents in a fixed order, passing the output of one directly to the next.
- **Concurrent**: It runs specialized agents in parallel and aggregates their outputs.
- **Group Chat**: It enables moderated, multi-party agent conversations, optionally with human participation.
- **Handoff**: It transfers task control between agents, based on pre-defined conditions.
- **Magnetic**: It dynamically assigns tasks across agents over multiple iterations, and is well-suited to open-ended problem-solving.

These patterns provide abstract coordination, state handling, and error management, reducing the operational complexity of multi-agent workflows.

Process Framework

For workflows involving business logic, human-in-the-loop steps, or long-running operations, Process Framework of SK structures execution into discrete, versionable steps. These enable auditing, retries, branching, and conditional execution. Processes can incorporate both local SK agents and connected Azure AI Foundry agents, providing hybrid execution with centralized governance and observability.

Multi-Agent Control Protocol (MCP)

MCP defines a standardized communication model for inter-agent and agent-system interactions, ensuring interoperability across different platforms and programming languages. By adhering to MCP, SK orchestrations can coordinate with Azure AI Foundry agents, local agents, and even agents hosted in non-Microsoft environments without custom integration code. This is particularly relevant for distributed enterprise scenarios requiring cross-system coordination.

Agent-to-Agent Integration (A2A) with Connected Agents

Azure AI Foundry Agent Service supports **Connected Agents**, which allows one managed agent to invoke another as if it were a built-in tool. This design eliminates the need for manual API integration between agents and simplifies modular system design.

When configuring Connected Agents in the **Azure AI Foundry portal**:

1. Open the configuration page of the primary agent.
2. Add a new tool, selecting **Connected Agent** from the list.
3. Choose the secondary (connected) agent from the available managed agents in the project.
4. Provide a descriptive name and optional usage notes so that the invoking agent can reason about when to use it.

Once configured, the connected agent appears in the toolset of the primary agent. During execution, the primary agent can select it automatically through the reasoning process of the model, or it can be explicitly targeted in orchestrations such as the **Sequential** or **Handoff** patterns of SK. Inputs, outputs, and run steps, from the connected agent are fully traceable in the Observability view of the portal.

Operational Advantages

- **Modularity**: Each agent can focus on a specific domain (for example, research, compliance, drafting) which can be re-used in multiple solutions.
- **Governance**: All calls between agents pass through the same identity, RBAC, content safety, and logging controls as other tools.
- **Hybrid orchestration**: Connected agents can be combined with local SK agents in the same workflow without any additional integration code.

Example usage scenario: A content pipeline uses a local SK research agent, a managed Foundry writer agent, and a connected compliance agent. The SK orchestration invokes the connected compliance agent as if it were a local, while Foundry handles secure invocation, logging, and monitoring.

Example: Hybrid SK and Foundry Agent Orchestration (Python)

```
# Requirements:
# pip install "semantic-kernel>=1.0.0" "azure-ai-projects>=1.0.0"
"azure-identity>=1.17.0"
import asyncio
import os
from azure.identity import DefaultAzureCredential
from azure.ai.projects import AIProjectClient
from semantic_kernel.agents.orchestration import Sequential
Orchestration, InProcessRuntime
from semantic_kernel.agents.chat_completion import
ChatCompletionAgent
from semantic_kernel.agents.azure_ai.azure_ai_agent import
AzureAIAgent, AzureAIAgentSettings
```

```
PROJECT_ENDPOINT = os.environ["PROJECT_ENDPOINT"]
MODEL_DEPLOYMENT = os.environ["MODEL_DEPLOYMENT_NAME"]
asyncdefmain():
    # Local SK agent for research
    researcher = ChatCompletionAgent(
        name="research_agent",
        instructions="Collect exactly 3 relevant facts with short
references."
    )
    # Foundry project client for managed agents
project_client = AIProjectClient(endpoint=PROJECT_ENDPOINT,
credential=DefaultAzureCredential())
    # Managed Foundry agent for writing
writer_def = project_client.agents.create_agent(
        model=MODEL_DEPLOYMENT,
        name="writer_agent",
        instructions="Draft clear, well-structured text using
provided facts."
    )
    writer = AzureAIAgent(client=project_client, definition
=writer_def)
    # Orchestration: research → writing
    orchestration = SequentialOrchestration(members=[researcher,
writer])
    runtime = InProcessRuntime()
    await runtime.start()
    result = await orchestration.invoke(
        task="Summarize current advances in multi-agent AI
systems.",
        runtime=runtime
    )
print(await result.get())
    await runtime.stop_when_idle()
if __name__ == "__main__":
asyncio.run(main())
```

Resilience, Governance, and Observability

When implementing complex multi-agent solutions:

- Keep agent responsibilities isolated to avoid recursion loops.
- Use OpenTelemetry tracing and Application Insights for real-time performance and error visibility.
- Implement circuit breakers, fallback logic, and escalation paths to human operators.

- Capture context snapshots for replay and diagnostics.

Combining the orchestration and process framework of SK with the managed runtime of Azure AI Foundry ensures consistent governance, security, and monitoring across both local and cloud-hosted agents.

Managing Multi-Agent Workflows and Interactions

The value of an agent-based architecture extends beyond the design of individual agents. True operational impact is achieved when multiple agents collaborate, share context, delegate tasks, and execute within structured workflows. Azure AI Foundry Agent Service, combined with Semantic Kernel (SK), provides the tools and frameworks to design, run, and govern multi-agent workflows that blends locally hosted SK agents with managed cloud agents.

Hybrid Composition of Agents

Hybrid architectures combine the flexibility of local SK agents with the scalability, governance, and observability of managed Foundry agents.

A local SK agent can consume a Foundry agent as a connected tool, while Foundry agents can invoke each other through **Connected Agents (A2A)**. This modular approach allows specialized capabilities to be encapsulated in dedicated agents and reused across workflows.

Typical roles in hybrid multi-agent systems are:

- **Domain Expert Agents**: Specialized in areas such as compliance, analytics, or search
- **Coordinator Agents**: Direct task distribution and workflow orchestration
- **Bridge Agents**: Facilitate integration between the agent ecosystem and external systems or APIs

Interaction Patterns and Dynamic Delegation

Multi-agent workflows can leverage the orchestration patterns described earlier (see *Orchestration Patterns*) to define collaboration models without re-defining them here. Dynamic delegation is particularly valuable in adaptive workflows, where data conditions or business rules change mid-process. The Process Framework of SK supports conditional branching, asynchronous execution, retries, and human-in-the-loop approval steps.

MCP in Workflow Management

The **Multi-Agent Control Protocol (MCP)** standardizes message formats, state tracking, and invocation semantics across agents, regardless of where they are hosted. This allows a single workflow to span Azure AI Foundry agents, local SK agents, and even agents running on third-party platforms, all while maintaining interoperability and traceability.

Example: Multi-Agent Pipeline with Delegation

The following example demonstrates a pipeline where a coordinator SK agent delegates tasks to both a local research agent and a managed Foundry validation agent using Connected Agents.

```
# Requirements:
# pip install "semantic-kernel>=1.0.0" "azure-ai-projects>=1.0.0"
"azure-identity>=1.17.0"
import asyncio
import os
from azure.identity import DefaultAzureCredential
from azure.ai.projects import AIProjectClient
from semantic_kernel.agents.orchestration import SequentialOr
chestration, InProcessRuntime
from semantic_kernel.agents.chat_completion import
ChatCompletionAgent
from semantic_kernel.agents.azure_ai.azure_ai_agent import
AzureAIAgent, AzureAIAgentSettings
PROJECT_ENDPOINT = os.environ["PROJECT_ENDPOINT"]
MODEL_DEPLOYMENT = os.environ["MODEL_DEPLOYMENT_NAME"]
asyncdefmain():
    # Local SK agent for research
research_agent = ChatCompletionAgent(
        name="research_agent",
        instructions="Collect three verified facts with references."
    )
    # Managed Foundry agent for compliance validation
project_client = AIProjectClient(endpoint=PROJECT_ENDPOINT,
credential=DefaultAzureCredential())
validation_def = project_client.agents.create_agent(
        model=MODEL_DEPLOYMENT,
        name="validation_agent",
        instructions="Validate facts for accuracy and compliance
with corporate policy."
    )
validation_agent = AzureAIAgent(client=project_client, definition
=validation_def)
    # Coordinator orchestration (research → validation)
```

```
    orchestration = SequentialOrchestration(members=[research_
agent, validation_agent])
    runtime = InProcessRuntime()
    await runtime.start()
    result = await orchestration.invoke(
        task="Prepare a compliance-checked summary of recent AI
regulations.",
        runtime=runtime
    )
print(await result.get())
    await runtime.stop_when_idle()
if __name__ == "__main__":
asyncio.run(main())
```

Governance and Monitoring Considerations

Multi-agent workflow governance requires enforcing role isolation to prevent uncontrolled recursion, implementing retry and timeout policies per agent, and storing shared context in secure repositories such as Azure Cosmos DB. Observability should capture per-agent metrics, including success rate, latency, cost, and tool error frequency. MCP-based message logs, combined with SK and Foundry tracing, provide a unified operational view for audits and optimization.

Evaluation, Optimization, and Deployment of Agent-Based Solutions

The effectiveness of an agent-based system is determined not only by the sophistication of its individual agents or orchestration patterns, but also by its ability to be measured, optimized, and deployed reliably in production environments. Azure AI Foundry and Semantic Kernel provide integrated capabilities for evaluation, performance tuning, and secure deployment pipelines that align with enterprise operational standards.

Comprehensive Evaluation

Evaluation is the process of measuring an agent or a workflow against defined performance and quality criteria. This process should capture both operational metrics and qualitative outcomes.

Core operational metrics:

- Latency per run and per agent
- Token usage and associated cost

- Tool call frequency and success rate
- Error rate and root cause distribution

Quality and compliance metrics:

- Task adherence (Did the agent fulfill the request?)
- Tool call accuracy (Did the agent use the correct tool?)
- Content safety compliance

Azure AI Foundry integrates with the **Azure AI Evaluation SDK** to transform real Agent Service runs into evaluation datasets, which can then be scored automatically using built-in or custom evaluators. Evaluations can run locally, in staging environments, or as part of CI/CD pipelines for continuous quality monitoring.

Example: Agent Evaluation in Python

```
# Requirements:
# pip install "azure-ai-evaluation>=1.7.0" "azure-ai-projects>
=1.0.0" "azure-identity>=1.17.0"
from azure.identity import DefaultAzureCredential
from azure.ai.projects import AIProjectClient
from azure.ai.evaluation import evaluate, TaskAdherenceEvaluator
from azure.ai.evaluation.integrations.agent_service import
AgentServiceRunConverter
PROJECT_ENDPOINT = "https://<your-foundry>.services.ai.azure.com/
api/projects/<ProjectName>"
THREAD_ID = "<thread_id>"  # Captured from a real Agent Service
run
RUN_ID = "<run_id>"        # Captured from a real Agent Service
run
# Project client to access Agent Service data
project = AIProjectClient(endpoint=PROJECT_ENDPOINT, creden-
tial=DefaultAzureCredential())
# Convert a run to structured evaluation rows
converter = AgentServiceRunConverter(project_client=project)
rows = converter.to_evaluation_rows(thread_id=THREAD_ID, run_
id=RUN_ID)
# Evaluate with one or more evaluators
metrics = evaluate(
    data=rows,
    evaluators=[TaskAdherenceEvaluator()]
)
print(metrics)  # Dictionary with per-row scores and aggregate
results
```

Optimization Strategies

Optimization involves improving cost efficiency, reducing latency, and enhancing resilience without sacrificing quality. Common techniques include:

- **Prompt and context management**: Controlling token usage by summarizing historical context and removing unnecessary data.
- **Caching**: Storing outputs from idempotent tool calls to avoid repeated computation.
- **Parallelization**: Using the Concurrent orchestration of SK for independent subtasks.
- **Parameter tuning**: Adjusting model parameters such as temperature and top-p for stability and determinism.
- **Circuit breakers and fallback logic**: Ensuring graceful degradation by routing to alternative agents or human operators when necessary.

The impact of these strategies can be monitored in the Azure AI Foundry Observability dashboard, therefore, allowing data-driven tuning.

Deployment Practices

Deployment pipelines should promote separation between development, staging, and production environments, with automated validation at each stage. Agents and workflows can be packaged for deployment as managed services in Azure AI Foundry or as containerized SK applications.

Key deployment considerations include:

- **Access control**: Leveraging Microsoft Entra RBAC to manage permissions per environment.
- **Network isolation**: Implementing Private Link to restrict public exposure.
- **Content safety enforcement**: Enabling appropriate filtering policies for both input and output streams.
- **Geographic distribution**: Deploying to multiple Azure regions to reduce latency and ensure availability.

These practices, combined with MCP for cross-environment agent coordination, enable distributed deployment models where agents operate across organizational and geographic boundaries.

Continuous Operations

In production, agent-based systems require ongoing monitoring, logging, and evaluation:

- **Observability**: Integrate OpenTelemetry tracing with Application Insights for near real-time monitoring.
- **Traceability**: Use MCP message logging to audit cross-agent interactions.
- **Continuous evaluation**: Automate quality and compliance checks in CI/CD pipelines to detect regressions.

Hence, by combining these practices with robust orchestration in SK and secure execution in Azure AI Foundry, organizations can sustain high-quality, cost-efficient agent systems at scale.

Conclusion

The implementation of agent-based solutions using Azure AI Foundry and Semantic Kernel establishes a robust framework for both individual and multi-agent deployments. By leveraging managed runtimes, integrated tool ecosystems, and advanced orchestration patterns, these solutions achieve operational efficiency while adhering to enterprise standards for governance, security, and compliance.

The convergence of Semantic Kernel and AutoGen, combined with capabilities such as Connected Agents and the Multi-Agent Control Protocol (MCP), enables organizations to design modular, interoperable, and adaptable AI architectures. Through consistent evaluation, optimization, and structured deployment practices, agent-based systems can scale from prototype to production with predictable performance and clear traceability.

In the next chapter, we shift the focus from agent-based architectures to applied artificial intelligence scenarios centered on visual data. The chapter explores how to implement computer vision solutions using Azure AI Vision, Custom Vision, and Azure AI Video Indexer, covering image analysis, custom model training, and advanced video intelligence to transform images and audiovisual content into structured, actionable insights.

Points to Remember

- Azure AI Foundry Agent Service combines model, instructions, tools, and governance into a single managed runtime.
- Threads, runs, and run steps provide full traceability of agent execution.

- Tool integration includes Code Interpreter, Azure AI Search, Bing Grounding, OpenAPI, Azure Functions, Logic Apps, Connected Agents, and MCP.
- Semantic Kernel is the recommended production framework for multi-agent orchestration, with built-in patterns and Process Framework support.
- Connected Agents (A2A) enable managed agents to invoke each other as tools without custom orchestration logic.
- MCP standardizes communication across agents and platforms for interoperability.
- Observability is achieved through OpenTelemetry, Application Insights, and built-in Foundry dashboards.
- Evaluation can be automated via the Azure AI Evaluation SDK for both quality and safety.
- Optimization strategies include prompt/context management, caching, and circuit breakers.
- Deployment best practices include RBAC, network isolation, content safety, and staged rollouts across environments.

CHAPTER 5
Implementing Computer Vision Solutions

Introduction

Computer vision has become one of the most transformative areas of artificial intelligence, enabling machines to interpret and reason about visual content in ways that were once limited to human perception. From recognizing objects and reading text to generating natural-language descriptions of images, these capabilities open the door to a wide range of practical applications across industries such as retail, healthcare, manufacturing, media, and accessibility. Microsoft Azure provides a robust suite of services—Azure AI Vision, Custom Vision, Face API, and Azure AI Video Indexer—that allow developers to build powerful vision-driven applications without needing deep expertise in machine learning.

This chapter introduces the core building blocks for implementing computer vision solutions using Azure AI Services. We will begin with image analysis, covering tagging, object detection, OCR, and advanced features available in Azure AI Vision. Next, we will explore how to develop and deploy custom vision models for classification and object detection, ensuring that solutions can be tailored to domain-specific needs. Finally, we will dive into Azure AI Video Indexer, a comprehensive service that extracts multimodal insights from video and audio content, showing how to transform unstructured media into structured, searchable, and actionable data.

Structure

In this chapter, we will cover the following topics:

- Image Analysis using Azure AI Vision
    - Image Analysis with Azure AI Vision

  - Comparing API v3.2 and v4.0
  - Practical Use Cases
  - Face API: Beyond People Detection
  - Face API Complementing Image Analysis
  - Real-Word Scenarios
  - Best Practices
- Developing Custom Vision Models
  - Understanding Classification in Azure Custom Vision
  - Object Detection Models in Azure Custom Vision
- Advanced Video Intelligence Using Azure AI Video Indexer
  - Introduction to Azure AI Video Indexer
  - Core Features and Capabilities
  - Setting Up and Using Video Indexer
  - Advanced Scenarios and Customization
  - Evaluating and Interpreting Results
  - Deployment and Integration in Enterprise Solutions
  - Consuming Insights via the REST API

Image Analysis Using Azure AI Vision

The Image Analysis service of Azure AI Vision is the central building block for extracting structured meaning from images. In its current form, it brings together capabilities such as **tagging, object detection, Optical Character Recognition (OCR), and advanced visual features** that once required multiple endpoints and separate calls. With a single unified request, developers can ask for descriptive tags, localized objects, recognized text, and even natural language captions.

The philosophy of Image Analysis is to bridge computer vision and real application needs. Metadata such as tags are useful for search engines; bounding boxes allow interfaces to highlight or count detected items; OCR turns signs, documents, and tickets into usable text; captions enable accessibility tools to narrate images to visually impaired users; and smart crops ensure consistent visual design. In practice, this means an e-commerce platform can automatically enrich its product catalog, a news site can generate thumbnails adapted to social media layouts, and a compliance team can digitize and index scanned contracts, all through the same API call.

Image Analysis with Azure AI Vision

Version 4.0 consolidates the core visual capabilities into a single **Analyze** operation. Instead of orchestrating different endpoints, developers simply decide which **features** to enable – **`tags`**, **`objects`**, **`read`**, **`caption`**, **`denseCaptions`**, **`people`**, or **`smartCrops`**–and the service returns them in a structured JSON payload. The operation is synchronous: the client sends an image and receives results directly, avoiding the asynchronous polling loops required in version 3.2.

The REST endpoint is straightforward:

```
POST https://<your-resource>.cognitiveservices.azure.com/
computervision/ imageanalysis:analyze?api-version=2024-02-01
```

The body can either be a JSON object with a URL to the image or a binary stream with the file itself. Parameters such as *language* and *model version* allow you to control the localization and reproducibility of results.

Example: REST request

```
curl -X POST \
  "https://<your-resource>.cognitiveservices.azure.com/computer-
vision/ imageanalysis:analyze?api-version=2024-02-01&features=
tags,objects,read,caption,denseCaptions,people,smartCrops&
language=en" \
  -H "Ocp-Apim-Subscription-Key: <VISION_KEY>" \
  -H "Content-Type: application/json" \
  -d '{"url":"<IMAGE_URL>"}'
```

This single request will return multiple sections: **`captionResult`**, **`tagsResult`**, **`objectsResult`**, **`readResult`**, **`denseCaptionsResult`**, **`peopleResult`**, and **`smartCropsResult`**.

Before reviewing the Python SDK example, we will use an image captured in a *Star Wars*-inspired setting – an ideal context to illustrate the capabilities of intelligent image analysis.

The following image highlights a person standing in front of a formation of Star Wars stormtroopers, captured in a themed environment with strong lighting and visual contrast. The scene provides a rich mix of human presence, recognizable characters, and contextual elements, making it well suited for demonstrating tagging, people detection, object recognition, and caption generation with Azure AI Vision.

Figure 5.1: *Example Image Used for Testing the Code in the Following Snippet*

Example: Python SDK:

```
import os
from azure.core.credentials import AzureKeyCredential
from azure.ai.vision.imageanalysis import ImageAnalysisClient
from azure.ai.vision.imageanalysis.models import VisualFeatures
# Read environment variables for the Azure AI Vision resource
endpoint = os.environ["VISION_ENDPOINT"]
key = os.environ["VISION_KEY"]
# Create client
client = ImageAnalysisClient(endpoint=endpoint, credential=Azure-
KeyCredential(key))
# Select visual features (simple)
features = [
    VisualFeatures.TAGS,
    VisualFeatures.OBJECTS,
    VisualFeatures.READ,
    VisualFeatures.CAPTION,
    VisualFeatures.DENSE_CAPTIONS,
    VisualFeatures.SMART_CROPS,
    VisualFeatures.PEOPLE,
]
# Analyze image from public URL
```

```
result = client.analyze_from_url(
    image_url="https://raw.githubusercontent.com/ppiova/Azure-
ComputerVision-BackgroundRemoval/main/Images/RiseoftheResistance.
jpg",
visual_features=features,
       language="en",
       gender_neutral_caption=True,
       model_version="latest"
)
# Print main caption
print("Caption:", result["captionResult"]["text"])
# Print tags
for t in result["tagsResult"]["values"]:
    print("Tag:", t["name"], t["confidence"])
# Print dense captions
print("\nDense Captions:")
for dc in result["denseCaptionsResult"]["values"]:
    print(f"- '{dc['text']}' (confidence: {dc['confidence']},
bounding box: {dc['boundingBox']})")
```

The following image highlights the console output produced by the Azure AI Vision Image Analysis service when processing the sample image. It shows the generated global caption, detected tags with confidence scores, and multiple dense captions describing different regions of the image along with their corresponding bounding boxes.

```
Caption: a person standing in front of a group of white storm troopers
Tag: clothing 0.9772326946258545
Tag: person 0.9629377722740173
Tag: concert 0.9584404230117798
Tag: man 0.9234851002693176
Tag: standing 0.7660043239593506

Dense Captions:
- 'a person standing in front of a group of white storm troopers' (confidence: 0.8122022747993469, bounding box: {'x': 0, 'y': 0, 'w': 960, 'h': 720})
- 'a person standing in front of a group of white and black storm troopers' (confidence: 0.7274222373962402, bounding box: {'x': 459, 'y': 227, 'w': 327, 'h': 484})
- 'a picture of the earth and planets' (confidence: 0.6481895446777344, bounding box: {'x': 539, 'y': 392, 'w': 156, 'h': 182})
- 'a blurry image of a person in a white uniform' (confidence: 0.8147698044776917, bounding box: {'x': 54, 'y': 310, 'w': 80, 'h': 171})
- 'a person standing in a room' (confidence: 0.6585175395011902, bounding box: {'x': 0, 'y': 449, 'w': 948, 'h': 231})
- 'a person in a white suit' (confidence: 0.6778044700622559, bounding box: {'x': 387, 'y': 307, 'w': 69, 'h': 174})
- 'blur blurry image of a white object' (confidence: 0.6808965802192688, bounding box: {'x': 9, 'y': 312, 'w': 53, 'h': 163})
- 'a person in a white suit' (confidence: 0.7085853815078735, bounding box: {'x': 818, 'y': 301, 'w': 91, 'h': 184})
- 'a close-up of a pair of legs' (confidence: 0.7300141453742981, bounding box: {'x': 270, 'y': 307, 'w': 78, 'h': 370})
- 'a blurry image of a person in a white suit' (confidence: 0.747745156288147, bounding box: {'x': 269, 'y': 309, 'w': 80, 'h': 172})
```

Figure 5.2: *Output from Running the Python Code*

This is the output generated by the service for the selected image. The model not only produces a global caption–"*a person standing in front of a group of white storm troopers*"–but also provides tags such as *clothing*, *concert*, *person*, and *standing*, each with confidence scores. In addition, the dense captions feature goes further by describing multiple regions of the image and drawing bounding boxes around them, such as "*a person in a white suit*" or "*a blurry image of a person in a white uniform*."

What makes this particularly powerful is that Image Analysis 4.0 is built on a foundation model, which gives it the ability to open word recognition. Unlike older versions constrained by a fixed dictionary of categories, this approach enables the system to generate free-text labels and descriptions, even for cultural references or specialized entities that were not part of a predefined taxonomy. That is why in this example, the model is able to identify *stormtrooper* characters, associating them with the Star Wars universe. The same capability extends to other domains as well, allowing the system to recognize names of characters, places, or concepts that it has learned through massive multimodal training.

Comparing API v3.2 and v4.0

The move from **Computer Vision 3.2** to **Image Analysis 4.0** represents a fundamental change. Version 3.2 offered breadth: its **`/analyze`** endpoint returned categories, tags, descriptions, faces with age and gender estimates, **`adult/racy/gore`** scores, color schemes, brands, and domain models for landmarks and celebrities. OCR required a separate */read/analyze* endpoint, which was asynchronous: developers had to send the image, then poll until the operation finished. Thumbnails were generated by yet another endpoint, **`/generateThumbnail`**, which returned a cropped binary image.

By contrast, version 4.0 narrows the scope but greatly improves usability. It unifies all essential tasks into the synchronous **`imageanalysis:analyze`** call. Instead of a thumbnail image, it returns **smart crop coordinates** so developers can apply crops locally. Instead of face attributes, it offers **people detection** without demographic information, aligning with stronger privacy commitments. Some features–such as brands, **`adult/racy/gore`**, color, and landmarks–are not part of 4.0 and require other services.

The following table compares the key features and capabilities between Azure Computer Vision API version 3.2 and version 4.0, highlighting differences in endpoints, supported features, and output formats:

Aspect	Version 3.2	Version 4.0
Endpoint	**`/vision/v3.2/analyze plus /read/analyze, /generateThumbnail`**	**`/computervision/imageanalysis:analyze`**
Call pattern	Mix of **`sync`** (analyze) and **`async`** (read)	Single synchronous call
Tags	Yes	Yes
Objects	Yes	Yes
OCR	Async /read/analyze + polling	Sync **`readResult`**
Captions	Yes (via Description)	Yes (**`captionResult`**, English-only)
Dense captions	-	Yes

People/Faces	Faces with attributes	People bounding boxes only
Brands	Yes	-
Color and ImageType	Yes	-
Adult/Racy/Gore	Yes	-
Landmarks/Celebrities	Yes (domain models)	-
Thumbnails	Yes (binary)	Smart crops (coordinates only)

Table 5.1: *Comparison of Computer Vision API Versions 3.2 and 4.0*

Practical Use Cases

The Image Analysis service lends itself to a wide variety of scenarios where images must become actionable data. One of the most significant domains is accessibility. By combining captions with OCR, an application can provide screen readers with a natural-language description of an image and any visible text. This helps visually impaired users interact with content in a way that was previously inaccessible.

In the field of e-commerce, tags and object detection enrich product listings with searchable metadata. A product image no longer remains a static asset: once processed, it can be indexed by keywords, related products can be recommended based on shared tags, and catalogs can become far easier to navigate. Smart crops complement this by allowing a single product photo to adapt across responsive thumbnails for mobile, web, and social media previews without manual editing.

Document digitization and compliance workflows also benefit from Image Analysis. Legal teams, for example, can upload scanned contracts or receipts, and the OCR results provide a searchable text layer that feeds directly into knowledge bases. This turns large archives of paper documents into digital repositories where clauses, amounts, and names can be queried.

Even media and publishing platforms gain value from advanced features. Captions and dense captions can generate text for preview cards or social shares, making it possible to automate summaries for news articles or blogs. Meanwhile, safety and surveillance systems make use of people detection to flag human presence in an environment without requiring personal identification, striking a balance between security and privacy.

Face API: Beyond People Detection

While Image Analysis 4.0 includes a *people* feature, it deliberately stops at drawing bounding boxes around human figures. No personal information is returned, and this is by design: Microsoft has limited identity-level insights in Image Analysis to preserve privacy. However, for scenarios that demand more advanced face-specific capabilities, developers can turn to the **Face API**.

The Face API is a dedicated service of Azure for working with human faces in images. It is capable of detecting and framing individual faces, returning not only the bounding box but also detailed facial landmarks such as the positions of the eyes, nose, and mouth. These landmarks enable downstream applications such as overlaying augmented reality elements or ensuring alignment in face comparison tasks. Unlike Image Analysis, the Face API is explicitly designed to handle biometric scenarios such as verifying whether two faces belong to the same person or identifying an individual within a group.

Responsible AI Changes

It is important to note that the Face API today is not the same as it was a few years ago. In mid-2022, Microsoft announced a major realignment of its vision services in line with its **Responsible AI Standard**. As part of that commitment, the API retired several attribute-inference capabilities that attempted to predict sensitive traits such as gender, age, smile, facial hair, hair color, makeup, or emotional state. These attributes are no longer available to new customers, and the existing users were required to discontinue them by 2023.

This decision reflects a broader recognition that inferring personal characteristics from facial images can be inaccurate and potentially harmful if misused. By limiting access to sensitive features, Microsoft has repositioned the Face API around responsible, well-justified use cases. Advanced operations such as identification and verification now fall under a **Limited Access policy**, requiring developers to apply and justify their intended usage before Microsoft grants approval.

Current Capabilities

One must note that what remains available by default are **deterministic and non-sensitive features**. Developers can detect one or more faces in an image and obtain:

- The **face rectangle** (bounding box)
- A set of **landmarks** (for example, eyes, nose, mouth)
- **Image quality and context metrics** such as blur, exposure, occlusion, and head pose
- Whether or not the person is wearing **glasses**

These outputs may not reveal identity or personal attributes, but they still provide meaningful signals. For instance, blur and exposure help determine whether an image is usable for recognition, while occlusion indicates whether a face is partially blocked.

Glasses detection can improve accuracy in verification systems by adjusting pre-processing strategies.

Example: REST request (Face API):

```
curl -X POST \
  "https://<your-resource>.cognitiveservices.azure.com/face/v1.0/
detect?returnFaceAttributes= blur,exposure,glasses,headPose,
occlusion" \
  -H "Ocp-Apim-Subscription-Key: <FACE_KEY>" \
  -H "Content-Type: application/json" \
  -d '{"url":"<IMAGE_URL>"}'
```

Sample response:


```
[
  {
    "faceId": "abcd-1234",
    "faceRectangle": { "top": 120, "left": 200, "width": 130,
"height": 130 },
    "faceLandmarks": {
      "pupilLeft": {"x": 135.2, "y": 155.4},
      "pupilRight": {"x": 168.7, "y": 154.8}
    },
    "faceAttributes": {
      "blur": {"blurLevel": "low", "value": 0.1},
      "exposure": {"exposureLevel": "goodExposure", "value":
0.72},
      "glasses": "NoGlasses",
      "headPose": {"roll": 1.2, "yaw": 0.5, "pitch": -0.3},
      "occlusion": {"foreheadOccluded": false, "eyeOccluded":
false, "mouthOccluded": false}
    }
  }
]
```


Face API Complementing Image Analysis

The two services serve different purposes, and together they cover the full spectrum of visual intelligence. Image Analysis provides contextual understanding–objects, tags, captions, text, and the mere presence of people–without stepping into identity-sensitive territory. Face API, on the other hand, provides individual-level insights, such as accurate face localization, landmarks for alignment, and controlled access to identity verification features.

This combination allows developers to build applications that respect privacy yet remain powerful. For example, an image moderation system could use Image Analysis to describe the scene and detect people, while Face API could be used under Limited Access to verify identity only when strictly necessary.

Real-World Scenarios

In practice, the Face API is used in scenarios where the focus is on the face itself rather than the surrounding context. Secure facilities and smart buildings use it for **access control**, verifying whether the person at the door matches an enrolled profile. Marketing and retail environments rely on **landmark detection** and quality metrics to ensure that captured customer images are clear enough for further processing. Photo management platforms leverage face detection and landmarks for clustering and tagging, even without attributes such as age or gender.

Another important use case is **privacy protection**. Organizations that process photos or videos at scale can automatically detect faces and apply anonymization techniques, such as blurring, before storing or publishing the material. This ensures compliance with data protection regulations, while retaining the value of visual content.

Best Practices

Working effectively with the vision services of Azure is not only about knowing how to call the APIs, but also about using them responsibly and efficiently. A first rule of thumb is to request only the features you actually need. Every additional capability adds cost and latency, so tailoring your call to tags, objects, or OCR alone when that is all you require will keep your application lean. Another best practice is to pin the *model-version* parameter to guarantee reproducible results. This becomes critical in production scenarios where small changes in model behavior could otherwise introduce inconsistencies.

Language support is another consideration. While tags and OCR support multiple languages, captions and dense captions remain English-only and are restricted to specific regions. Applications targeting multilingual audiences should plan for integration with translation services or fallback mechanisms.

Security must always be treated as a primary concern. Keys should be stored in **Azure Key Vault** or protected with **managed identities**, never embedded directly in code. These practices reduce the risk of leaks and simplify rotation.

Finally, developers should stay aware of the **Responsible AI commitments by Microsoft**. In Image Analysis, privacy-preserving design means that the *people* features only indicate human presence. In Face API, sensitive attributes such as age, gender, and emotion have been replaced, and identity-level operations such as verification and identification now require **Limited Access approval**. This ensures that biometric data is handled with the scrutiny and justification it deserves. By combining Image Analysis

4.0 with the Face API and, where necessary, by services like Azure Content Safety, you can build vision-powered applications that are both technically effective and ethically aligned.

Developing Custom Vision Models

Azure Custom Vision enables developers to create domain-specific computer vision models tailored to their own data and business scenarios. Unlike prebuilt vision services designed for general-purpose recognition, Custom Vision allows organizations to define exactly what the model should recognize by providing labeled examples and iteratively improving performance.

This approach is particularly valuable in scenarios where generic models fall short–such as recognizing industry-specific products, specialized equipment, or unique visual patterns–making custom image classification and object detection essential tools for real-world applications.

Understanding Classification in Azure Custom Vision

In computer vision, **classification** refers to the process of assigning an image to one or more predefined categories. Unlike object detection, which attempts to locate items in an image, classification looks at the image as a whole and predicts the most likely label(s).

In the context of **Azure Custom Vision**, classification models are particularly powerful because they allow organizations to create tailored recognition systems without requiring expertise in machine learning. Microsoft provides the infrastructure, algorithms, and APIs; developers only need to supply training data and decide which categories they want to recognize.

For instance, imagine a company in the agricultural sector that wants to automatically recognize whether a crop leaf is healthy or affected by a specific disease. A traditional prebuilt image recognition model would not understand these specialized categories, but a Custom Vision classification model can be trained specifically for this purpose.

Project Setup: Domains, Tags, and Iterations

When creating a classification project in **Custom Vision**, the first step is to define its **domain**. Domains are pre-optimized model templates that Microsoft provides to accelerate training:

- **General**: Suitable for a wide variety of images

- **Food**: Optimized for food recognition tasks
- **Retail**: Good for product identification in retail contexts
- **Landmarks**: Useful for buildings, natural structures, and similar categories

The domain choice subtly influences the feature extraction process and ensures that the model architecture is tuned for your scenario.

Within a project, you define **tags**. Tags represent the categories you want the model to recognize. For a fruit classification system, you might have tags such as *Apple*, *Banana*, *Orange*, and *Mango*.

Every time you train the project, Custom Vision creates a new **iteration** of the model. Iterations are versioned, which allows you to experiment, compare, and roll back to a previous version, if needed.

Preparing and Labeling Data

Data preparation is arguably the most critical part of building a classification model. Azure recommends starting with at least 50 images per class for baseline performance, though production-grade models typically require hundreds or thousands.

Key guidelines for effective training images:

- **Variety**: Capture images under different conditions – lighting, background, perspective, resolution.
- **Balance**: Ensure that each class has a roughly similar number of images. If one class has 1,000 samples and another only 50, the model may become biased toward the larger class.
- **Quality**: Images should clearly depict the subject. Blurry or ambiguous images should be avoided unless they represent real-world conditions the model must handle.

Labeling is the process of assigning each image to one or more tags. In classification, labeling is straightforward: every image belongs to a class (or possibly multiple classes if you choose a **multilabel** project).

Labeling can be done:

- Via the Custom Vision Portal (drag-and-drop images and apply tags)
- Programmatically using the Training API, which supports uploading labeled images in batches

Training via Portal: A Step-by-Step Example

1. Sign in to the `Custom Vision portal` at https://www.customvision.ai.

2. Create a **`new project`**, select *Classification*, and choose the **`General`** domain.
3. Create tags: *Goku, Piccolo, Goku-Super Saiyan.*
4. Upload images to each tag.
5. Click **`Train`**. You can choose between *Quick Training* (fast, suitable for prototyping) or *Advanced Training* (slower but higher accuracy).
6. After training, an **`iteration`** is produced. You can then test it directly in the portal by uploading new images or providing a URL.

The following image highlights the Azure Custom Vision portal during the training workflow, showing a classification project with labeled training images and the option to start model training. The interface illustrates how developers can choose between quick and advanced training modes directly from the portal.

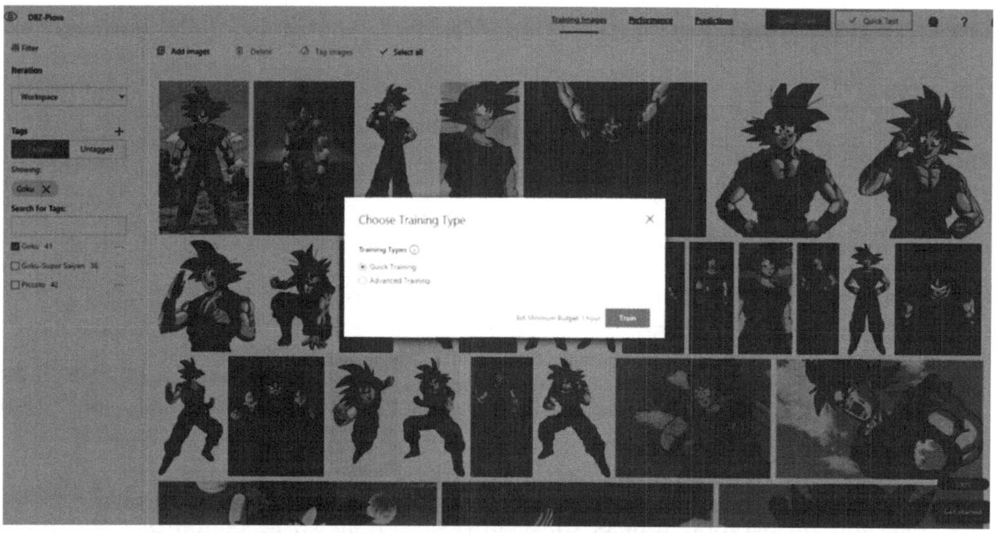

Figure 5.3: *Custom Vision Portal, Used to Upload, Tag, and Train Custom Image Recognition Models*

Training via API in Python

The following is a more complete example in Python, showing project creation, tag definition, image upload, training, and prediction:

```
from azure.cognitiveservices.vision.customvision.training import
CustomVisionTrainingClient
from azure.cognitiveservices.vision.customvision.prediction
import CustomVisionPredictionClient
from msrest.authentication import ApiKeyCredentials
import time
# Replace with your own keys and endpoint
```

```
ENDPOINT = "https://<your-custom-vision-endpoint>.cognitiveser-
vices.azure.com/"
training_key = "<your-training-key>"
prediction_key = "<your-prediction-key>"
project_name = "FruitClassifier"
# Authenticate with the training API
training_credentials = ApiKeyCredentials(in_headers
={"Training-key": training_key})
trainer = CustomVisionTrainingClient(ENDPOINT,
training_credentials)
# Create a new classification project
project = trainer.create_project(project_name, domain_id=None)
# Define tags
goku_tag = trainer.create_tag(project.id, "Goku")
piccolo_tag = trainer.create_tag(project.id, "Piccolo")
goku-super_tag = trainer.create_tag(project.id, "Goku-Super
Saiyan")
# Upload images with labels
defupload_image(tag, filepath):
    with open(filepath, "rb") as image_contents:
trainer.create_images_from_data(project.id, image_contents,
[tag.id])
upload_image(goku_tag, "goku1.jpg")
upload_image(goku_tag, "goku2.jpg")
upload_image(piccolo_tag, "piccolo1.jpg")
upload_image(goku-super_tag, "goku-supersaiyan1.jpg")
# Train the model
iteration = trainer.train_project(project.id)
while (iteration.status != "Completed"):
    iteration = trainer.get_iteration(project.id, iteration.id)
time.sleep(10)
print(f"Training complete. Iteration: {iteration.id}")
```

Prediction with REST API: Once trained and published, predictions can be requested using the **Prediction API**.

Request:

```
POST https://<your-endpoint>/customvision/v3.0/Prediction/
{projectId}/classify/iterations/{iterationName}/url
Content-Type: application/json
Prediction-Key: <your-prediction-key>
```

Body:

```
{
  "Url": "https://example.com/goku-image.jpg"
}
```

Response:


```
{
  "id": "d2f9c620-1d7b-4bfb-9a6e-1b223a5d9a9f",
  "project": "dbz-project-id",
  "iteration": "Iteration1",
  "created": "2025-06-01T15:45:00Z",
  "predictions": [
{ "tagId": "123", "tagName": "Goku", "probability": 0.85 },
{ "tagId": "456", "tagName": "Goku-Super Saiyan", "probability":
0.14 },
{ "tagId": "789", "tagName": "Piccolo", "probability": 0.01 }
  ]
}
```


Practical Considerations:

- **Multiclass versus Multilabel**: By default, projects are *multiclass*—the model assigns one label per image. However, multilabel classification is supported, allowing multiple tags per image. This is useful, for example, if an image could contain both *Healthy* and *Leaf* tags.
- **Iteration Management**: Always version your iterations. Keep track of which iteration is in production and which are experimental.
- **Continuous Improvement**: Retraining with new data over time is essential. Azure allows you to upload misclassified images and retrain iteratively.

Object Detection Models in Azure Custom Vision

While classification assigns a single label to an image as a whole, object detection goes further by identifying where specific objects are located within an image and labeling them accordingly. This involves not only recognizing the type of object but also drawing a bounding box around each detected instance.

For many real-world business applications, this distinction is crucial. Consider a factory scenario: it is not enough to know that an image contains a defective part—you need to know which part is defective and where it is located. Similarly, in retail shelf monitoring, a model must not only detect that cereal boxes are present, but also count how many are on a given shelf, and whether any are misplaced or missing.

Thus, object detection models provide both classification and localization capabilities, making them far more versatile for operational use cases.

Use Cases for Object Detection in Industry:

- **Retail shelf analysis**: Detecting and counting specific products (for instance., soda cans, snack packages) to verify compliance with planograms.

- **Manufacturing quality control**: Identifying defective components, scratches, or assembly errors at specific locations on a product.
- **Logistics and inventory**: Recognizing and counting packages in warehouses, verifying labels or barcode presence.
- **Healthcare**: Locating and classifying anomalies in medical images (for example, lesions in X-rays or MRI scans).
- **Agriculture**: Detecting pests on leaves, estimating fruit yield by counting visible produce.

The Labeling Process: Bounding Boxes

Training an object detection model in Azure Custom Vision requires images where each region of interest is annotated. This is typically done through **bounding boxes**: rectangular regions drawn around each object. Each box is assigned a tag corresponding to the object class.

In practice, bounding boxes must be as precise as possible, tightly surrounding the object. Poorly drawn or inconsistent annotations can significantly degrade the accuracy of the model. For example, when building a model that detects *logos* such as **Xamarin**, **MSBuild**, or even pop culture figures like **Grogu**, each instance of the object must be clearly enclosed within a bounding box and labeled accordingly.

An annotation in JSON format may look like this:

```
{
  "tagName": "Xamarin",
  "boundingBox": {
    "left": 0.15,
    "top": 0.25,
    "width": 0.30,
    "height": 0.40
  }
}
```

These normalized coordinates (values between 0 and 1) indicate the position and size of the object relative to the image dimensions.

Building an Object Detection Solution with Azure Custom Vision

1. **Preparing the Dataset:** The foundation of any successful object detection model lies in the training images. Unlike classification, which only needs a tag for each image, object detection requires both the **images** and **bounding box annotations** for each object instance.

When preparing a dataset for objects such as *logos, icons, or characters* (for instance., Xamarin, MSBuild, or Grogu), consider the following principles:

- **Balance across classes**: Aim for a similar number of annotated examples for each tag. A common recommendation is at least 50 images per class, though more samples yield better performance in real-world deployments.
- **Variety in context**: Include objects under different lighting conditions, angles, and scales. If Grogu is always centered with the same background, the model may fail in diverse settings.
- **Multiple instances per image**: Object detection benefits from images containing more than one object, possibly from different classes, to help the model generalize to cluttered environments.
- **Annotation precision**: Draw bounding boxes tightly around the object. Boxes that are too loose or inconsistent across samples reduce localization quality.

2. **Creating and Configuring a Project in the Portal:** Azure Custom Vision provides a streamlined workflow through the **`Custom Vision portal`** (**https://www.customvision.ai**). The steps for object detection are:

   a. **Create a new project** and choose *Object Detection* as the project type. Select an appropriate domain, such as *General (compact)* if you plan to deploy on edge devices, or *General* for cloud-hosted scenarios.

   b. **Define tags** for each class you want to detect, such as *Grogu*, *MSBuild*, and *Xamarin*.

   c. **Upload images** into the project.

   d. **Annotate each object** using the bounding box tool. Every instance of Grogu, MSBuild, and Xamarin in the image must be enclosed and tagged.

The following image highlights the Azure Custom Vision portal during the object annotation process, showing how bounding boxes are drawn around detected objects and associated with specific tags. The interface demonstrates how each instance of an object is precisely labeled to train an object detection model.

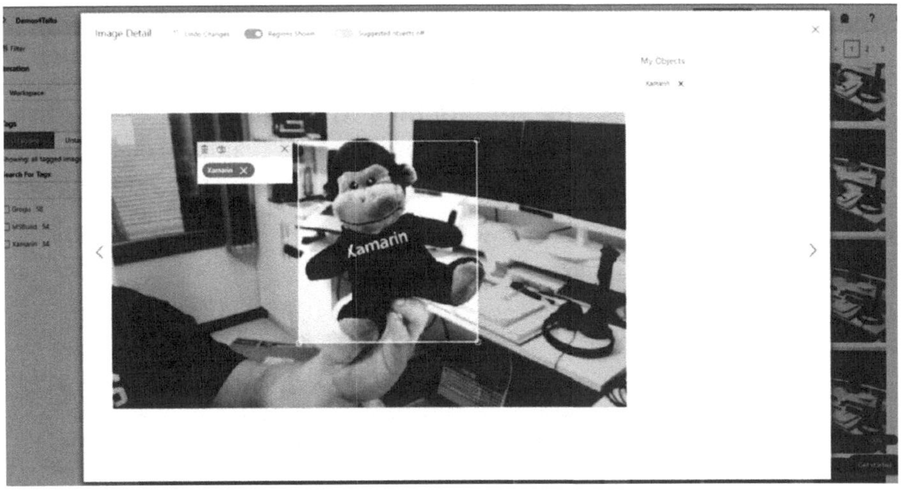

Figure 5.4: *Custom Vision Portal, Annotating Objects with Bounding Boxes in the Portal*

e. **Train the project**. Select **`Quick Training`** for rapid iterations or Advanced Training for deeper optimization.

f. **Evaluate performance** using the metrics provided (precision, recall, and average precision).

The following image highlights the performance evaluation view of an Azure Custom Vision object detection model after training. It displays key metrics such as precision, recall, and mean average precision (mAP), along with per-tag performance results used to assess model quality.

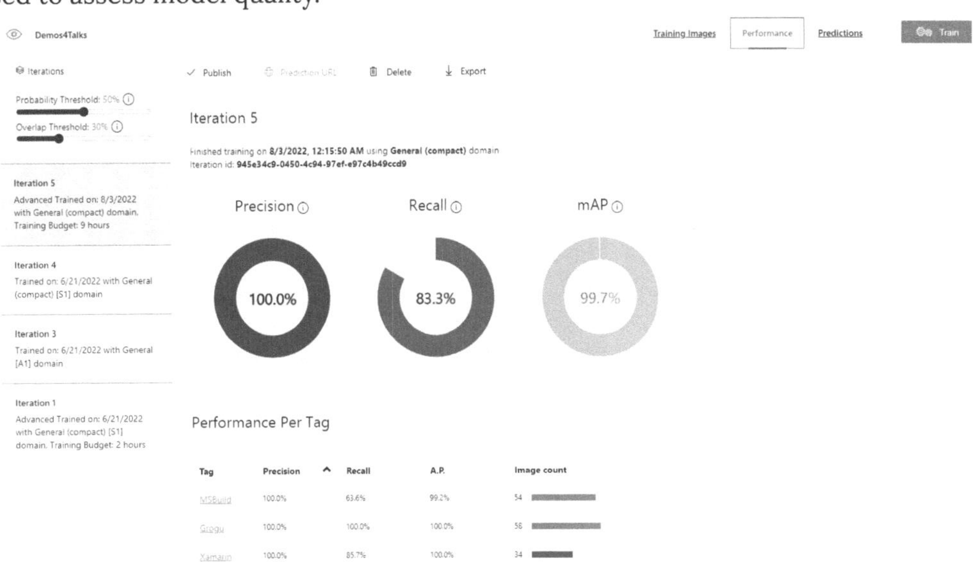

Figure 5.5: *Custom Vision Portal, Evaluating Performance Metric for the Trained Model*

g. **Publish the iteration** once you are satisfied with performance, making it available through the **Prediction API**.

3. **Automating the Workflow with the Training API:** While the portal is useful for exploration and manual labeling, most production teams prefer to automate training and iteration management through the **Custom Vision Training API**.

The following Python example shows how to upload an annotated image with bounding boxes, train the model, and publish the iteration:

```
from azure.cognitiveservices.vision.customvision.training import
CustomVisionTrainingClient
from azure.cognitiveservices.vision.customvision.training.models
import ImageFileCreateEntry, Region
from msrest.authentication import ApiKeyCredentials
import time
# Replace with your Custom Vision keys and project details
ENDPOINT = "https://<your-endpoint>.cognitiveservices.azure.com/"
TRAINING_KEY = "<your-training-key>"
PROJECT_ID = "<your-project-id>"
trainer = CustomVisionTrainingClient(
    ENDPOINT,
ApiKeyCredentials(in_headers={"Training-key": TRAINING_KEY})
)

# Example: upload one image with bounding boxes for Grogu and
MSBuild
with open("training_images/scene1.jpg", "rb") as image_contents:
    entry = ImageFileCreateEntry(
        name="scene1.jpg",
        contents=image_contents.read(),
        regions=[
            Region(tag_id="<grogu-tag-id>", left=0.10, top=0.18,
width=0.28, height=0.40),
            Region(tag_id="<msbuild-tag-id>", left=0.55,
top=0.25, width=0.22, height=0.30)
        ]
    )
trainer.create_images_from_files(PROJECT_ID, [entry])
# Train the project
iteration = trainer.train_project(PROJECT_ID)
while iteration.status != "Completed":
time.sleep(10)
    iteration = trainer.get_iteration(PROJECT_ID, iteration.id)
# Publish the iteration
PUBLISHED_NAME = "prod-v1"
trainer.publish_iteration(PROJECT_ID, iteration.id, PUBLISHED_
```

```
NAME, prediction_resource_id=None)
print(f"Iteration {iteration.id} trained and published as
'{PUBLISHED_NAME}'")
```

This script demonstrates how bounding box annotations are represented in the API. Each *Region* object specifies the coordinates and the tag ID corresponding to the labeled object.

4. **Consuming the Prediction API:** Once an iteration is published, you can access it through the **Prediction API**. Predictions return a list of detected objects with probabilities and bounding box coordinates.

Example request (URL-based image):

```
POST https://<your-endpoint>/customvision/v3.0/Prediction/
{projectId}/detect/iterations/prod-v1/url
Prediction-Key: <your-prediction-key>
Content-Type: application/json
{
  "Url": "https://example.org/test-scene.jpg"
}
Example response:
{
  "id": "6f9a2a30-45f1-4caa-917c-efb5a2c84a22",
  "project": "project-id",
  "iteration": "prod-v1",
  "created": "2025-03-10T14:25:00Z",
  "predictions": [
    {
      "probability": 0.95,
      "tagId": "guid-grogu",
      "tagName": "Grogu",
      "boundingBox": { "left": 0.12, "top": 0.18, "width": 0.28,
"height": 0.40 }
    },
    {
      "probability": 0.83,
      "tagId": "guid-xamarin",
      "tagName": "Xamarin",
      "boundingBox": { "left": 0.55, "top": 0.25, "width": 0.20,
"height": 0.32 }
    }
  ]
}
```

The client application can use these normalized bounding boxes to draw rectangles over the original image, enabling visualization of detected objects.

Best Practices

- **Confidence thresholds**: Apply a cutoff (for example, 0.6 or 0.7) to filter out low-confidence predictions.
- **Non-maximum suppression**: When the model outputs overlapping boxes for the same object, apply suppression to keep the best candidate.
- **Continuous improvement**: Collect false positives and false negatives from real-world usage, re-label them, and retrain the model to improve accuracy.
- **Domain selection**: For edge deployment, use a "`compact`" domain to export models to TensorFlow, ONNX, or Docker containers.

Advanced Video Intelligence Using Azure AI Video Indexer

Azure AI Video Indexer (AVI) sits at the intersection of media engineering and applied AI. It orchestrates more than thirty speech, vision, and language models to transform raw audio-video into a time-aligned "*insights graph*" you can search, visualize, and wire into downstream systems. In this section, we will move beyond a quickstart and build a developer-centric understanding of what AVI can do, how its REST API works, and how to deploy it as a reliable building block inside enterprise solutions.

Introduction to Azure AI Video Indexer

Azure AI Video Indexer is a cloud (and Arc-enabled edge) application in the Azure AI Services family. When you upload a video, AVI runs a pipeline of AI models across audio and frames: automatic speech recognition with diarization, language identification and translation, topic inference, OCR of on-screen text, brand and entity detection, face and person insights, scene/shot/keyframe segmentation, and text-based sentiment/emotion over the transcript. The results are returned as a single JSON document with timestamps for every detected element, which is the foundation for search, recommendation, accessibility, and compliance workflows. The public documentation of Microsoft describes AVI as "running 30+ AI models" and producing comprehensive, time-aligned insights JSON; it also provides a feature inventory that includes transcripts, OCR, faces, topics, emotions/sentiment, and more.

AVI is delivered as a managed web portal and a fully documented REST API. The developer portal exposes the endpoints for uploading media, retrieving insights, generating captions, redacting faces, and managing custom models, and shows an example upload that uses an OAuth-style bearer token in the Authorization header to call **POST *https://api.videoindexer.ai/{Region}/Accounts/{AccountId}/Videos*** with query parameters such as **`name`**, **`privacy`**, **`language`**, **`indexingPreset`**, and **`streamingPreset`.**

Two access patterns exist today:

- **Developer-portal ("`classic`") key → account access token** You obtain a short-lived access token by calling the Video Indexer Auth endpoint with your subscription key, then call the data plane APIs with that bearer token. The developer portal outlines this flow and surfaces the endpoints.

The following image highlights the Azure Video Indexer developer portal, presenting the main onboarding flow for working with the Video Indexer API. It illustrates the high-level steps for obtaining access tokens, adding media content, and extracting video insights through the portal or REST APIs.

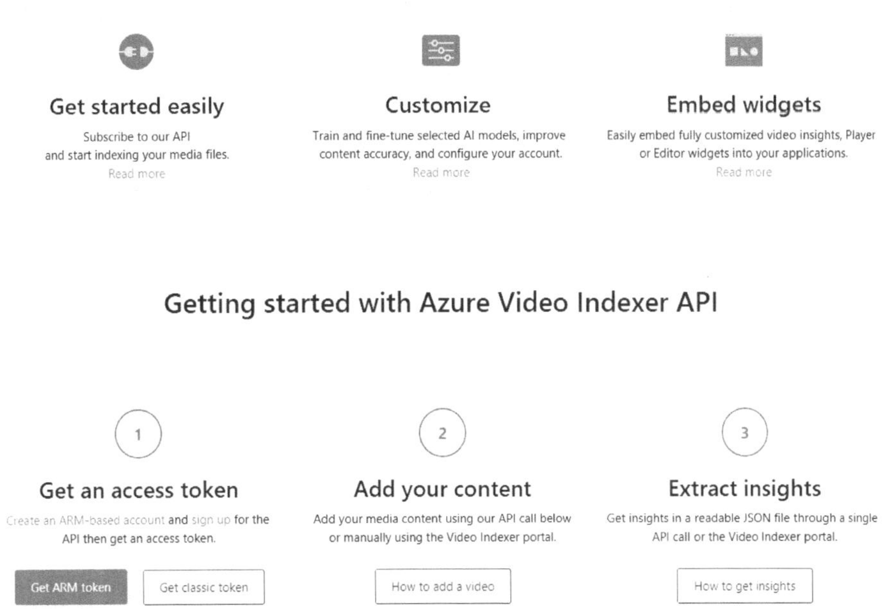

Figure 5.6: *Azure Video Indexer Developer Portal*

- **ARM-based accounts:** For ARM resources, you call the management plane to generate an account/video-scoped access token via **`POST` *https://management.azure.com/subscriptions/{subscriptionId}/resourceGroups/{rg}/providers/Microsoft.VideoIndexer/accounts/{accountName}/generateAccessToken?api-version=2025-04-01*.** This token can then be used against the data plane.

From an architectural point of view, the value of AVI is threefold. First, it unifies multimodal analysis into a single, consistent JSON you can treat as a schema for "what happened when" in your media. Second, it is configurable: you can choose languages and presets, enable custom models (person/brand/speech/language), and fine-tune behavior at scale. Third, it integrates easily with search engines, BI tools, and content management systems through standard web APIs and web widgets.

Core Features and Capabilities

This section explains the major insight types AVI generates, when to use them, and practical caveats.

- **Speech-to-text and transcript generation**: AVI transcribes speech, identifies languages, and can translate to target languages. It emits closed captions in VTT, SRT, and TTML, and provides speaker-attributed transcripts when diarization is available. The transcript is the backbone for search, captions, and downstream NLP. You can download captions or access them via the API; the connector and docs describe parameters such as **`format=vtt and language`**. Accuracy depends on audio quality, domain terminology, and language model selection; for specialized domains, train a custom speech model and set the linguistic model on upload.
- **Speaker identification (diarization)**: AVI segments that can speak, and can attach editor-assigned speaker names across a single file. For cross-video recognition, couple diarization with person/face models (below) or your own identity systems. Typical diarization limits include overlapping speech and far-field audio; leverage two-channel processing where available to improve attribution.
- **Object, label, and activity detection**: AVI classifies visual content into a large label set ("labels" in the JSON), detects shots, scenes, and keyframes, and extracts entities such as brands and landmarks. Remember that visual classes are broad and not exhaustive; for domain-specific concepts (for example., medical instruments), incorporate Custom Vision on top of the keyframes in AVI.
- **Facial recognition and person models**: AVI detects faces and can recognize celebrities (limited access) and user-trained persons through account-scoped person models. Person recognition requires model training with face images, and the documentation provides APIs to customize person models and patch thresholds. As with all Azure facial capabilities, certain uses are limited-access and subject to responsible AI policies; ensure you have legal grounds and end-user consent.
- **Sentiment and text-based emotion analysis**: AVI computes sentiment and labels emotions over the **transcript text**, not by inferring facial emotion. That distinction matters for compliance and fairness: text-based models are intended to characterize the tone in language (for example, positive/negative/

neutral or categorical emotions such as joy and sadness) and should not be used to assess the individual emotional state or performance.

- **On-screen text (OCR)**: AVI extracts text from slides, lower thirds, and any on-screen text, merges it with speech, and exposes combined entities and topics over a unified timeline. OCR accuracy depends on font, size, motion blur, and contrast (AVI also provides the raw locations and timestamps in the JSON).
- **Content moderation**: AVI exposes visual explicit-content indicators and offers a **Face Redaction** preset to automatically blur faces—useful for privacy and compliance. For text moderation of transcripts or comments, combine AVI with Azure AI Content Moderator; for static image moderation, you can also use the adult/racy/gore detection of Azure AI. One should always include human-in-the-loop reviews for high-stakes decisions.
- **Edge and Arc-enabled indexing**: For sovereign or low-latency scenarios, AVI can run on Arc-enabled Kubernetes, extracting the same insights without uploading files to the Azure cloud.

Limitations to keep in mind: STT quality tracks audio quality; diarization struggles with crosstalk; label coverage is broad but not exhaustive; person/celebrity recognition is gated and subject to policy; emotion detection is text-only; throttling and file-size limits apply (for instance., prefer URL/SAS uploads over multipart for large files). AVI guides at-scale indexing, including using callback URLs and respecting **retry-after**.

Setting Up and Using Video Indexer

This subsection walks through the end-to-end API flow—from authentication to retrieval of insights—with both C# and Python examples.

1. **Authentication: getting an access token**

   Classic (developer-portal key) → data-plane token:

   a. Sign in to the developer portal (**https://api-portal.videoindexer.ai/**) and subscribe to the API to get your primary/secondary keys.

   b. Call the Auth endpoint with your key to receive a short-lived account token. Typical pattern:

```
GET https://api.videoindexer.ai/Auth/{region}/Accounts/
{accountId}/AccessToken?allowEdit=true
Ocp-Apim-Subscription-Key: {your_api_key}
```

This token is then used in the Authorization: Bearer header on subsequent data-plane calls.

ARM-based account:

Enterprises often prefer ARM flow and RBAC. Use:

```
POST https://management.azure.com/subscriptions/{subscriptionId}/
resourceGroups/{rg}/providers/Microsoft.VideoIndexer/accounts/
{accountName}/generateAccessToken?api-version=2025-04-01
```

Include a body with **permissionType** and scope (for example., account/video), and use the returned **accessToken** against data-plane APIs.

2. **Uploading media and indexing: Choosing the upload method:** For files up to many GB, prefer **URL/SAS** upload (AVI pulls your blob) rather than posting byte arrays; it scales better and avoids multipart timeouts. You can also provide a **callbackUrl** so AVI calls back when indexing state changes.

C# – authenticate, upload via URL, and poll (or use callback)

```
using System;
using System.Net.Http;
using System.Net.Http.Headers;
using System.Threading.Tasks;
using System.Web;

class AviUploadSample
{
    static async Task Main()
    {
var region    = "trial";            // e.g., "westus2" or "trial"
varaccountId = "<your-account-id>";
varapiKey    = "<your-dev-portal-key>";
varvideoUrl  = "<https-or-sas-url-to-media>";
var name      = "Contoso Product Demo";
varcallback  = "https://example.com/avi-callback"; // optional

        // 1) Get account access token (classic flow)
var http = new HttpClient();
http.DefaultRequestHeaders.Add("Ocp-Apim-Subscription-Key",
apiKey);
vartokenResp = await http.GetStringAsync(
            $"https://api.videoindexer.ai/Auth/{region}/Accounts/
{accountId}/AccessToken?allowEdit=true");
var token = tokenResp.Trim('"'); // endpoint returns a JSON
string literal
        // 2) Upload: POST .../Videos with bearer token
varqs = $"name={Uri.EscapeDataString(name)}" +
                  $"&videoUrl={HttpUtility.UrlEncode(videoUrl)}" +
                  "&privacy=Private&indexingPreset=Default&
streamingPreset=None" +
```

```
                    $"&callbackUrl={HttpUtility.UrlEncode
(callback)}";
varuploadUri = $"https://api.videoindexer.ai/{region}/Accounts/
{accountId}/Videos?{qs}";

varreq = new HttpRequestMessage(HttpMethod.Post, uploadUri);
req.Headers.Authorization = new AuthenticationHeaderValue
("Bearer", token);
var upload = await http.SendAsync(req);
upload.EnsureSuccessStatusCode();
varjson = await upload.Content.ReadAsStringAsync();   // contains
videoId and initial state

Console.WriteLine(json);
    }
}
```

That upload pattern matches the example in the developer's portal (bearer token in header, **POST …/Videos** with query-string options).

Python – authenticate (classic), upload, and fetch insights

```
import requests, urllib.parse, time
region    = "trial"            # e.g., 'westus2'
accountId = "<your-account-id>"
apiKey    = "<your-dev-portal-key>"
videoUrl  = "<https-or-sas-url>"
name      = "Quarterly Update"
session   = requests.Session()
# 1) get access token
r = session.get(f"https://api.videoindexer.ai/Auth/{region}
/Accounts/{accountId}/AccessToken",
params={"allowEdit":"true"},
    headers={"Ocp-Apim-Subscription-Key": apiKey},
    timeout=30)
r.raise_for_status()
token = r.text.strip('"')
# 2) upload
qs = {
    "name": name,
    "videoUrl": videoUrl,
    "privacy": "Private",
    "indexingPreset": "Default",
    "streamingPreset": "None"
}
u = f"https://api.videoindexer.ai/{region}/Accounts/{accountId}/
Videos"
u = f"{u}?{urllib.parse.urlencode(qs, safe='')}"
```

```
r = session.post(u, headers={"Authorization": f"Bearer {token}"},
timeout=60)
r.raise_for_status()
video = r.json()
video_id = video["id"]
# 3) poll (or rely on callbackUrl)
state = video.get("state")
while state not in ("Processed","Failed"):
time.sleep(10)
    r = session.get(f"https://api.videoindexer.ai/
{region}/Accounts/{accountId}/Videos/{video_id}/Index",
                    headers={"Authorization": f"Bearer {token}"},
timeout=30)
r.raise_for_status()
idx = r.json()
    state = idx.get("state")
print(f"Video {video_id} is {state}")
```

The same upload works with **ARM tokens** by skipping the **Ocp-Apim-Subscription-Key** step and calling the ARM **`generateAccessToken`** endpoint; you then pass the bearer token exactly as above.

Callback instead of polling: To avoid polling, specify **`callbackUrl=...`** on upload; AVI posts **the ID** and **state** when indexing state changes (Processed/Failed) and can also notify on person identification events. This pattern integrates cleanly with Azure Functions or Logic Apps.

3. **Retrieving insights and captions**

Insights JSON. After indexing, call:

```
GET https://api.videoindexer.ai/{region}/Accounts/{accountId}/
Videos/{videoId}/Index
Authorization: Bearer {accessToken}
```

The response contains the insights graph: **faces**, **labels**, **ocr**, **topics**, **shots**, **scenes**, **keyframes**, **sentiments/emotions**, **speakers**, and more, each with arrays of instances and **start/end** timestamps. Docs emphasize using the full "**`insights`**" object rather than legacy summarized insights.

Captions, to fetch VTT/SRT captions programmatically:

```
GET https://api.videoindexer.ai/{region}/Accounts/{accountId}/
Videos/{videoId}/Captions?format=vtt
Authorization: Bearer {accessToken}
```

The connector docs highlight the **format** and optional **language** parameters for caption retrieval.

Face redaction and media processing: Beyond analysis, AVI exposes media operations like face redaction via a preset; you submit a redaction job and retrieve the processed asset.

Advanced Scenarios and Customization

While the majority of applications can be built directly on top of the insights JSON had produced by Video Indexer, some scenarios benefit from extending its capabilities or combining it with other Azure services. In this section, we will briefly examine three common patterns.

- **Integrating Video Indexer with enterprise search**: Organizations often need to make large video archives searchable at the level of spoken words, on-screen text, faces, and topics. A recommended approach is to extract the Video Indexer insights JSON, normalize key elements (transcript lines, OCR results, face appearances), and push them into **Azure AI Search**. This enables keyword and semantic search, and allows users to jump directly to the relevant moment within a video.
- **Building recommendation engines**: The structured metadata extracted by Video Indexer–topics, labels, entities, and people–can serve as features for recommendation systems. By computing similarity between videos based on these attributes, or by tracking which topic users engage with most organizations can deliver personalized content suggestions. This is particularly relevant in media streaming, education, and corporate knowledge management.
- **Extending with Custom Vision**: For highly specialized domains where built-in object detection of Video Indexer does not provide sufficient coverage, developers can export **keyframes** from indexed videos and run them through a **Custom Vision** classifier. Detected domain-specific tags (such as industrial tools, medical instruments, or branded products) can then be merged back into the Video Indexer insights and made searchable alongside the default labels.

These extension scenarios illustrate that Video Indexer is not an isolated tool but a foundation for broader intelligent media solutions. By combining it with Azure AI Search, Custom Vision, or recommendation frameworks, developers can tailor video intelligence to the exact needs of their organization, without reinventing the indexing pipeline.

Evaluating and Interpreting Results

JSON of AVI is rich, but getting value requires understanding the structure, confidence, coverage, and the limits of each model.

- **The insights schema:** The top-level **videos** array describes your asset(s). **insights** contain the meat: arrays such as **faces, labels, brands, topics, ocr, speakers, sentiments/emotions, shots, scenes**, each with **instances** that include **start/end** (or `startTime/endTime`), and often **confidence**. For captions, use the **Captions** API; for global stats and timelines, the portal mirrors fields found in the JSON.
- **Confidence and acceptance thresholds:** Treat confidences as ranking signals, not ground truth. Build per-feature acceptance heuristics per your scenario. For instance, you might accept brand matches ≥0.8 if they co-occur with OCR or audio mentions; for face/person, use the person-model threshold and configure it via the person-model API (release notes highlight this).
- **Precision/recall tradeoffs in practice:** For speech-driven search, you want high recall; for compliance redaction, you want high precision. Build a validation set and compute P/R on transcript segments, face appearances, and brands. Then set post-filters (for instance, minimum duration, multi-channel evidence) to reduce false positives.
- **Diarization and speakers:** Map speakers to readability in your UI ("Speaker 1", and so on). If you need true identities across videos, train a person model and link diarized time ranges to recognized faces (or use your HR/CRM identities). The docs call out that editing a speaker name in a single video does not propagate across the account automatically.
- **Sentiment and emotions:** Since the emotion model of AVI is transcript-based, it is robust to camera angle but sensitive to translation and sarcasm. Use it for **content tone analytics** and **highlight reels**, not to evaluate individuals; the transparency note of Microsoft states this explicitly.
- **Moderation and redaction:** Face redaction is a separate preset; if you rely on it for privacy, and test on your content and keep a manual override path for missed faces (for instance, allow editors to add faces by time range).
- **Automated evaluation in CI:** Treat model output drift as you would any ML system: maintain a small benchmark set of videos; after system updates, run a job that re-indexes them and computes deltas of: WER on transcripts (if ground truth available), P/R on face/brand detections (checked by QA annotators), and time-coverage of labels. Fail your pipeline if deviations exceed tolerance.

Deployment and Integration in Enterprise Solutions

Deploying Azure AI Video Indexer in enterprise-grade applications requires more than simply calling its REST API. It involves designing a complete architecture that ensures scalability, security, monitoring, and integration with the broader Azure ecosystem. In this section, we will explore how Video Indexer can be embedded into web, mobile, and backend systems, and how its insights can be combined with other Azure services such as Azure AI Search, Power BI, and Azure Functions.

Architectural Considerations

When integrating Video Indexer into enterprise solutions, developers must account for three primary dimensions:

- **Scalability**: Video Indexer is designed to handle both ad-hoc video uploads and large-scale batch processing. For high-volume ingestion scenarios, it is recommended to orchestrate uploads through **Azure Functions** or **Azure Logic Apps**, using the **callbackUrl** parameter to trigger downstream workflows when indexing is complete. This avoids continuous polling and reduces unnecessary API calls.
- **Security**: Authentication is handled using either the classic developer portal keys or Azure Resource Manager (ARM)-based access tokens. In enterprise deployments, the ARM model is preferred because it integrates with **Azure EntraID** and enables granular Role-Based Access Control (RBAC). This ensures that only authorized services and users can generate access tokens and interact with Video Indexer resources.
- **Data governance**: Video Indexer produces sensitive metadata such as transcripts, detected faces, and recognized entities. Enterprises must enforce compliance with data protection regulations (GDPR, HIPAA, and so on) by defining retention policies, securing insight storage in **Azure Blob Storage** or **Cosmos DB**, and, where necessary, using the **Face Redaction** preset to protect privacy.

By addressing these dimensions early, organizations can ensure that Video Indexer becomes a trusted component of their media analytics architecture.

Integration Patterns

Different applications require different integration patterns, but most deployments fall into one of the following categories:

- **Web and mobile applications**: A common requirement is to enrich video players with search and navigation features powered by Video Indexer. Developers can use the Video Indexer widgets, which provide embeddable playback experiences with timeline insights, or build custom players that consume the insights JSON. For example, a corporate training portal can display a transcript panel next to the video player, enabling learners to search for keywords and jump directly to relevant moments.

- **Backend systems and content management**: For Digital Asset Management (DAM) or Enterprise Content Management (ECM) platforms, Video Indexer serves as an automated enrichment engine. After the media is ingested, an Azure Function or Logic App uploads the file to Video Indexer, waits for processing to complete, and then persists the resulting JSON in a metadata repository. This enriched metadata can be indexed in **Azure Cognitive Search**, making the entire video library searchable not only by title or tags but also by spoken words, topics, and detected entities.
- **Analytics and dashboards**: Business stakeholders often require aggregate insights across a catalog of videos. By exporting Video Indexer data to **Azure Data Lake Storage** or **Azure SQL Database**, organizations can build dashboards in **Power BI** that display sentiment trends, brand exposure metrics, or speaker participation over time. This transforms unstructured video content into structured, decision-ready data.

Consuming Insights via the REST API

The REST API of Video Indexer provides straightforward endpoints for accessing insights. A typical workflow involves retrieving the full analysis JSON, and then projecting the relevant fields into your application.

Retrieve insights for a processed video:

```
GET https://api.videoindexer.ai/{region}/Accounts/{accountId}/
Videos/{videoId}/Index
Authorization: Bearer {accessToken}
```

Sample response excerpt:

```
{
  "videos": [
    {
      "id": "abcd1234",
      "insights": {
        "faces": [
          {
            "name": "PablitoPiova",
            "appearances": [
{ "startTime": "0:01:23", "endTime": "0:02:05" }
            ]
          }
        ],
        "labels": [
          {
```

```
                "name": "Laptop",
                "appearances": [
      { "startTime": "0:00:15", "endTime": "0:00:30" }
                ]
              }
            ],
            "sentiments": [
              {
                "sentimentType": "positive",
                "instances": [
      { "startTime": "0:03:00", "endTime": "0:03:20" }
                ]
              }
            ]
          }
        }
      ]
    }
```


In this example, the JSON indicates when a person, object, or sentiment appears in the video. Applications can consume this information to highlight entities in the player, build search indexes, or trigger workflows (for example, flagging negative sentiment segments for editorial review).

Conclusion

Implementing computer vision solutions with Azure services shows how applied AI can transform visual data into structured, actionable information. From extracting tags, objects, text, and captions with Azure AI Vision to training custom classification and object-detection models with Custom Vision, developers can build applications that not only automate tasks but also enable more accessible, secure, and domain-adapted experiences.

Azure AI Video Indexer extends these capabilities to audiovisual content, providing transcripts, entity detection, OCR, sentiment over text, and compliance tools. Integrating these services into enterprise architectures turns large volumes of content into high-value assets for search, analysis, and strategic decision-making. Together, these solutions demonstrate how responsibly scaled computer vision becomes a cornerstone for digital innovation.

In the next chapter, we will explore **Natural Language Processing (NLP) solutions**, including translation, sentiment analysis, language detection, and PII recognition. We will also cover speech-to-text, text-to-speech, avatars, and conversational AI with CLU and custom question answering, as well as building custom translation models and integrating real-time speech processing into applications.

Points to Remember

- Azure AI Vision 4.0 unifies multiple features in a single synchronous call, simplifying development by allowing tags, objects, OCR, and captions to be requested together in one API request.
- Tags, objects, OCR, and captions enrich catalogs and improve accessibility, turning images into searchable assets while also making content more usable for people with visual impairments.
- Smart crops return coordinates instead of images, increasing flexibility, so developers can apply consistent cropping across devices and screen formats without relying on pre-generated thumbnails.
- Face API offers face detection and landmarks while limiting sensitive attributes, ensuring applications can localize and analyze faces without exposing demographic or personal identity data.
- Custom Vision lets you train domain-specific models with your own labeled data, enabling highly specialized recognition systems tailored to industries such as healthcare, retail, or agriculture.
- Classification assigns global labels, while detection localizes specific objects, meaning one approach is best for broad categorization, while the other is essential for pinpointing items within images.
- Balanced, high-quality labeling is critical for model accuracy, since inconsistent or unevenly distributed training samples can bias predictions and weaken real-world performance.
- Azure AI Video Indexer combines 30+ models to produce multimodal insights, generating transcripts, OCR, sentiment, and face detection results in a unified, time-aligned JSON.
- Integrations with Azure AI Search and Power BI make videos easily searchable, turning unstructured audiovisual content into interactive data that can power dashboards and discovery tools.
- Security, data governance, and responsible use are essential for implementation, ensuring compliance with privacy regulations and alignment with the Responsible AI guidelines of Microsoft.

CHAPTER 6
Implementing Natural Language Processing (NLP) Solutions

Introduction

In this chapter, we shall turn natural language processing into deployable solutions on Azure. We will start with Azure AI Language and Translator to detect language, translate, analyze sentiment, and identify PII, with examples in REST and the Python SDK. Gradually, you will see how to quickly validate capabilities in Language Studio and Azure AI Foundry Playgrounds, and how to take those tests into production services with endpoints and keys. We will then proceed to explore Azure AI Speech for voice: Speech-to-Text (real-time, Fast Transcription, and batch), Text-to-Speech, real-time speech translation, and TTS Avatars, along with selection criteria, operational limits, and quality considerations.

You will also learn how to design and deploy conversational models with Conversational Language Understanding (CLU) and Custom Question Answering (CQA), and how to tailor translation using custom models and glossaries (both in Text Translation and Document Translation). We shall integrate reference architectures, required resources, quotas, observability with Azure Monitor, and security controls (RBAC, Private Link, loggingOptOut) to meet compliance requirements. Finally, we close with production patterns—such as orchestration routing, A/B testing, blue/green deployments, and error handling—so you can move from demos to robust, measurable, and maintainable systems.

Structure

In this chapter, we will cover the following topics:

- Language Detection, Translation, Sentiment Analysis, and PII Identification

- Architecture and Required Resources
- Language Detection
- Translation
- Sentiment Analysis
- PII Identification
- Observability and Security

- Speech Processing Solutions
  - Speech-to-Text (STT)
  - Real-Time Speech Translation
  - Text-to-Speech (TTS)
  - TTS Avatars
  - Observability and Security
- Conversational AI with CLU and CQA
  - When to use CLU versus Custom Question Answering
  - Architecture and Authoring Workflow
  - Custom Language Understanding (CLU)
  - Custom Question Answering (CQA)
  - Orchestration with CLU and CQA
  - Observability and Security
- Creating and Deploying Custom Translation Models
  - Limits and Quotas

Language Detection, Translation, Sentiment Analysis, and PII Identification

Azure AI Language and Translator empower organizations to analyze, translate, and safeguard textual content across multiple languages. These capabilities enable the creation of global applications that comply with security and privacy requirements while enhancing user experience through sentiment analysis and automatic translation.

This section explains in detail the services for language detection, translation, sentiment analysis, and Personally Identifiable Information (PII) recognition, along with usage examples in **REST** and the **Python SDK**.

Architecture and Required Resources

Before diving into the APIs, it is important to understand the underlying resources. Two main Azure resources are required:

- **Azure AI Language (Analyze Text Runtime)**: It provides APIs for language detection, sentiment analysis, PII recognition, and other text analytics tasks.
- **Azure AI Translator**: It specializes in automatic translation, integrated language detection, and transliteration.

Each service is consumed through specific endpoints and subscription keys. Both support **synchronous requests** (short text) and **asynchronous jobs** (longer text or multiple tasks in one request).

The following table summarizes the key limits and quotas that apply to Azure AI Language service of Azure AI Foundry:

Concept	**Value**
Max. characters per document (synchronous)	5,120
Max. characters per request (asynchronous)	125,000 (max. 25 documents)
Documents per request - Language Detection	1,000
Documents per request - Sentiment / Opinion Mining	10
Documents per request - PII	5
Maximum request size	1 MB

***Table 6.1**: Limits and Quotas in Azure AI Foundry Azure AI Language*

In synchronous requests, individual documents exceeding the limit fail. In asynchronous jobs, the entire request is rejected.

Language Detection

Multilingual applications often need to know what language the user is typing in before deciding how to respond. The Language Detection API handles this automatically, returning the language name, ISO 639-1 code, and confidence score. This is essential for scenarios such as chatbots, which can decide to either reply in the language of the user or translate the input for internal processing.

From the portal: You can test this visually in **Language Studio or in Azure AI Foundry Language Playground** and selecting the `Detect language` tile. Paste sample text such as "*Bonjour à tous!*" or "*¿Cómo estás?*" and the portal immediately shows the detected language and confidence score.

The following image highlights the Azure AI Foundry Language Playground configured for language detection, showing how a short text input is analyzed to identify the language, ISO code, script, and confidence score in real time:

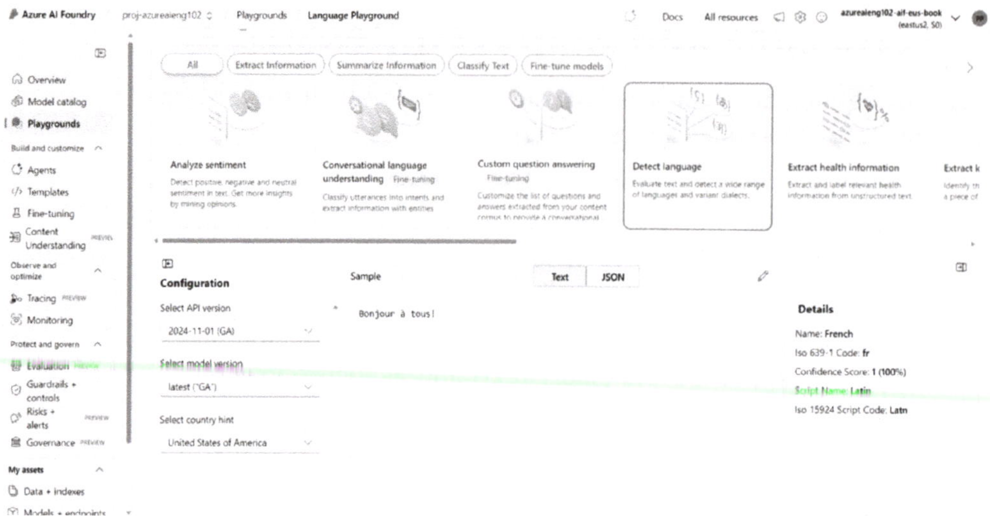

Figure 6.1: *Azure AI Foundry – Language Playground – Detect Language*

REST

```
curl -s -X POST "$AZURE_LANGUAGE_ENDPOINT/language/:analyze-
text?api-version=2024-11-01" \
  -H "Ocp-Apim-Subscription-Key: $AZURE_LANGUAGE_KEY" \
  -H "Content-Type: application/json" \
  -d '{
    "kind": "LanguageDetection",
    "analysisInput": {
      "documents": [
        { "id": "1", "text": "Bonjour à tous!" },
        { "id": "2", "text": "¿Cómo estás?" }
      ]
    }
  }'
```

Python SDK

```
from azure.core.credentials import AzureKeyCredential
from azure.ai.textanalytics import TextAnalyticsClient
client = TextAnalyticsClient(
    os.environ["AZURE_LANGUAGE_ENDPOINT"],
    AzureKeyCredential(os.environ["AZURE_LANGUAGE_KEY"])
)
docs = ["Bonjour à tous!", "¿Cómo estás?"]
for r in client.detect_language(docs, country_hint="none"):
    print(r.primary_language.name, r.primary_language.iso6391_
name, r.confidence_score)
```

Translation

Automatic translation converts text from a source language into one or more target languages. Azure AI Translator can automatically detect the source language, return sentence length information, and perform transliteration between writing systems (for example, Arabic to Latin).

This service is widely used in customer support portals, global e-commerce, internal communications across regions, and any application that requires multilingual accessibility in real time.

From the portal: You can test this visually in **Azure AI Foundry** to go to **Playgrounds** and then navigate **Translator playground** option to test translations directly. Enter a sentence in Spanish, choose English and French as target languages, and the portal instantly shows the translations. For full document scenarios, you can configure **Document Translation** in the portal by connecting Blob Storage containers for input and output.

The following image highlights the Translator Playground in Azure AI Foundry, where text is translated from a source language to one or more target languages, displaying the original text alongside the translated output:

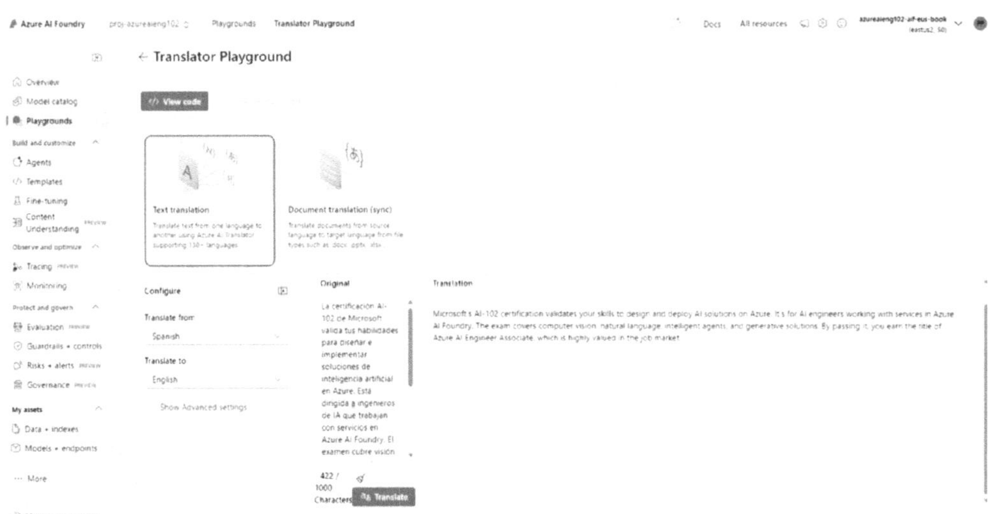

Figure 6.2: *Azure AI Foundry – Translator Playground – Text Translation*

REST

```
curl -s -X POST "https://api.cognitive.microsofttranslator.com/
translate?api-version=3.0&to=en&to=fr" \
  -H "Ocp-Apim-Subscription-Key: $TRANSLATOR_KEY" \
  -H "Ocp-Apim-Subscription-Region: $TRANSLATOR_REGION" \
```

```
-H "Content-Type: application/json; charset=UTF-8" \
-d '[{ "Text": "Hola, ¿qué tal estuvo el Microsoft Build?"}] '
```

In this example, the Spanish sentence is automatically translated into English and French.

Sentiment Analysis

Understanding how users feel about a product or service is vital for organizations. Sentiment analysis classifies text as positive, neutral, or negative, and with opinion mining enabled, it can highlight specific aspects of the text. For example, "*the shipping was late*" may be negative, while "*the support was excellent*" is positive.

This capability is especially valuable for social media monitoring, customer satisfaction surveys, product review analysis, and any scenario where understanding user perception is critical.

From the portal: You can explore this feature in **Azure AI Foundry Language Playground** in **Analyze sentiment** or **Language Studio** by opening the **Analyze sentiment and opinions** tile. Enter sample reviews or feedback and view the sentiment classification, confidence scores, and highlighted positive/negative phrases.

The following image highlights sentiment analysis in the Azure AI Foundry Language Playground, illustrating how text is classified into positive, negative, and neutral sentiment with sentence-level breakdown and confidence scores:

Figure 6.3: *Azure AI Foundry – Language Playground – Analyze Sentiment*

REST

```
curl -s -X POST "$AZURE_LANGUAGE_ENDPOINT/language/:analyze-
text?api-version=2024-11-01" \
  -H "Ocp-Apim-Subscription-Key: $AZURE_LANGUAGE_KEY" \
  -H "Content-Type: application/json" \
  -d '{
    "kind": "SentimentAnalysis",
    "parameters": { "opinionMining": true, "stringIndexType":
"TextElements_v8" },
    "analysisInput": {
      "documents": [
        { "id": "1", "language": "en", "text": "Shipping was
late, but support was excellent." }
      ]
    }
  }'
Python SDK
result = client.analyze_sentiment(
    ["Shipping was late, but support was excellent."],
    show_opinion_mining=True
)
for doc in result:
    print(doc.sentiment, doc.confidence_scores)
    for s in doc.sentences:
        print("-", s.sentiment, s.confidence_scores)
```

PII Identification

Personally Identifiable Information (PII) detection locates sensitive personal information within text, such as names, phone numbers, email addresses, tax identifiers, or bank account numbers.

The service not only returns the detected entities with their category and confidence score but also generates a version of the text where sensitive data is masked (`redactedText`). This is particularly relevant for compliance scenarios (such as GDPR or HIPAA) and for processes that require anonymizing data before storage or analysis.

From the portal: In **Language Studio**, open the **Extract PII** tile or in **Azure AI Foundry Language Playground** in **Extract PII from text** tile, paste text containing personal information, and observe how the portal highlights sensitive entities and shows the redacted version. This simple UI makes it easy to explain the feature visually.

The following image highlights PII extraction in Azure AI Foundry, showing how sensitive entities such as names, dates, addresses, and email addresses are detected, labeled, and optionally redacted within unstructured text:

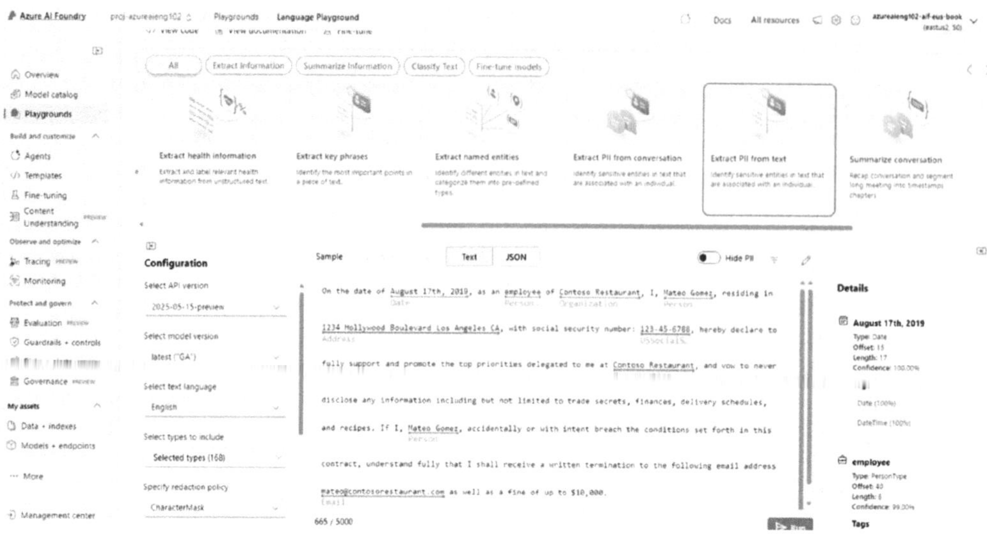

Figure 6.4: *Azure AI Foundry – Language Playground – Extract PII from Text*

REST

```
curl -s -X POST "$AZURE_LANGUAGE_ENDPOINT/language/:analyze-
text?api-version=2024-11-01" \
  -H "Ocp-Apim-Subscription-Key: $AZURE_LANGUAGE_KEY" \
  -H "Content-Type: application/json" \
  -d '{
    "kind": "PiiEntityRecognition",
    "parameters": {
      "domain": "none",
      "piiCategories": ["Person", "PhoneNumber", "Email"],
      "stringIndexType": "TextElements_v8",
      "loggingOptOut": true
    },
    "analysisInput": {
      "documents": [
        { "id": "1", "language": "es", "text": "Llama a Pablo
Piovano al 3493415005 o ppiova@hotmail.com" }
      ]
    }
  }'
```

Python SDK

```
res = client.recognize_pii_entities(
    ["Llama a Pablo Piovano al 3493415005 o ppiova@hotmail.com"],
language="es"
)
for r in res:
```

```
        print("Redacted:", r.redacted_text)
        for e in r.entities:
            print(e.text, e.category, e.confidence_score)
```

Observability and Security

Both services integrate with **Azure Monitor**, exposing metrics such as latency, successful calls, and errors. These can be visualized in dashboards or used to configure proactive alerts.

From a security perspective, Azure AI Language and Translator include:

- RBAC with Microsoft Entra ID to control access.
- Private Link to isolate the service from public internet exposure.
- Encryption in transit and at rest by default.
- The ability to disable content logging (**`loggingOptOut`**) when processing sensitive information.

Speech Processing Solutions

This section covers Azure AI Speech capabilities for voice processing: speech-to-text (STT), text-to-speech (TTS), real-time speech translation, and TTS Avatars. You'll find concepts, high-level architecture notes, operational limits, and practical examples in **Python (SDK)** and **REST (cURL)** suitable for production integrations.

Speech-to-Text (STT)

Speech-to-Text converts spoken audio into written text. Azure offers three main options:

- **Short audio (REST):** Single HTTP request for brief clips. No partial hypotheses; limit ≤ 60 seconds per request.
- **Fast Transcription (REST, synchronous):** "*Faster-than-real-time*" transcription for single files, without managing jobs. Typical constraints are **< 250 MB** and **< 2 hours** per file.
- **Batch Transcription (REST, asynchronous):** Jobs over one or many files stored in Azure Storage (SAS). It enables diarization, word-level timestamps, and post-processing. Common storage constraints for input containers include up to **10,000 blobs**, **5 GB per container**, and **2.5 GB per blob**.

How it works: Audio is decoded, normalized, and processed through acoustic and language models. Results include recognized text and confidence scores. Accuracy can be improved with **phrase lists** (SDK) or **Custom Speech**.

Use cases: This technology can be applied in various scenarios such as captioning, call center analytics, searchable media archives, medical dictation, and conversational agents.

From the portal: After creating a Speech resource, open **Speech Studio** and select **Real-time speech to text** or in **Azure AI Foundry in Speech Playground** in **Real-time transcription** tile. From here you can upload a sample audio file or record directly, and the portal will display the recognized text in real time. For larger files, use the **Batch transcription** option, which lets you upload audio, configure speaker diarization, and view detailed transcripts.

The following image highlights real-time speech-to-text transcription in the Azure AI Foundry Speech Playground, where an uploaded or recorded audio file is transcribed with configurable language, output format, and diarization options:

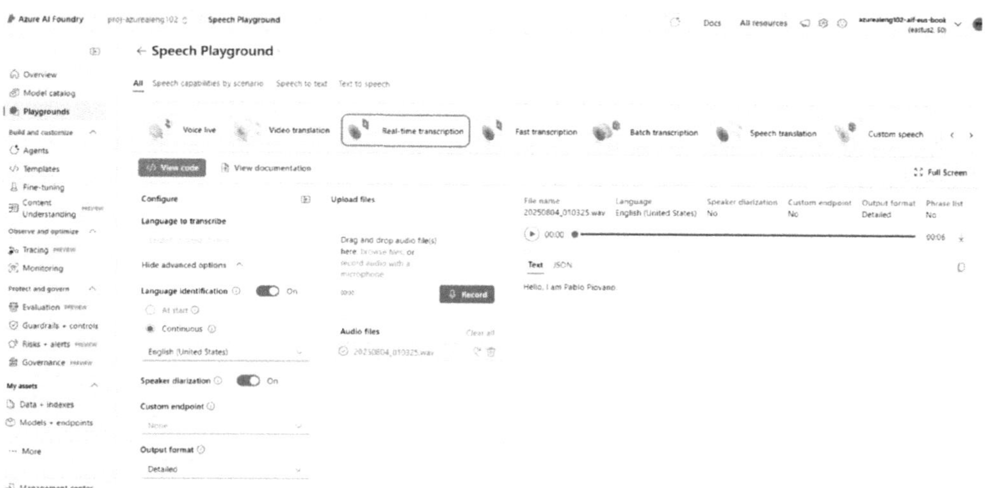

Figure 6.5: *Azure AI Foundry – Speech Playground – Real-Time Transcription*

Python SDK Example

```
import os
import azure.cognitiveservices.speech as speechsdk
speech_key = os.getenv("SPEECH_KEY")
service_region = os.getenv("SPEECH_REGION")
speech_config = speechsdk.SpeechConfig(subscription=speech_key, 
region=service_region)
speech_config.speech_recognition_language = "es-ES"
audio_config = speechsdk.AudioConfig(filename="sample.wav")
recognizer = speechsdk.SpeechRecognizer(speech_config=speech_
config, audio_config=audio_config)
result = recognizer.recognize_once()
if result.reason == speechsdk.ResultReason.RecognizedSpeech:
```

```
        print("Text:", result.text)
    else:
        print("Error:", result.reason)
```

Practical usage: Use **start_continuous_recognition[_async]** for live captioning, wire the recognizing/recognized/canceled events for partials and final results, and add a **PhraseListGrammar** with brand names or jargon to boost accuracy.

REST (cURL) Examples

- **Short audio (≤60s)**

```
REGION="eastus"
KEY="$SPEECH_KEY"
curl -s -X POST "https://${REGION}.stt.speech.microsoft.com/
speech/recognition/conversation/cognitiveservices/v1?language
=es-ES&format=detailed" \
  -H "Ocp-Apim-Subscription-Key: ${KEY}" \
  -H "Content-Type: audio/wav; codecs=audio/pcm; samplerate
=16000" \
  --data-binary "@sample_16k_mono.wav"
```

- **Fast Transcription (synchronous)**

```
REGION="eastus"
KEY="$SPEECH_KEY"
API="2024-11-15"
curl -s -X POST "https://${REGION}.api.cognitive.microsoft.com/
speechtotext/transcriptions:transcribe?api-version=${API}" \
  -H "Ocp-Apim-Subscription-Key: ${KEY}" \
  -H "Content-Type: multipart/form-data" \
  -F 'definition={"locales":["es-ES"],"profanityFilterMode"
:"Masked"};type=application/json' \
  -F audio=@sample.wav;type=audio/wav
```

Batch Transcription (asynchronous)

```
REGION="westeurope"
KEY="$SPEECH_KEY"
API="2024-11-15"
curl -s -X POST "https://${REGION}.api.cognitive.microsoft.com/
speechtotext/transcriptions:submit?api-version=${API}" \
  -H "Ocp-Apim-Subscription-Key: ${KEY}" \
  -H "Content-Type: application/json" \
  -d '{
        "displayName": "batch-es",
        "locale": "es-ES",
        "contentContainerUrl": "https://<storage>.blob.core.
windows.net/input?sv=...&sp=rl&se=...",
        "properties": {
```

```
        "wordLevelTimestampsEnabled": true,
        "diarization": { "enabled": true, "maxSpeakers": 4 },
        "timeToLiveHours": 48
    }
}'
```

Real-Time Speech Translation

It is the live translation from a source spoken language to one or more target languages, optionally with **speech-to-speech** output (synthesized audio in the target language). It is further exposed via the Speech **SDK** for low-latency streaming.

The SDK captures audio, recognizes source text, applies neural translation, and emits translated text (and optionally TTS output), with latencies suitable for interactive experiences.

Common use cases: This technology can be applied in various scenarios such as multilingual customer support, hybrid meetings, subtitling/interpretation, kiosks, and tourism.

From the portal: In **Speech Studio**, open the **Speech translation** page or in **Azure AI Foundry** in **Speech Playground** in **Speech translation** tile. You can select a source language (for instance, Spanish), one or more target languages, and even generate audio output in a synthetic voice. Upload a recording or speak live, and the portal shows both the transcribed source text and the translated text.

The following image highlights real-time speech translation in the Azure AI Foundry Speech Playground, demonstrating automatic language detection, live transcription, and translation of spoken audio into a target language:

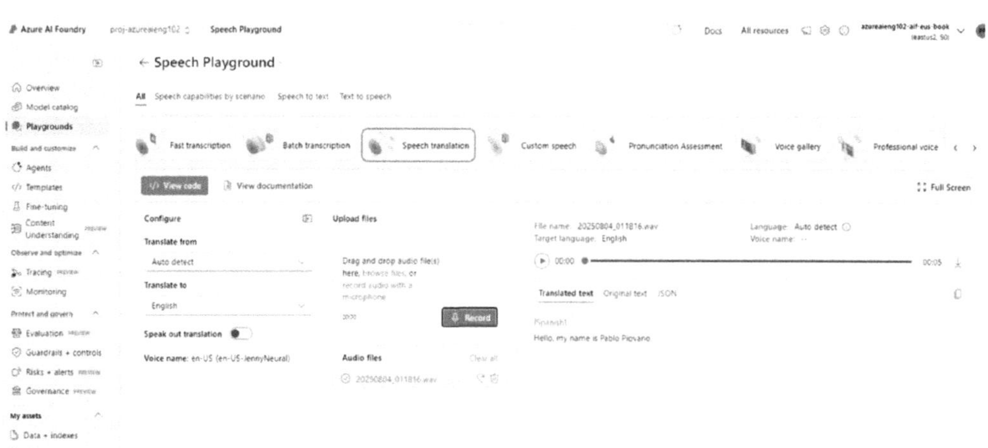

Figure 6.6: *Azure AI Foundry – Speech Playground – Speech Translation*

Python SDK Example

```
import os
import azure.cognitiveservices.speech as speechsdk
speech_key = os.getenv("SPEECH_KEY")
region = os.getenv("SPEECH_REGION")
tconfig = speechsdk.translation.SpeechTranslationConfig
(subscription=speech_key, region=region)
tconfig.speech_recognition_language = "es-ES"
tconfig.add_target_language("en")
tconfig.voice_name = "en-US-JennyNeural"  #optional TTS voice for
translation
audio = speechsdk.AudioConfig(filename="meeting_es.wav")
translator = speechsdk.translation.TranslationRecognizer
(translation_config=tconfig, audio_config=audio)
res = translator.recognize_once()
print("Source (ES):", res.text)
print("Translation (EN):", res.translations.get("en"))
```

Text-to-Speech (TTS)

It refers to the neural synthesis of natural-sounding speech from text or SSML, with voice styles (for example., news, chat), prosody control, and broad locale coverage. It is also accessible via **SDK** or **REST**.

The Neural TTS engine generates audio (WAV/MP3/OGG) from text or **SSML**. A single REST request typically produces up to **~10 minutes** of audio; longer content should be chunked.

Common use cases: Screen readers and accessibility, branded voices for virtual agents, notifications, audio guides, and dubbing.

REST (cURL) Example

```
REGION="eastus"
KEY="$SPEECH_KEY"
# 1) Obtain access token (~10 minutes validity)
TOKEN=$(curl -s -X POST "https://${REGION}.api.cognitive.
microsoft.com/sts/v1.0/issueToken" \
  -H "Ocp-Apim-Subscription-Key: ${KEY}" -d "")
# 2) List voices
curl -s -X GET "https://${REGION}.tts.speech.microsoft.com/
cognitiveservices/voices/list" \
  -H "Authorization: Bearer ${TOKEN}" > voices.json
# 3) Synthesize to WAV using SSML
curl -s -X POST "https://${REGION}.tts.speech.microsoft.com/
cognitiveservices/v1" \
  -H "Authorization: Bearer ${TOKEN}" \
```

```
  -H "Content-Type: application/ssml+xml" \
  -H "X-Microsoft-OutputFormat: riff-24khz-16bit-mono-pcm" \
  --data '<speak version="1.0" xml:lang="es-ES">
<voice name="es-ES-ElviraNeural">Hola, este es un ejemplo de
síntesis.</voice>
</speak>' \
  --output tts.wav
```

Python SDK Example

```
import os
import azure.cognitiveservices.speech as speechsdk
speech_key = os.getenv("SPEECH_KEY")
region = os.getenv("SPEECH_REGION")
speech_config = speechsdk.SpeechConfig(subscription=speech_key,
region=region)
speech_config.speech_synthesis_voice_name = "es-ES-ElviraNeural"
audio_config = speechsdk.AudioConfig(filename="output.wav")
synth = speechsdk.SpeechSynthesizer(speech_config=speech_config,
audio_config=audio_config)
result = synth.speak_text_async("Hola, este es un ejemplo de
síntesis con Azure AI Speech.").get()
print(result.reason)
```

TTS Avatars

Generates video of a speaking avatar synchronized with TTS audio. Two modes:

- **Batch Avatars (REST)**: Renders clips (WebM/MP4) from text/SSML. You control voice, character, style, crop, background, and bitrate.
- **Real-time Avatars (WebRTC):** Low-latency streaming of video+audio; typically consumed from a browser or mobile client (SDK JS). A REST call can provide ICE/TURN credentials before establishing the session.

Use cases: Training/e-learning, kiosks and signage, self-service portals, marketing campaigns, on-screen digital agents.

From the portal: Once access to this limited feature is approved, you will see **Avatars** in **Speech Studio** or **Azure AI Foundry Speech Playground**. In batch mode, you configure text, voice, and avatar style, and the service renders a video file. In real-time mode, the portal provides WebRTC connection details for interactive sessions.

The following image highlights the Text-to-Speech Avatar capability in Azure AI Foundry, where synthesized speech is combined with a selectable digital avatar to generate a synchronized video output:

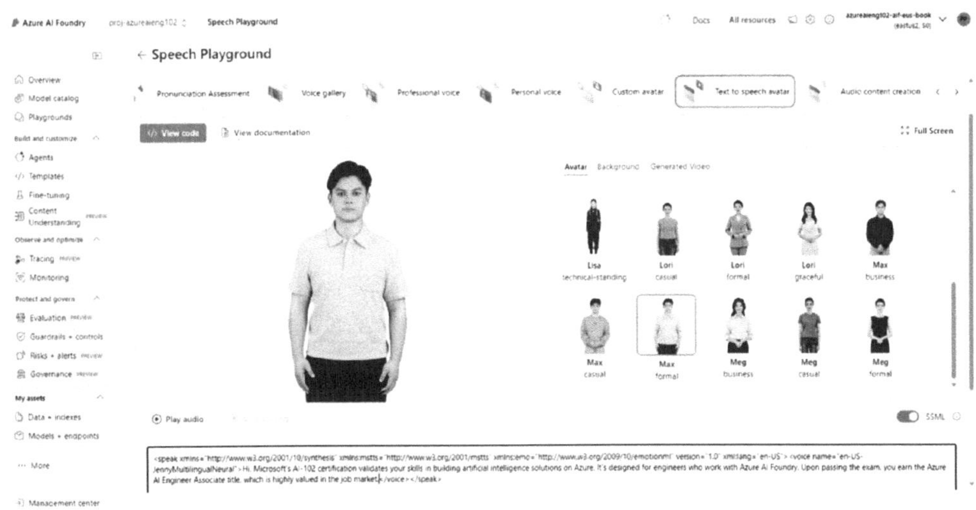

Figure 6.7: Azure AI Foundry – Speech Playground – Text-to-Speech Avatar

REST (cURL) – create a Batch Avatar job

```
REGION="eastus"
KEY="$SPEECH_KEY"
API="2024-08-01"
JOB_ID="demo-avatar-job-001"
curl -s -X PUT "https://${REGION}.api.cognitive.microsoft.com/
avatar/batchsyntheses/${JOB_ID}?api-version=${API}" \
  -H "Ocp-Apim-Subscription-Key: ${KEY}" \
  -H "Content-Type: application/json" \
  -d '{
        "inputKind": "PlainText",
        "synthesisConfig": { "voice": "es-ES-ElviraNeural" },
        "inputs": [ { "content": "Hola, soy tu avatar de Azure."
} ],
        "avatarConfig": {
          "talkingAvatarCharacter": "lisa",
          "talkingAvatarStyle": "casual-sitting",
          "videoFormat": "webm",
          "videoCodec": "vp9",
          "subtitleType": "soft_embedded",
          "backgroundColor": "transparent"
        }
      }' -D - | tee headers.txt
```

Check the Operation-Location header to poll status and download the video when completed. Typical request payload limits for creation are **up to ~500 KB**.

REST (cURL) – retrieve ICE/TURN token for Real-time Avatar

```
REGION="westus2"
KEY="$SPEECH_KEY"
curl -s -X GET "https://${REGION}.tts.speech.microsoft.com/
cognitiveservices/avatar/relay/token/v1" \
  -H "Ocp-Apim-Subscription-Key: ${KEY}"
```

Practical usage: In production, render batches for scripted content (courses, onboarding). For live assistants, your backend issues short-lived ICE tokens to a browser client, while Speech + your NLU layer orchestrate the conversation.

The following table outlines the principal limits and quotas associated with the Azure AI Speech capabilities of the Azure AI Foundry:

Capability	**Primary limit**	**Notes**
STT REST **short audio**	≤ **60 s** per request	No partial results; use stt.speech.microsoft.com with correct codec and sample rate.
Fast Transcription (synchronous REST)	**< 2 h** and **< 300 MB** per file	multipart/form-data with audio and definition.
Batch Transcription	Up to **10,000** blobs; **5 GB** per container; **2.5 GB** per blob	Supply SAS (r,l) and enable diarization/timestamps as needed.
TTS REST	Output ≤ **~10 min** of audio	Chunk longer content; prefer SSML.
STS tokens	**~10 min** validity	Endpoint /sts/v1.0/issueToken.
Batch Avatars	**~500 KB** creation payload	Track via Operation-Location.

Table 6.2: *Limits and Quotas in Azure AI Foundry Azure AI Speech*

Putting it into Production (Quick Patterns)

- **Call analytics and summaries:** Record calls (with consent), run **`Batch Transcription`** with diarization and timestamps; push transcripts into a search index and run downstream sentiment/entity analysis. This avoids real-time coupling and optimizes cost.
- **Express captioning/dubbing:** For short videos, use **`Fast Transcription`**→ translate text → synthesize with **Neural TTS** (consistent voice/style). For longer videos, segment and orchestrate via Batch.
- **Visual agent on a kiosk**: Front-end uses **Real-time Avatar (WebRTC)** and TTS; back-end handles NLU and orchestration. For network isolation, adopt **Private Link** with a custom domain and update endpoints accordingly.

Observability and Security

- **Monitoring with Azure Monitor:** Speech resources (**`Microsoft.CognitiveServices/accounts`**) emit **metrics** (for instance, total calls, client errors, throttling) and **logs** via **Diagnostic settings**. Route them to **Log Analytics**, Event Hubs, or Storage. Build dashboards with:
    - **Success rate** (100% - 5xx) and **client error rate** (4xx/429).
    - **Latency** from your app (SDK timings) correlated with service metrics.
    - **`OperationName`** split (for example., STT short audio vs. TTS synth) to spot hotspots.
    - Set **alerts** (Metric/Log) for **`BlockedCalls`** > 0, **`ClientErrors spikes`**, or *throttling thresholds.*
- **Role-Based Access Control (RBAC):** Prefer **Cognitive Services Speech User** for runtime clients and **Cognitive Services Speech Contributor** for operational tasks. Avoid broad Owner/Contributor for least privilege. For AAD integration, obtain OAuth2 tokens (Microsoft Entra ID) and use Authorization: Bearer <token> where supported; and, classic keys were kept only for tightly controlled scenarios.
- **Private Link and Network Isolation:** Create a **Private Endpoint** for the Speech account and integrate **private DNS**. If you enable a **custom domain** on the resource, update SDK/REST base URLs to the custom endpoint (and verify name resolution from private networks). Validate egress rules if your app runs in restricted environments (AKS, App Service with VNet integration).

`loggingOptOut` and data handling.

Adopt a **privacy-first default**:

- Do not enable audio logging in SDK sessions unless you have explicit consent (in SDKs, "**`audio logging`**" is opt-in).
- For **`Custom Speech`** endpoints, keep *content logging* disabled unless needed for quality improvement.
- If your application exposes a per-request privacy toggle (for instance, **`loggingOptOut`**), ensure it bypasses any logging hooks and that downstream storage honors it (no audio/transcript persistence).
- Store secrets in **Azure Key Vault**; rotate keys; prefer **managed identity** for data-plane access where supported.

- **Audit and Evidence:** Log **correlation IDs** across STT/TTS/Avatar calls, persist **who/what/when** for each request, and retain the **exact SSML** used for TTS in a secure store when required by **compliance**. Combine **Activity Log** (control plane) with **service logs** (data plane) to reconstruct events.

Conversational AI with CLU and CQA

This section describes how to design, train, and operate conversational AI with **Azure AI Language**, combining **Conversational Language Understanding (CLU)**–for intent classification and entity extraction–and **Custom Question Answering (CQA)**–for knowledge-grounded answers from your own content. The structure uses clear subsections and dedicated **Practical Use Blocks** after each code example, avoiding the "title-with-dot-then-text" style you do not want.

When to Use CLU versus Custom Question Answering

CLU focuses on understanding the goal of the user (what the user wants to do) and extracting structured fields (dates, amounts, IDs, locations) from free text to drive transactional flows and API calls.

CQA focuses on informational prompts where answers must be derived from enterprise knowledge bases (FAQs, manuals, policies) with confidence scores, optional short answer spans, and source references.

A combined pattern uses a **CLU Orchestration** project as a router. Informational prompts are delegated to CQA; transactional prompts are routed to business skills. Your client calls one endpoint and receives a unified payload.

Architecture and Authoring Workflow

- **Data and Labeling:** For CLU, define intents and entities and label representative utterances for training and validation, including **hard negatives** to reduce confusion between similar intents.

  For CQA, connect sources (URLs, PDF/HTML/Markdown) and attach metadata (product, region, effective dates) to enable query-time filtering.

- **Training and Evaluation:** For CLU, review precision/recall/F1 per intent and entity, rebalance examples, and inspect the confusion matrix to resolve overlaps.

  For CQA, validate with a hold-out question set, track coverage and confidence, split very long documents, and normalize content (headings, anchors) for better retrieval.

- **Deployment and Runtime:** Publish named deployments (for example, *staging* and *production*).
  - Consume CLU/Orchestration with `:analyze-conversations` and CQA with `:query-knowledgebases`.

- Integrate telemetry, alerts, and access controls from day one.

Custom Language Understanding (CLU)

CLU provides Natural Language Understanding (NLU) for intent classification and entity extraction across conversational inputs. A typical lifecycle moves from labeled examples, to training and validation, to deployment, and finally inference that returns top intent, confidence distribution, and extracted entities with types, values, and offsets.

From the portal: In **Language Studio**, create a **Conversational Language Understanding project** by selecting it from the main dashboard. The portal guides you through adding **intents**, defining **entities**, and labeling sample utterances. You can then train the model and deploy it to a production or staging environment. The built-in **Test** panel lets you type a sentence and see the recognized intent and entities.

The following image highlights the model performance dashboard for a Conversational Language Understanding (CLU) project in Language Studio, displaying evaluation metrics such as precision, recall, F1 score, and training/test dataset distribution:

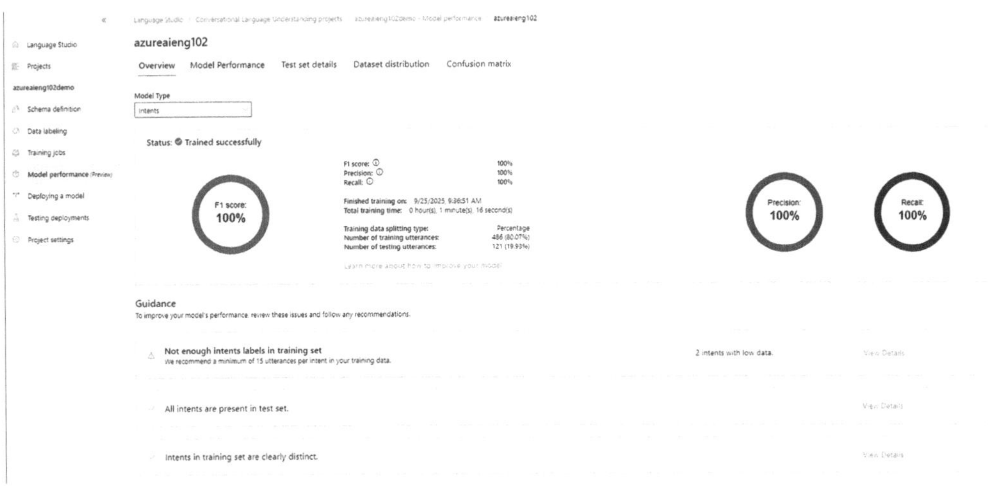

Figure 6.8: *Azure AI Language Studio – Conversational Language Understanding Projects- Model Performance*

REST (cURL) - analyze-conversations

Replace placeholders with your endpoint, key, and active API version.

```
ENDPOINT="https://<your-endpoint>"
API_VERSION="<your-api-version>"
KEY="<your-key>"
```

```
curl -sS -X POST "$ENDPOINT/language/:analyze-conversations?
api-version=$API_VERSION" \
  -H "Content-Type: application/json" \
  -H "Ocp-Apim-Subscription-Key: $KEY" \
  -d '{
    "kind": "Conversation",
    "analysisInput": {
      "conversationItem": {
        "id": "1",
        "participantId": "user1",
        "modality": "text",
        "language": "en",
        "text": "Book a table for two tomorrow at 8 pm"
      }
    },
    "parameters": {
      "projectName": "restaurant-bot",
      "deploymentName": "production",
      "verbose": true,
      "stringIndexType": "TextElement_V8"
    }
  }'
```

Practical use: Normalize extracted values (for example, convert "tomorrow 8 pm" to an ISO-8601 datetime and "two" to 2) and apply business rules (capacity, cut-off times) before invoking downstream APIs. The confidence distribution of the response can drive fallbacks such as clarification prompts or agent handoff.

Runtime (Python SDK): `ConversationAnalysisClient`

```
import os
import time
from azure.core.credentials import AzureKeyCredential
from azure.ai.language.conversations import ConversationAnalysis-
Client
endpoint = os.environ["AZURE_LANGUAGE_ENDPOINT"]
key = os.environ["AZURE_LANGUAGE_KEY"]
client = ConversationAnalysisClient(endpoint, AzureKeyCreden-
tial(key))
def analyze_text(text: str):
    task = {
        "kind": "Conversation",
        "analysisInput": {
            "conversationItem": {
                "id": "1",
                "participantId": "user",
                "language": "en",
                "modality": "text",
```

```
                "text": text
            }
        },
        "parameters": {
            "projectName": "restaurant-bot",
            "deploymentName": "production",
            "verbose": True,
            "stringIndexType": "TextElement_V8"
        }
    }
    for attempt in range(3):
        try:
            return client.analyze_conversation(task=task)
        except Exception:
            if attempt == 2:
                raise
            time.sleep(2 ** attempt)
result = analyze_text("Book a table for two tomorrow at 8 pm")
pred = result["result"]["prediction"]
print(pred["topIntent"])
for ent in pred.get("entities", []):
    print(ent["category"], ent.get("text"), ent.get
("confidenceScore"))
```

Practical use: Use retries with exponential backoff for transient network or throttling errors, and add timeouts and request-ID correlation in production. A/B test different deployments (for instance, *staging* vs. *production*) and enforce validators (future dates, numeric ranges, required fields) before triggering business actions.

Deploying CLU (Authoring REST)

```
ENDPOINT="https://<your-endpoint>"
API_VERSION_AUTH="<your-authoring-api-version>"
KEY="<your-key>"
curl -sS -X PUT \
  "$ENDPOINT/language/authoring/analyze-conversations/projects/
restaurant-bot/deployments/production?api-version=$API_VERSION_
AUTH" \
  -H "Ocp-Apim-Subscription-Key: $KEY" \
  -H "Content-Type: application/json" \
  -d '{
        "trainedModelLabel": "<your-trained-model-label>"
      }'
# Poll the Operation-Location header for deployment status.
```

Practical use: Automate promotion in CI/CD after regression and business checks. Adopt blue/green rollouts and keep a rollback target to mitigate risk in accuracy or latency regressions.

Custom Question Answering (CQA)

CQA builds a question-answering layer over your enterprise content and returns ranked answers with confidence, optional short spans, and follow-up prompts for multi-turn flows. Projects ingest and index sources (often via Azure AI Search), publish a deployment, and expose a query endpoint. Metadata enables filtering by attributes such as product, region, or effective dates.

From the portal: In **Language Studio**, create a **Custom Question Answering project**. You'll connect your **Azure AI Search resource** if not already linked, then add content sources such as URLs, PDFs, or Markdown files. Once ingestion completes, you can test the knowledge base directly in the portal by asking natural language questions.

The following image highlights the Custom Question Answering authoring experience in Azure AI Language Studio, showing how question-answer pairs are edited, validated, and managed within a knowledge base:

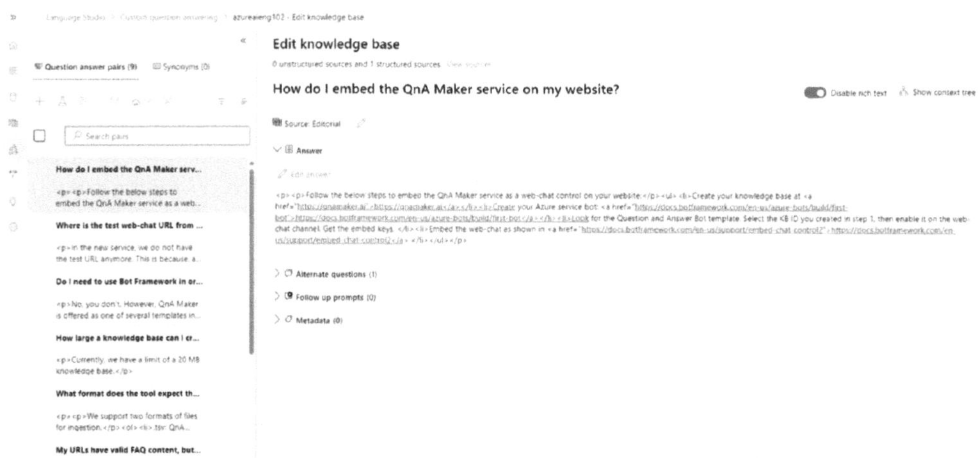

***Figure 6.9**: Azure AI Language Studio – Custom Question Answering – Edit Knowledge Base*

REST (cURL): query-knowledgebases

```
ENDPOINT="https://<your-endpoint>"
API_VERSION="<your-api-version>"
KEY="<your-key>"
PROJECT="helpcenter"
DEPLOYMENT="production"
curl -sS -X POST \
```

```
  "$ENDPOINT/language/:query-knowledgebases?api-version=$API_
VERSION&projectName=$PROJECT&deploymentName=$DEPLOYMENT" \
  -H "Content-Type: application/json" \
  -H "Ocp-Apim-Subscription-Key: $KEY" \
  -d '{
        "question": "How do I request a refund?",
        "top": 3,
        "rankerType": "Default",
        "includeUnstructuredSources": true,
        "userId": "user-123"
      }'
```

Practical use: Display the answer with its source, apply a confidence threshold (for example, 0.60), and offer clarification or multiple candidates when below threshold. Use metadata filters (country, product) to restrict eligible sources for regulated scenarios.

Python SDK: `QuestionAnsweringClient`

```
import os
from azure.core.credentials import AzureKeyCredential
from azure.ai.language.questionanswering import Question
AnsweringClient
endpoint = os.environ["AZURE_LANGUAGE_ENDPOINT"]
key = os.environ["AZURE_LANGUAGE_KEY"]
qa = QuestionAnsweringClient(endpoint, AzureKeyCredential(key))
response = qa.get_answers(
    question="How do I request a refund?",
    project_name="helpcenter",
    deployment_name="production",
    top=3
)
THRESHOLD = 0.60
candidates = [a for a in response.answers if a.confidence >=
THRESHOLD]
if not candidates:
    print("No answer meets the confidence threshold; ask for
clarification or show alternatives.")
else:
    for ans in candidates:
        print(f"{ans.confidence:.2f}  {ans.answer}  [{ans.
source}]")
```

Practical use: Implement policy-based routing: answer above the threshold; otherwise, elicit clarification or present alternatives. Log anonymized feedback signals (**`helpfulness`**, "**`did this answer your question?`**") to drive active learning and content improvements.

Authoring (REST): update project sources

```
ENDPOINT="https://<your-endpoint>"
API_VERSION_AUTH="<your-authoring-api-version>"
KEY="<your-key>"
curl -sS -X PATCH \
  "$ENDPOINT/language/authoring/query-knowledgebases/projects/
helpcenter/sources?api-version=$API_VERSION_AUTH" \
  -H "Ocp-Apim-Subscription-Key: $KEY" \
  -H "Content-Type: application/json" \
  -d '[
        {
          "op": "add",
          "value": {
            "displayName": "Refund policy",
            "sourceKind": "url",
            "sourceUri": "https://contoso.com/policies/refunds"
          }
        },
        {
          "op": "replace",
          "value": {
            "displayName": "Terms",
            "refresh": true,
            "sourceKind": "url",
            "sourceUri": "https://contoso.com/terms"
          }
        }
      ]'
# Use Operation-Location to track ingestion progress.
```

Practical use: Schedule a recurring job that syncs from your CMS, applies source updates, and republishes the deployment. Monitor knowledge coverage with a control question set and alert when coverage or confidence drops.

Orchestration with CLU and CQA

A CLU Orchestration project centralizes routing decisions so the client calls only **`:analyze-conversations`**. The prediction includes the target (for example, **`QuestionAnswering`**) and either a knowledge answer (with confidence and source) or an intent plus entities. Apply per-target thresholds, consistent fallbacks, and business rules for a predictable user experience.

REST (cURL): Orchestration as a router

```
ENDPOINT="https://<your-endpoint>"
API_VERSION="<your-api-version>"
```

```
KEY="<your-key>"
curl -sS -X POST "$ENDPOINT/language/:analyze-conversations?a-
pi-version=$API_VERSION" \
  -H "Content-Type: application/json" \
  -H "Ocp-Apim-Subscription-Key: $KEY" \
  -d '{
    "kind": "Conversation",
    "analysisInput": {
      "conversationItem": {
        "id": "1",
        "participantId": "user1",
        "language": "en",
        "modality": "text",
        "text": "How do I request a refund?"
      }
    },
    "parameters": {
      "projectName": "orchestrator",
      "deploymentName": "production",
      "verbose": true
    }
  }'
```

Practical use: Inspect the target and payload to either surface the CQA answer or execute transactional skills with CLU entities. Implement target-specific thresholds and generalized fallbacks (clarify intent, show alternatives, or escalate to a human).

Limits and quotas: Values vary by region, SKU, and API version and can change. Treat these as operational guides and confirm in your subscription before go-live.

Conversational Language Understanding (CLU)

The following table summarizes the typical limits and configuration guidelines for Conversational Language Understanding (CLU) projects in Azure AI Foundry:

Category	**Typical limit/guide**
Utterances per project	`Up to tens of thousands (≈50k)`
Intents per project	`Hundreds (≈500)`
Entities per project	`Hundreds (≈300+)`
Input length (inference)	Thousands of characters (order of magnitude)
Trained models per project	`≈10 (for A/B versioning)`
Deployments per project	`≈10`
Throughput	**Subject to SKU; scale out with replicas/regions**

Table 6.3: *Limits and Quotas in Conversational Language Understanding*

A practical capacity plan establishes P95 latency targets, burst handling (queues + exponential backoff), and per-endpoint rate limits. In blended workloads (for example, 70% CQA / 30% CLU), retrieval often dominates latency; scale **Azure AI Search** replicas for reads and partitions for data size.

Custom Question Answering (CQA) and Azure AI Search

The following table highlights the main limits and operational guidelines for Custom Question Answering (CQA) and Azure AI Search within Azure AI Foundry:

Category	Limit/guide
Sources per project	No strict hard cap; free plans limit files
Deep links per URL	Dozens (useful for fine-grained navigation)
Query throughput	Scale with Azure AI Search (replicas for reads; partitions for data volume)
File size	Connector-dependent; prefer clean, well-structured PDF/HTML
Typical latency	Sub-second to a few seconds depending on KB size and load

***Table 6.4**: Limits and Quotas in Custom Question Answering*

MLOps Patterns for Conversational AI

Use explicit versioning with labeled model and deployment artifacts. Roll out via blue/green and canary, comparing success rate and latency before full promotion. Close the loop with active learning: harvest low-confidence queries, re-label, retrain, and re-deploy. For CLU, add **contract tests** to ensure critical entity structures remain stable across versions. For CQA, automate ingestion and deployment when content changes.

Error Handling and Resilience

Implement timeouts and retries with exponential backoff and jitter. Respect Retry-After headers on 429 throttling and smooth bursts with queues. Ensure idempotency for transactional actions using request IDs and de-duplication. Track business-level outcomes (task success, answer deflection, and CSAT) in addition to technical metrics.

Observability and Security

- **Monitoring with Azure Monitor:** Track **Total Calls**, **Client Errors (4xx)**, **Server Errors (5xx)**, **Latency**, and **Throttled/Blocked Calls** on the Language resource. Filter by **ApiName** (for example, **`AnalyzeConversations`**, **`QueryKnowledgebases`**) for targeted alerts.

Enable **`Diagnostic settings`** to ship logs and metrics to **`Log Analytics`**, and optionally to **`Event Hub`** or **`Storage`** for extended retention. Use trace categories only if policy allows (CQA can log snippets of questions/answers).

```
// CLU intent distribution by hour
AzureDiagnostics
| where ResourceProvider == "MICROSOFT.COGNITIVESERVICES"
| where OperationName has "AnalyzeConversations"
| extend props = parse_json(properties_s)
| extend topIntent = tostring(props.topIntent), score
= todouble(props.score)
| summarize count(), avg(score) by topIntent, bin(TimeGenerated,
1h)
```

- **Access control with Azure RBAC:** Assign minimal roles per persona: *Cognitive Services Reader/User* for inference and *Cognitive Services Contributor* for resource management and deployments. Prefer **Managed Identity** or **Service Principal** for pipelines with least-privilege scopes (resource or resource group).
- **Network isolation with Private Link:** Set the **Language** resource to **Selected networks and private endpoints** and create a **Private Endpoint** in your VNet. Ensure DNS resolves to privatelink.cognitiveservices.azure.com via a **Private DNS Zone** linked to the VNet. If CQA depends on **Azure AI Search**, enable **Private Link** there as well and disable public access on both resources.
- **Data Handling:** Control logging to minimize sensitive payloads. For CLU requests that may include PII, avoid logging request bodies and apply data minimization (tokenization/masking) upstream. Where supported, enable **logging opt-out** at the account or request level. Keep CQA payload tracing disabled, unless you need quality analytics and meet privacy requirements.

Creating and Deploying Custom Translation Models

Custom models in Azure AI Translator allow you to adapt machine translation to your organizational vocabulary, terminology, and style. By providing parallel corpora and dictionaries, you can train and publish a model that is invoked through the same Translator API using a **Category ID**. This is particularly useful when the general models do not respect brand names, technical jargon, or internal conventions.

- **Architecture and Required Resources:** The solution builds on the same base resources as standard translation, with some additional components for authoring. **Azure AI Translator** provides inference, while the **Custom Translator portal** is used to create projects, upload data, and train models. Datasets are stored in **Azure Blob Storage**, and for batch scenarios **Document Translation** is available, supporting both model categories and optional glossaries.

- **High-level Workflow:** The process starts with preparing the training data, which is followed by creating a project in the portal, uploading corpora and dictionaries, and running training jobs. After evaluating with metrics such as BLEU, you publish the best-performing version and obtain the **Category ID**. Finally, the model is consumed by adding this identifier to each Translator API request.
- **Data Types and Preparation:** Parallel corpora consist of aligned sentence pairs in the source and target languages. At least 10,000 unique pairs are recommended to achieve consistent improvements. Dictionaries or glossaries, provided in TSV, CSV, or XLSX format, allow you to enforce translations for key terms. It is the best practice to split datasets into training, tuning, and testing sets to enable objective evaluation. File sizes should remain under 100 MB, and supported formats include TMX, XLIFF, aligned TXT, and ZIP files with naming conventions per language.
- **Training and Deployment:** Each project corresponds to a specific language pair and direction. When uploading datasets, you assign them to training, tuning, or testing. Once training is complete, the model is evaluated against a baseline using BLEU scores and then published to the chosen regions. Publishing returns a **Category ID**, which you include in API calls to route requests to the custom model. Each project can have only one model published at a time; if multiple models are required simultaneously, separate projects should be created.

Understanding Limits and Quotas

The following table provides general guidance on the recommended limits and configurations for **Custom Translation Models** in Azure AI Foundry:

Concept	**Typical value/guide**
Recommended sentence pairs	≥ 10,000
Training file size	< 100 MB
Concurrent published models per project	1
Text Translation usage	Same as general model, add category
Document Translation	category per target + optional glossaries

Table 6.5: *Limits and Quotas in Custom Translation Models*

REST – Text Translation with custom model

```
# Translate ES->EN using your model (no fallback to general model
allowed)
curl -s -X POST "https://api.cognitive.microsofttranslator.com/
translate?api-version=3.0&from=es&to=en&category=$CATEGORY_ID&
allowFallback=false" \
  -H "Ocp-Apim-Subscription-Key: $TRANSLATOR_KEY" \
  -H "Ocp-Apim-Subscription-Region: $TRANSLATOR_REGION" \
  -H "Content-Type: application/json; charset=UTF-8" \
  -d '[{ "Text": "El flujo de caja libre creció un 18%
interanual." }]'
# The X-MT-Systems header confirms whether the Custom model was
used.
```

REST – Document Translation with category and glossary

```
DT_ENDPOINT="https://<your-resource>.cognitiveservices.azure.com"
API="2024-05-01"
curl -i -X POST "$DT_ENDPOINT/translator/document/batches?
api-version=$API" \
  -H "Ocp-Apim-Subscription-Key: $TRANSLATOR_KEY" \
  -H "Ocp-Apim-Subscription-Region: $TRANSLATOR_REGION" \
  -H "Content-Type: application/json" \
  -d '{
        "inputs": [{
          "source": { "sourceUrl": "https://<storage>.blob.core.
windows.net/source?sv=..." },
          "targets": [{
            "targetUrl": "https://<storage>.blob.core.windows.
net/target?sv=...",
            "language": "en",
            "category": "'"$CATEGORY_ID"'",
            "glossaries": [{
              "glossaryUrl": "https://<storage>.blob.core.
windows.net/glossaries/es-en.tsv?sv=...",
              "format": "tsv"
            }]
          }]
        }]
      }'
# Use the Operation-Location header to poll status and results.
```

Python (requests) – Text API with category

```
import os, requests
endpoint = "https://api.cognitive.microsofttranslator.com/
translate"
params = {
```

```
        "api-version": "3.0",
        "from": "es",
        "to": "en",
        "category": os.environ["CATEGORY_ID"],
        "allowFallback": "false"
    }
    headers = {
        "Ocp-Apim-Subscription-Key": os.environ["TRANSLATOR_KEY"],
        "Ocp-Apim-Subscription-Region": os.environ["TRANSLATOR_
    REGION"],
        "Content-Type": "application/json; charset=UTF-8"
    }
    body = [{"Text": "El controlador se instaló correctamente en
    Contoso IoT."}]
    res = requests.post(endpoint, params=params, headers=headers,
    json=body, timeout=15)
    print("X-MT-Systems:", res.headers.get("X-MT-Systems"))
    print(res.json())
```

Practical use: When running A/B validation tests, it is recommended to set **allowFallback=false** to ensure that you are measuring your custom model rather than the general one. During operations, you should log the **X-MT-Systems** value together with a custom **clientTraceId** to achieve full traceability of each request. For document scenarios, glossaries in TSV format stored in Blob can enforce key term translations and maintain consistency across outputs. If you do not yet have enough parallel corpus data, you can begin with a dictionary-only approach–based solely on forced equivalences–and later evolve toward a full model as your dataset grows.

Observability and security: Azure Monitor can be used to track calls, latencies, and errors. With Document Translation you can query the status of each batch and obtain per-document metrics. For access and secret management, use Microsoft Entra ID with minimal roles and store keys in Azure Key Vault with periodic rotation. On the networking side, enabling Private Link ensures traffic isolation, and if you configure a custom domain, one should remember to update the SDK and REST endpoints. From a data perspective, apply minimization practices, and disable content logging when processing sensitive information.

Putting it into production (quick patterns): The typical production cycle includes training, evaluating with BLEU metrics, publishing, performing A/B testing, and promoting the new version to production. To ensure fair comparison across versions, keep a stable test set. Because only one model per project can be published at a time, it is advisable to create duplicate projects to enable blue/green rollouts with zero downtime. In mixed implementations, it is common to consume the Text Translation API with a category for chat and UI scenarios, while Document Translation with category and glossary is used for manuals and batch processing.

Conclusion

This chapter grounded the key NLP and voice components in Azure into real implementation patterns. We moved from quick tests in Language Studio and Azure AI Foundry Playgrounds to production-ready designs that cover language detection, translation, sentiment analysis, and PII recognition; as well as Speech-to-Text (real-time, Fast Transcription, and batch), Text-to-Speech, speech translation, and avatars. We also reviewed when to use CLU versus Custom Question Answering – and how to orchestrate them–to handle both transactional interactions and informational queries in a unified flow.

Throughout the chapter, we emphasized operational limits, security, and observability: RBAC with Microsoft Entra ID, Private Link, logging controls, and privacy practices, together with metrics and alerts in Azure Monitor. We closed with production patterns (retries with backoff, handling 429 errors, A/B testing, blue/green deployments, and traceability with correlation IDs) and with custom translation through personalized models and glossaries, enabling you to deliver multilingual experiences that are robust, measurable, and compliant.

In the next chapter, we will explore **Implementing Knowledge Mining and Information Extraction Solutions**. You will learn how to build intelligent search and extraction systems with Azure AI Search, Document Intelligence, and Content Understanding. The chapter covers semantic, vector, and hybrid search; OCR and layout analysis; summarization and chunking; and advanced data extraction using both prebuilt and custom models–along with evaluation, scalability, and governance to ground LLMs in enterprise content.

Points to Remember

- Azure AI Language and Azure AI Translator address different usage scenarios, with Language focused on text analytics and conversational understanding and Translator optimized for multilingual translation and batch document processing.
- Understanding the difference between synchronous and asynchronous requests is essential, as synchronous calls handle short text with per-document validation, while asynchronous jobs process larger workloads and reject the entire job if limits are exceeded.
- Language detection returns the detected language, ISO 639-1 code, and confidence score, enabling reliable chatbot routing and multilingual processing workflows.
- Azure AI Translator supports automatic source language detection, transliteration, and document translation for batch scenarios, while custom

translation models can be invoked using a Category ID and validated through controlled A/B testing.

- Sentiment analysis and opinion mining provide insights at both document and sentence level, including aspects and opinions, enabling deeper understanding of user feedback when configured with the appropriate string index type.
- Personally Identifiable Information (PII) detection identifies sensitive entities and produces redacted text, supporting compliance with regulations such as GDPR and HIPAA when combined with logging opt-out and data minimization practices.
- Azure AI Speech services offer multiple processing modes, including real-time speech-to-text, Fast Transcription, and batch transcription, allowing applications to balance latency, scale, and cost requirements.
- Text-to-Speech and avatar capabilities enable the creation of natural-sounding audio and visual digital agents, supporting both batch-generated content and real-time interactive experiences.
- Conversational solutions combine Conversational Language Understanding for intent and entity extraction with Custom Question Answering for knowledge-based responses, often orchestrated through a routing model to ensure consistent behavior.
- Secure and production-ready deployments rely on least-privilege access control, Managed Identity, Azure Key Vault, Private Link, and observability practices such as monitoring, alerting, correlation IDs, and controlled rollout strategies.

CHAPTER 7
Implementing Knowledge Mining and Information Extraction Solutions

Introduction

Here, we shall move from simply storing documents to turning knowledge into a product. This chapter introduces the foundations of *knowledge mining* and *information extraction* in Azure, showing how to transform heterogeneous repositories into searchable, verifiable, and generative-ready data. It focuses on the key components—semantic and vector search, skillset enrichment, advanced OCR, and structured extraction—so your solutions can respond with precision, context, and traceability across scenarios such as catalogs, financial back-office, or technical analysis.

We will explore these concepts across three main fronts: Azure AI Search, where you will design indexes, skillsets, and indexers, combine BM25, semantic, and vector retrieval in hybrid search, and extend these results to both, classic and agentic RAG. Azure AI Document Intelligence, that will be featuring pre-built and custom (template or neural) models, composition with classification, and large-scale batch processing; and Azure AI Content Understanding, which unifies advanced OCR, summarization, classification, and multimodal extraction. The chapter concludes with guidance on provisioning, security, and observability to help you operate production-grade solutions with quality and resilience.

Structure

In this chapter, we will cover the following topics:

- Implementing Azure AI Search
  - Core Concepts: Indexes, Enrichment, and Query
  - Provisioning, Security, and Networking
  - Skillsets and Enrichment Pipelines
  - Data sources and Indexes
  - Knowledge Store Projections
  - Implementing RAG with Azure AI Search
- Azure AI Document Intelligence
  - Provisioning, Security, and Networking
  - Prebuilt, Prebuilt Models and Layout Analysis
  - Implement a Custom Document Intelligence Model
  - Creating a Composed Model with Classification
  - Choosing the Right Model
  - Production Patterns
  - Observability and Resilience
- Azure AI Content Understanding
  - Architecture and Core Components
  - Limits, Quotas, and Scaling Considerations
  - Advanced OCR and Layout Analysis
  - Attribute Detection and Structured Data Extraction
  - Multimodal Analysis: Images, Audio, and Video

Implementing Azure AI Search

Azure AI Search turns heterogeneous content into a searchable corpus through indexes, skillsets for AI enrichment, and indexers for freshness, with optional Knowledge Store projections for analytics. On this foundation, applications query with keyword (BM25), semantic ranking (captions/answers), vector similarity, or hybrid retrieval.

Core Concepts: Indexes, Enrichment, and Query

This part focuses on provisioning the service, designing and building indexes, enriching content with skillsets, automating ingestion with indexers, projecting enrichments to Knowledge Store, querying with syntax and filters, combining semantic and vector retrieval, and closing with a short RAG bridge.

Provisioning, Security, and Networking

A successful deployment starts with a properly sized service and clear access boundaries. Create the Azure AI Search service in a region close to your data, and users. Following it, choose a pricing tier that matches your query throughput and corpus size, and plan identity and networking from day one. Enable role-based access control for the control plane, prefer managed identities for data access and enrichment calls, and use Private Endpoints if you require network isolation.

Creating the Azure AI Search Service from the Azure Portal

Open the Azure portal and create a new Azure AI Search resource. In the Basics tab, choose the subscription and resource group, provide a unique service name, select the region, and pick a pricing tier. In Networking, decide whether to keep public access for early testing or to enable Private Endpoints for a virtual network. In Review + create, confirm deployment and wait for the service to appear in your resource group.

The following image highlights the Azure portal experience for creating an Azure AI Search service, showing the selection of subscription, resource group, region, and pricing tier. It illustrates the initial provisioning step required before indexing and querying the enterprise data.

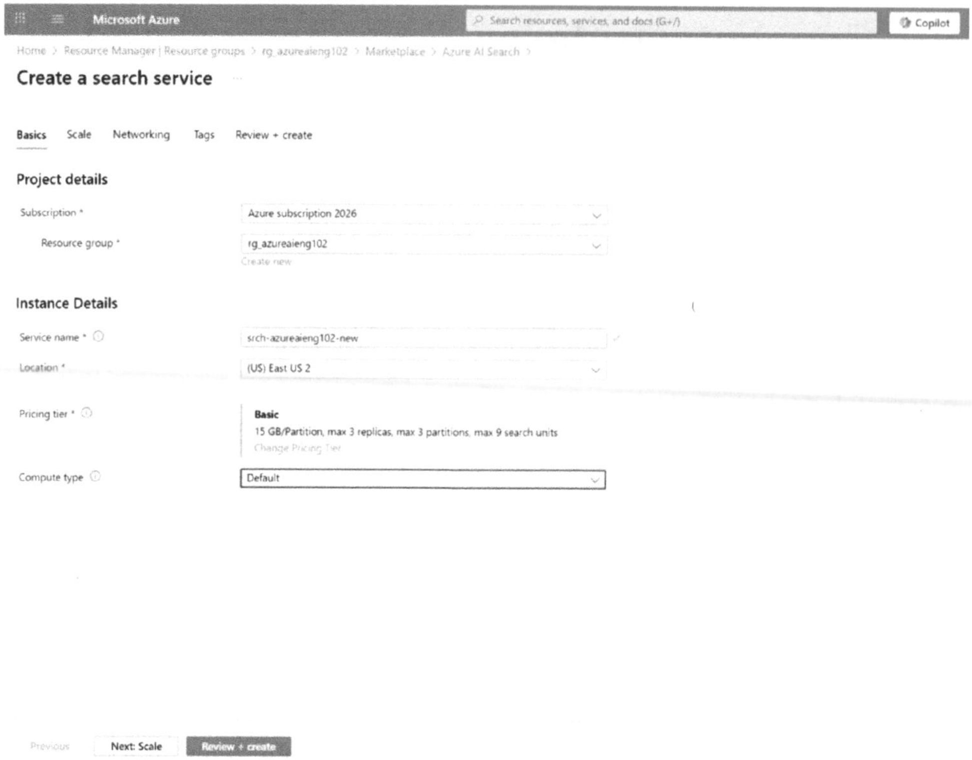

Figure 7.1: *Creating an Azure AI Search in Azure Portal*

Index Design: The Search Database

An index is a retrieval-optimized structure made of documents and fields. Field attributes determine behavior at query time: searchable, filterable, sortable, facetable, retrievable, and a unique key. Assign language analyzers (for example, **`en.microsoft`** or **`es.microsoft`**) on text fields that users will search and read. For vector search, add a vector field with the correct dimensions for your embedding model and associate a vector profile. Define semantic settings so the ranker knows which fields represent titles, keywords, and content.

Creating an Index from the Azure Portal

Open your Azure AI Search service and choose Import data (new). Connect to a source such as Azure Blob Storage, Azure SQL Database, Cosmos DB, or Azure Data Lake Storage Gen2. In the Add enrichment step, enable Split into chunks and Vectorize text and choose your embedding deployment. Review the generated schema, adjust analyzers and field attributes, configure a semantic configuration, and complete the wizard. The portal will create the data source, skillset, index, and indexer in a single operation.

The following image highlights the *Import data (new)* wizard in Azure AI Search, where users select the target scenario such as keyword search, RAG, or multimodal RAG. It demonstrates how the portal accelerates index, skillset, and indexer creation, based on common search and generative AI patterns.

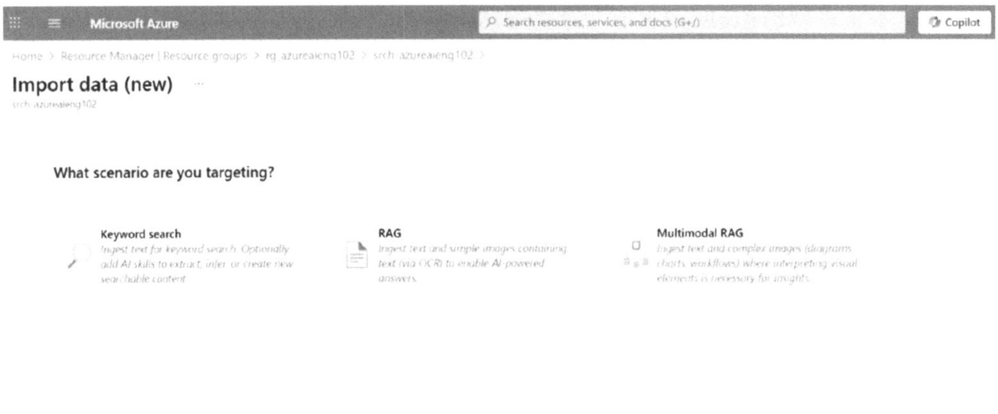

Figure 7.2: *Azure AI Search - Import Data (New) - Different Scenario Options*

Creating an Index with REST APIs

```
POST https://{service}.search.windows.net/indexes?api-version
={api-version}
Content-Type: application/json
api-key: {admin-key}
{
  "name": "docs-index",
  "fields": [
    { "name": "id", "type": "Edm.String", "key": true,
"filterable": true, "sortable": true },
    { "name": "title", "type": "Edm.String", "searchable": true,
"retrievable": true, "sortable": true, "analyzer": "en.microsoft"
},
    { "name": "content", "type": "Edm.String", "searchable":
true, "retrievable": true, "analyzer": "en.microsoft" },
    { "name": "category", "type": "Edm.String", "filterable":
true, "facetable": true, "sortable": true },
    {
      "name": "contentVector",
      "type": "Collection(Edm.Single)",
      "searchable": true,
      "retrievable": false,
      "dimensions": 1536,
      "vectorSearchProfile": "hnswProfile"
    }
```

```
    ],
    "semanticSettings": {
      "configurations": [{
        "name": "semantic-config",
        "prioritizedFields": {
          "titleField":   { "fieldName": "title" },
          "contentFields":[{ "fieldName": "content" }],
          "keywordsFields":[{ "fieldName": "category" }]
        }
      }]
    },
    "vectorSearch": {
      "algorithms": [
        { "name": "hnsw-default", "kind": "hnsw",
          "hnswParameters": { "m": 4, "efConstruction": 200,
  "efSearch": 100, "metric": "cosine" } }
      ],
      "profiles": [
        { "name": "hnswProfile", "algorithm": "hnsw-default",
  "vectorizer": "aoai-vec" }
      ]
    },
    "vectorizers": [
      {
        "name": "aoai-vec",
        "kind": "azureOpenAI",
        "azureOpenAIParameters": {
          "resourceUri": "https://{aoai}.openai.azure.com",
          "deploymentId": "text-embedding-3-small",
          "modelName": "text-embedding-3-small",
          "apiKey": "{use-managed-identity-or-key}"
        }
      }
    ]
  }
```

Model fields around how users will query (filters, facets, sorts), not just how data is stored at the source. Keep vector arrays out of responses with `retrievable:false`. Align dimensions and similarity metric with the embedding model used at ingestion and query time.

Before proceeding, it helps to have a compact reference of the field attributes, you will set most often.

Common Index Field Attributes

Use these attributes to balance query capabilities with payload size and performance.

Attribute	Purpose in queries and results
key	Unique identifier for each document.
searchable	Enables full-text analysis with a language analyzer.
filterable	Allows OData filters for hard constraints.
sortable	Enables ordering with `$orderby`.
facetable	Supports faceted navigation.
retrievable	Controls whether the field is returned in results.
Analyzer	Language/tokenization for searchable text (for example, `en.microsoft`, `es.microsoft`).

Table 7.1: *Common Index Field Attributes*

Skillsets and Enrichment Pipelines

A skillset is a declarative pipeline that runs during indexing to extract content, split it into chunks, generate embeddings, and produce additional signals. Use Text Split for chunking and the Azure OpenAI Embedding skill for vector generation; map those outputs into index fields and, optionally, into a Knowledge Store.

Built-in Skills: Text Splitting and Embeddings Minimal REST

```
{
  "name":"docs-skillset",
  "skills":[
    {"@odata.type":"#Microsoft.Skills.Text.SplitSkill",
"context":"/document/content","outputs":[{"name":"tex-
tItems","targetName":"chunks"}]},    {"@odata.type"
:"#Microsoft.Skills.Text.AzureOpenAIEmbeddingSkill","context":"/
document/chunks/*","inputs":[{"name":"text","source":"/document/
chunks/*"}],"outputs":[{"name":"embeddings","targetName"
:"embedding"}]}
  ]
}
```

Place Split before embeddings so vectors represent coherent passages. Size chunks for model token budgets and semantic-ranker limits. If you ingest scans or image-heavy PDFs, add OCR skills before splitting.

Custom Web API Skill

When built-in skills are not enough, insert a Custom Web API skill for domain-specific logic such as redaction, taxonomy tagging, or metadata normalization. The skill receives JSON from the enrichment tree and returns outputs that you can map to fields or projections.

Custom Web API skill - minimal REST

```
{
  "@odata.type":"#Microsoft.Skills.Custom.WebApiSkill",
  "uri":"https://<endpoint>/redact",
  "httpMethod":"POST",
  "context":"/document/chunks/*",
  "inputs":[{"name":"text","source":"/document/chunks/*"}],
  "outputs":[{"name":"outputText","targetName":"clean"}]
}
```

Host the endpoint behind Functions or API Management, secure it with managed identity or keys, and project both cleaned text and detected entities into the index or Knowledge Store for auditability.

Data Sources and Indexers

Indexers connect data sources to your index and skillset, run on demand or a schedule, and support change detection so only updated content is processed. Typical sources include Azure Blob Storage, Azure Data Lake Storage Gen2, Azure SQL Database, Cosmos DB, Azure Table Storage, and OneLake.

Creating Data Sources and Indexers with REST

```
PUT https://{service}.search.windows.net/datasources
('{dsName}')?api-version={api-version}
Content-Type: application/json
api-key: {admin-key}
{
  "name": "{dsName}",
  "type": "azureblob",
  "credentials": { "connectionString": "DefaultEndpointsProtocol
=..." },
  "container": { "name": "docs" }
}
PUT https://{service}.search.windows.net/indexers/{name}?
api-version={api-version}
Content-Type: application/json
api-key: {admin-key}
{
  "name": "docs-indexer",
  "dataSourceName": "{dsName}",
  "targetIndexName": "docs-index",
  "skillsetName": "docs-skillset",
  "schedule": { "interval": "PT15M" },
```

```
  "fieldMappings": [
    { "sourceFieldName": "metadata_storage_name", "targetField-
Name": "title" }
  ],
  "outputFieldMappings": [
    { "sourceFieldName": "/document/chunks/*", "targetFieldName":
"content" },
    { "sourceFieldName": "/document/chunks/*/embedding",
"targetFieldName": "contentVector" }
  ]
}
```

Pilot a small folder to validate change detection and throughput. Following it, schedule runs to meet freshness targets, and use Execution history to monitor duration, errors, and processed counts.

Scheduling and Monitoring Indexers from the Portal

Open your Search service and locate the indexer you created. Set an interval that fits your update cadence and review Execution history to confirm that runs complete successfully and to inspect errors if any appear.

Knowledge Store Projections

Knowledge Store persist selected outputs from the enrichment tree into Azure Storage for analytics or downstream systems. Projections can target tables (rows per chunk), objects (JSON documents), and files (artifacts such as images). Shapes defined in the skillset control the structure of each projection.

Add a Shaper skill that produces stable shapes for tables and objects. Apply lifecycle policies on the Storage account to control retention and cost.

Query Syntax Essentials

A compact set of query examples helps teams and students practice quickly. Use OData filter for hard constraints and **`$orderby`** for deterministic ordering; switch to **`queryType`**: "full" when you need Lucene-style wildcards, fuzzy matching, boolean operators, and proximity queries.

Keyword with filters and sorting -minimal REST

```
{ "search":"travel policy", "filter":"category eq 'HR'", "order-
by":"lastUpdated desc", "select":"id,title", "top":10 }
```

Hybrid + semantic with text-to-vector - minimal REST

This hybrid body fuses signals and gives the semantic ranker room to re-rank.

```
{
  "search":"travel policy",
  "queryType":"semantic",
  "semanticConfiguration":"sem",
  "vectorQueries":[{"kind":"text","text":"current reimbursement
rules","fields":"contentVector","k":50}],
  "hybridSearch":{"maxTextRecallSize":1000},
  "answers":"extractive|count-3","captions":"extractive|
highlight-true"
}
```

Hybrid plus semantic is a strong default for heterogeneous corpora. Increase vector k to give the semantic ranker enough candidates, and apply metadata filters to tighten precision. Use **$select** to return only the fields your UI needs.

Choosing the Right Search Mode

Before introducing RAG, the following table helps you choose a sensible default strategy for your content and users.

Use this mapping during design reviews to align retrieval choices with user goals.

Need in the application	Mode to use	Rationale
Precise lexical matching with facets and filters	Keyword (BM25) + filters	Affordable, predictable, and ideal for catalogs and documentation.
Passages and short answers from source text	Semantic ranking (captions/answers)	Improves UX with extractive highlights grounded in your content.
Concept-level retrieval beyond literal matches	Vector	Finds semantically related content for FAQs, R&D, and support knowledge.
Balanced coverage and precision	Hybrid (keyword + vector) + semantic	Fuses signals (RRF) and often yields the best overall relevance on complex queries

Table 7.2: *Search Modes and Typical Uses*

Implementing RAG with Azure AI Search

As discussed in *Chapter 3, Implementing Generative AI Solutions* in Data Grounding and RAG, it improves model accuracy by grounding responses in trusted enterprise data. This section focuses on how Azure AI Search powers the retrieval phase of RAG: it indexes and enriches documents, generates embeddings for semantic similarity, and executes hybrid queries that combine keyword and vector signals–

optionally with semantic ranking—to supply high-quality grounding context to the model.

Azure AI Search supports hybrid search as a single request that runs full-text (BM25) and vector queries in parallel and merges results using Reciprocal Rank Fusion (RRF). This fusion typically improves recall ability and robustness as compared to using a vector store alone, especially on mixed, real-world corpora.

Recent platform guidance distinguishes two complementary retrieval patterns for RAG: Agentic Retrieval uses a LLM to decompose complex questions into focused sub-queries, run them (often in parallel), and return structured results with citations—recommended for new solutions that need stronger coverage and traceability. Classic RAG issues a single retrieval call and forwards top-k passages to the model—simpler and fast, suitable when latency and minimal moving parts are the priority.

The following table contrasts these patterns so that you can choose a sensible default before you wire up prompts and evaluation:

RAG Patterns on Azure AI Search

Use this three-column summary to choose the retrieval pattern that best fits your solution.

Pattern	**How it works**	**Best for**
Agentic retrieval	LLM plans multiple focused sub-queries (optionally uses chat history), executes them, merges evidence, and returns structured results with citations; can include semantic re-ranking in the pipeline.	Complex or multi-step questions; maximum coverage with traceability and richer system telemetry.
Classic RAG	Single hybrid/semantic retrieval; top-k passages are injected into the prompt for generation.	Straightforward apps where low latency and operational simplicity outweigh advanced planning.
Hybrid retrieval (building block)	One request runs keyword + vector in parallel and fuses results with RRF; use filters and field selection to shape the context.	Heterogeneous corpora that benefit from both lexical precision and semantic similarity in the same flow.

Table 7.3: *RAG Retrieval Patterns on Azure AI Search*

Integration typically happens in your orchestration layer. Frameworks such as Microsoft Agent Framework, Semantic Kernel, LangChain, or LlamaIndex can call Azure AI Search as the retriever and Azure OpenAI (or another LLM) as the generator, keeping indexing and access control in Search, while prompts and conversation flow live in the app.

For continuous improvement, incorporate RAG evaluators to measure relevance, groundedness, and answer quality against your own datasets. Evaluations make it easier to compare retrieval settings (for example, top-k, hybrid weights, semantic rankers on/off) and to guard against drift as your corpus evolves.

Azure AI Document Intelligence

Azure AI Document Intelligence turns unstructured documents into structured data through ready-to-use pre-built models, custom extraction models (template or neural), and custom classification to route multi-document files–optionally composed under a single entry point. On this foundation, applications run single-document analysis or batch jobs, and can request searchable PDFs or cropped figures as outputs. Authoring and quick tests happen in Document Intelligence Studio, while production calls use the v4 REST API or SDKs

Provisioning, Security, and Networking

A successful deployment starts with the right resource and access boundaries. Create a Document Intelligence resource in the region closest to data and users. Prefer Microsoft Entra ID (managed identities or service principals) for runtime and pipelines and place the resource behind Private Endpoints if you need network isolation. The service supports secure connections from VNets and standard RBAC/ diagnostics like the rest of Azure AI Services.

Create the Document Intelligence resource from the Azure portal

1. Open the Azure portal and create a new resource of type Azure AI Services - Document Intelligence.
2. In Basics, select the subscription and resource group, choose a unique name, pick the region, and select the pricing tier.
3. In Networking, decide whether to keep public access during early testing or to restrict access through Private Endpoints in a virtual network.
4. Finally, review the settings and create the resource.
5. Once deployed, open Document Intelligence Studio from the blade of the resource to explore models and authoring options.

The following image highlights the creation of an Azure AI Document Intelligence resource in the Azure portal, including region selection and pricing tier configuration. This step establishes the service endpoint used for document analysis, extraction, and model training.

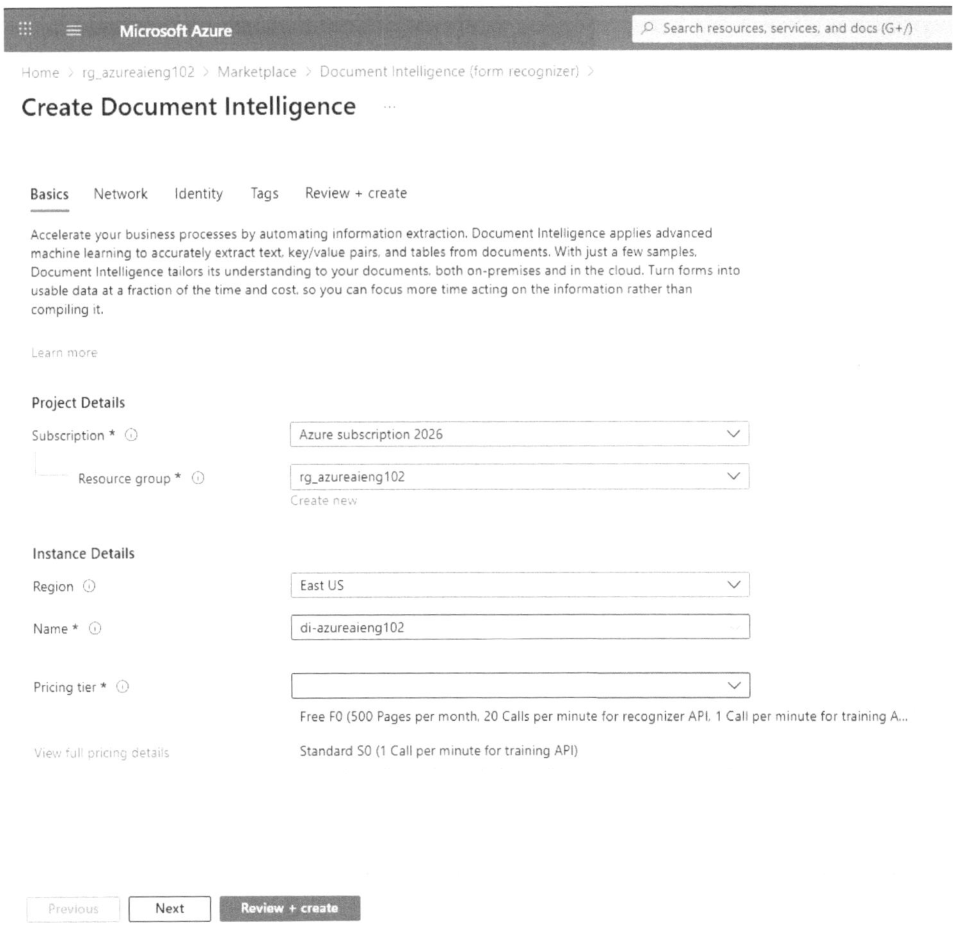

Figure 7.3: *Creating an Azure AI Document Intelligence Resource in the Azure Portal*

Prebuilt, Prebuilt Models and Layout Analysis

Prebuilt models extract structured data from common business documents such as invoices, receipts, IDs, contracts, and bank statements.

They provide an immediate way to start without training.

When only the document structure is required, or when you need to extend the extraction schema—you can use prebuilt-layout together with add-on features.

Extending Prebuilt Models with Query Fields

You can extend the response schema dynamically by using query fields, available in prebuilt and layout models.

Enable the `queryFields` feature and list additional keys to extract.

This option is ideal when you only need a few extra fields and want to avoid training a custom model.

REST Example – Prebuilt Invoice with Query Fields

```
ENDPOINT="https://<your-subdomain>.cognitiveservices.azure.com"
API="2024-11-30"
curl -sS -X POST \
  "$ENDPOINT/documentintelligence/documentModels/prebuilt-
invoice:analyze?_overload=analyzeDocument&api-version=$API&
features=queryFields&queryFields=InvoiceId,Total" \
  -H "Ocp-Apim-Subscription-Key:f $KEY" -H "Content-Type:
application/json" \
  -d '{ "urlSource": "https://<storage>/invoices/invoice-001.pd-
f?sv=..." }'
```

This calls the v4.0 REST endpoint and asks the prebuilt model to also return **`InvoiceId`** and **`Total`**, if present.

Python SDK – layout + key-value pairs + query fields

```
from azure.core.credentials import AzureKeyCredential
from azure.ai.documentintelligence import DocumentIntelligenceClient
from azure.ai.documentintelligence.models import DocumentAnalysis-
Feature
client = DocumentIntelligenceClient(
    endpoint="https://<your-subdomain>.cognitiveservices.azure.com",
    credential=AzureKeyCredential("<KEY>")
)
with open("form.pdf", "rb") as f:
    poller = client.begin_analyze_document(
        "prebuilt-layout",
        body=f,
        features=[DocumentAnalysisFeature.KEY_VALUE_PAIRS,
                  DocumentAnalysisFeature.QUERY_FIELDS],
        query_fields=["CustomerId", "OrderNumber"]
    )
result = poller.result()
print([d.doc_type for d in result.documents])
```

The Python client exposes features and `query_fields` so you can enable KVP extraction on layout and request additional fields without re-training.

When you only need text structure and a few fields, *layout plus* `keyValuePairs` *and* `queryFields` provides a fast, training-free solution.

Implement a Custom Document Intelligence Model

When prebuilt models are insufficient, a custom model is trained. Two build modes are available:

- Custom Template: It is best for fixed, stable layouts.
- Custom Neural: It is deep learning-based, more tolerant to layout variations, and recommended for most production cases.

Authoring from the Portal

1. Open Document Intelligence Studio and select Custom Extraction.
2. Connect an Azure Blob Storage container that holds your training documents and labels.
3. Define or import field labels, train the model, and test it with hold-out samples to inspect confidence levels before publishing.
4. As a starting point, prepare at least five documents per type, then expand the dataset to improve generalization.

The following image highlights the configuration workflow for a custom extraction model in Document Intelligence Studio, where a service resource, subscription, and API version are selected. It shows how projects are bound to a Document Intelligence resource before connecting training data.

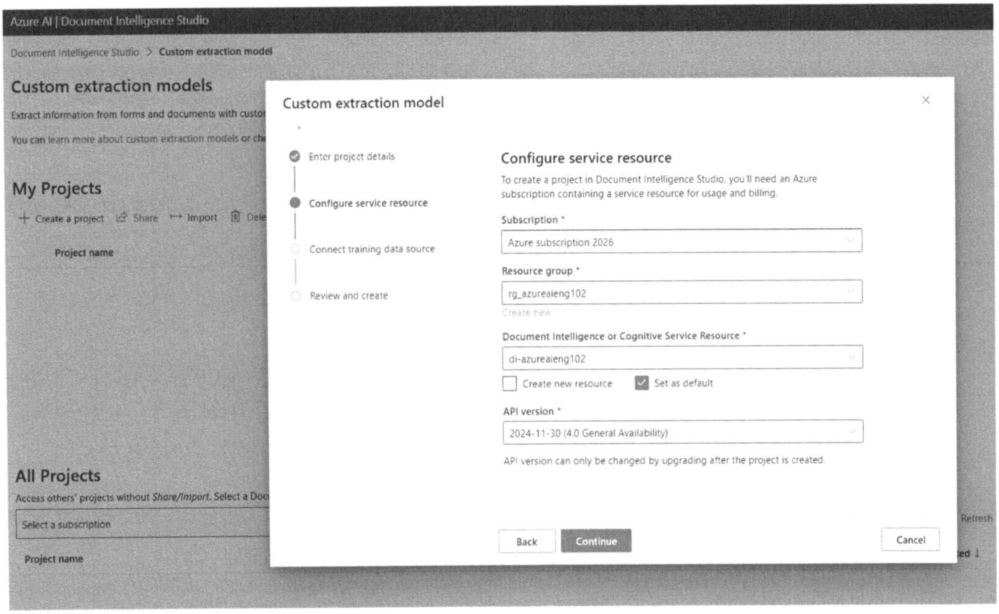

Figure 7.4: *Document Intelligence Studio - Create Custom Extraction Model*

Python Example – Train and Use a Custom Neural Model

```
import os, uuid
from azure.core.credentials import AzureKeyCredential
from azure.ai.documentintelligence import (
    DocumentIntelligenceAdministrationClient, Document
IntelligenceClient
)
from azure.ai.documentintelligence.models import (
    BuildDocumentModelRequest, DocumentBuildMode, AzureBlob
ContentSource
)
endpoint, key = os.environ["DI_ENDPOINT"], os.environ["DI_KEY"]
admin = DocumentIntelligenceAdministrationClient(endpoint, Azure-
KeyCredential(key))
req = BuildDocumentModelRequest(
    model_id=f"po-neural-{uuid.uuid4().hex[:6]}",
    build_mode=DocumentBuildMode.NEURAL,
    azure_blob_source=AzureBlobContentSource(container_url=os.
environ["TRAIN_SAS"])
)
model = admin.begin_build_document_model(req).result()
client = DocumentIntelligenceClient(endpoint, AzureKeyCredential
(key))
with open("po_sample.pdf", "rb") as f:
    result = client.begin_analyze_document(model.model_id,
body=f).result()
print(model.model_id, [d.doc_type for d in result.documents])
```

This uses the v4 SDKs to build a neural model and then analyze a PDF with that model.

Training, Testing, and Publishing

- Data: It collects representative samples (including edge cases and negatives).
- Labeling: It maintains clear field names and consistent regions/semantics.
- Evaluation: It keeps a separate test set; measure field-level precision/recall and coverage.
- Promotion: It versions your model IDs (for example, invoices-neural-v3) and promotes after hitting business thresholds. Studio and the REST admin APIs expose build, copy, compose, and list operations to manage the lifecycle.

Creating a Composed Model with Classification

For scenarios involving multiple document types or mixed files, create a custom classifier and combine it with extraction models into a composed model.

In v4, composition uses an explicit classifier, and you can enable split mode to automatically separate multi-document files so that each section is routed to the proper extractor.

REST Example – Compose with Classifier

```
ENDPOINT="https://<your-subdomain>.cognitiveservices.azure.com"
API="2024-11-30"
curl -sS -X POST \
 "$ENDPOINT/documentintelligence/documentModels:compose?
api-version=$API" \
 -H "Ocp-Apim-Subscription-Key: $KEY" -H "Content-Type:
application/json" \
 -d '{
   "modelId": "finance-compose-v1",
   "classifierId": "finance-classifier-v1",
   "split": "auto",
   "docTypes": {
     "invoice": { "modelId": "invoices-neural-v1" },
     "receipt": { "modelId": "receipts-template-v2" },
     "po":      { "modelId": "po-neural-v3" }
   }
 }'
```

Treat the confidence of the classifier as a routing signal: if it falls below your threshold, send the document to manual review or to a general fallback such as layout plus query fields.

Batch Processing and Additional Outputs

For high-volume workloads, use **Analyze Batch Documents**. Provide an input container (with optional prefixes or file lists) and an output container. You can request `output=pdf` to produce searchable PDFs, or **`output=figures`** to generate image crops of figures.

REST Example – Batch Processing with Searchable PDF

```
ENDPOINT="https://<your-subdomain>.cognitiveservices.azure.com"
API="2024-11-30"
curl -sS -X POST \
 "$ENDPOINT/documentintelligence/documentModels/prebuilt-read:
analyzeBatch?api-version=$API&output=pdf" \
 -H "Ocp-Apim-Subscription-Key: $KEY" -H "Content-Type:
application/json" \
 -d '{
   "azureBlobSource": { "containerUrl": "https://<storage>/input?
sv=...", "prefix": "docs/" },
   "resultContainerUrl": "https://<storage>/output?sv=...",
```

```
    "resultPrefix": "run-2025-10-20/"
  }'
```

Follow the *Operation-Location* header for status, and respect the *Retry-After* interval when polling.

Python Example – Retrieve PDF and Figure Outputs

```
from azure.ai.documentintelligence.models import AnalyzeOutput
Option
# Searchable PDF
with open("scan.pdf", "rb") as f:
    poller = client.begin_analyze_document(
        "prebuilt-read", body=f, output=[AnalyzeOutputOption.
PDF])
result = poller.result()
pdf_stream = client.get_analyze_result_pdf(
    model_id=result.model_id, result_id=poller.details
["operation_id"])
open("scan_searchable.pdf","wb").writelines(pdf_stream)
# Figures
with open("paper.pdf", "rb") as f:
    p2 = client.begin_analyze_document(
        "prebuilt-layout", body=f, output=[AnalyzeOutputOption.
FIGURES])
r2 = p2.result()
for fig in r2.figures or []:
    stream = client.get_analyze_result_figure(
        model_id=r2.model_id, result_id=p2.details["operation_
id"], figure_id=fig.id)
    open(f"{fig.id}.png","wb").writelines(stream)
```

Testing and Authoring from the Portal

Open Document Intelligence Studio to experiment with Prebuilt, Layout, Custom Extraction, and Custom Classification models. The portal allows you to toggle add-ons such as *query fields* during testing, label data, and export ready-to-use SDK snippets.

Choosing the Right Model

Requirement	Model Type	Rationale
Rapid start with standard forms	Prebuilt	Immediate extraction without training.
Need for text structure and a few custom fields	Layout + `keyValuePairs` + `queryFields`	Structure plus limited field extraction.

One fixed layout requiring high precision	Custom Template	Template-based extraction for rigid forms.
Highly variable formats across suppliers	Custom Neural	Robust to layout diversity; best for variability.
Mixed document types in a single file	Classifier + Composed Model with Split Mode	Automatically classifies, splits, and routes each section.

Table 7.4: *Model Selection Guidelines*

Production Patterns

- **Financial Back-Office (Purchase Orders, Invoices, or Receipts):** Use a classifier combined with a composed model to route each document type. Run neural models for invoices, template models for fixed receipts, and schedule nightly batch processing. Archive searchable PDFs for compliance.
- **KYC Onboarding:** Apply the prebuilt ID model with query fields for region-specific identifiers. Validate by confidence thresholds and business rules and route low-confidence cases for human review.
- **Engineering and Technical Documents:** Use the layout model with *figures* output to extract diagrams while preserving the text structure for indexing.

Observability and Resilience

- **Monitoring:** It enables diagnostics and export metrics to Azure Monitor. To note further, it tracks total calls, latency, success rate, and throttling.
- **Retry Policy:** It implements exponential backoff and respects the *Retry-After* header when polling asynchronous operations.
- **Security:** It uses Entra ID or managed identities for clients, store secrets in Key Vault, and keep the resource behind a Private Endpoint. It also encrypts content in transit and at rest.

Azure AI Content Understanding

Azure AI Content Understanding is an advanced service designed to convert unstructured information–such as text, documents, images, audio, and video–into structured and analyzable data.

It unifies Optical Character Recognition (OCR), summarization, classification, attribute detection, and structured data extraction within a single, consistent framework. This capability enables organizations to process large volumes of enterprise content automatically and generate enriched data suitable for analytics, search, and generative AI solutions.

In contrast to Azure AI Document Intelligence, which is optimized for template-based and trainable models, Content Understanding uses foundation models and generative reasoning to identify structure within any content, even when the layout or language is unfamiliar. The service offers both prebuilt analyzers, which are ready to use without configuration, and custom analyzers, which can be extended by defining schemas that describe the fields to be extracted, generated, or classified.

Analyzers can be tested and deployed directly in Azure AI Foundry, and consumed programmatically through asynchronous REST APIs or the Python SDK.

Architecture and Core Components

Before using the APIs, it is helpful to understand the key architectural components involved:

- Azure AI Foundry Resource hosts and authenticates analyzers. All content documents, images, audio, and video—share the same endpoint and key.
- Analyzers are logical units describing how each item of content is processed. Prebuilt analyzers include prebuilt-documentAnalyzer, prebuilt-imageAnalyzer, prebuilt-audioAnalyzer, and prebuilt-videoAnalyzer. Custom analyzers allow developers to specify field schemas that define which information is extracted or generated.
- Operating modes determine scope. *Standard mode* handles single-file analysis, while *Pro mode* (currently in preview) supports multi-file jobs, cross-document reasoning, and validation against external sources.
- Execution model is asynchronous. Each analysis request is initiated through a POST call ending in `:analyze`, and progress is retrieved by polling the Operation-Location header, until the status becomes *Succeeded*.

Limits, Quotas, and Scaling Considerations

Each Azure AI Content Understanding analyzer operates within specific technical limits that define schema complexity and maximum job size.

Understanding these limits helps prevent processing failures and supports efficient scaling when analyzing high-volume workloads.

Concept	Typical value or guideline
Fields per analyzer	Up to 1,000
Classification categories per field	Up to 300
Supported methods	extract, generate, classify

Maximum input size	Approximately 500 MB (Pro mode)
Execution model	Asynchronous with polling via Operation-Location
Pricing units	Content Extraction (input) and Field Extraction (output)

Table 7.5: *Limits and Quotas in Azure AI Content Understanding*

Advanced OCR and Layout Analysis

The prebuilt document analyzer provides detailed text and layout extraction. Results include hierarchical elements such as pages, paragraphs, lines, words, and tables, each with bounding boxes, spans, and confidence scores. Output can be returned as plain text, Markdown, or HTML tables for straightforward integration.

Testing Document Analysis from the Portal

In the *Documents* section of Content Understanding, upload a scanned invoice or contract and choose Analyze with prebuilt analyzer.

The interface presents detected text regions, table boundaries, and geometric coordinates.

The following image highlights the Content Understanding playground analyzing a document with the prebuilt document analyzer, displaying extracted text, layout structure, and tables. It illustrates how advanced OCR and layout analysis produce structured, reviewable results directly in Azure AI Foundry.

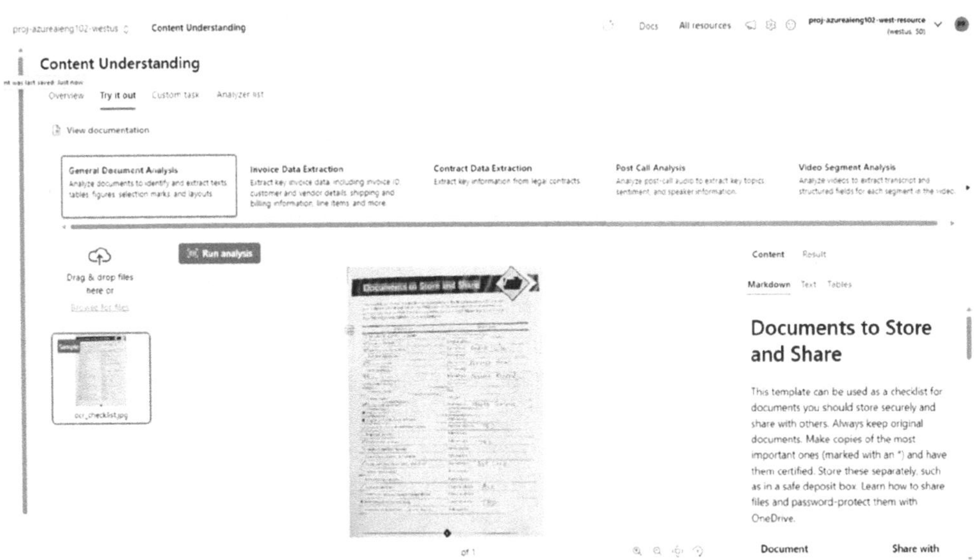

Figure 7.5: *Azure AI Foundry – Content Understanding Playground – Document Layout Analysis View*

REST Example – Prebuilt Document Analyzer

```
curl -i -X POST "{endpoint}/contentunderstanding/analyzers/prebuilt
-documentAnalyzer:analyze?api-version=2025-05-01-preview" \
  -H "Ocp-Apim-Subscription-Key: {key}" \
  -H "Content-Type: application/json" \
  -d '{"url":"https://github.com/Azure-Samples/azure-ai-
content-understanding-python/raw/main/data/invoice.pdf"}'
```

To retrieve the results, poll the Operation-Location URL until the status indicates *Succeeded.*

```
curl -i -X GET "{endpoint}/contentunderstanding/analyzerResults/
{request-id}?api-version=2025-05-01-preview" \
  -H "Ocp-Apim-Subscription-Key: {key}"
```

Python Example – Polling for Results

```
import os, time, requests
endpoint = os.environ["CU_ENDPOINT"]
key = os.environ["CU_KEY"]
headers = {"Ocp-Apim-Subscription-Key": key, "Content-Type":
"application/json"}
response = requests.post(
    f"{endpoint}/contentunderstanding/analyzers/prebuilt-
documentAnalyzer:analyze?api-version=2025-05-01-preview",
    headers=headers,
    json={"url": "https://.../invoice.pdf"}
)
operation = response.headers["Operation-Location"]
while True:
    result = requests.get(operation, headers=headers).json()
    if result.get("status") in ("Succeeded", "Failed",
"Canceled"):
        break
    time.sleep(1)
print(result["result"]["contents"][0]["tables"][0]["cells"][0]
["content"])
```

Practical guidance: When exporting tabular results, the HTML table format provides a reliable structure for dashboards or reporting tools. Retaining the spans and source attributes is useful for traceability and for linking extracted content back to its visual position in the original document. To achieve higher OCR accuracy on scanned materials, correct page orientation and ensure a resolution of at least 200 DPI before submission.

Summarization: Generative fields enable automatic summarization of textual or multimedia content. Each generative field is declared as a string with the generated method and produces concise summaries along with token-usage metrics.

This is valuable for meeting transcripts, lengthy reports, or policy documents where quick comprehension is needed.

Exploring summarization from the Portal: Upload a long document, audio transcript, or video in the Content Understanding workspace and enable a generative field of type *Summary*.

The preview panel displays a concise version of the original material, demonstrating how generative fields condense large inputs.

The following image highlights audio analysis using Azure AI Content Understanding, including transcription, summarization, topic extraction, and sentiment detection from a recorded call. It demonstrates how unstructured audio content is transformed into structured insights through generative and analytical fields.

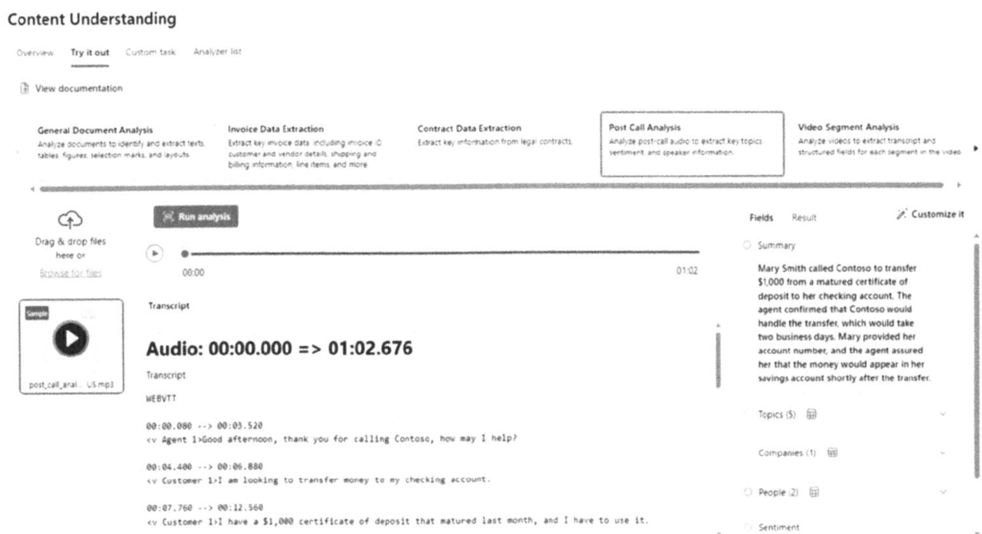

Figure 7.6: *Azure AI Foundry – Content Understanding Playground – Audio Summarization*

Classification

The classification capability in Azure AI Content Understanding enables the automatic identification of the category of a document or type within a dataset. It can operate on single documents or on compound files that contain multiple embedded documents of various types.

This feature serves as an early routing mechanism in a content-processing workflow. For example, when the analyzer recognizes that a file is an *Invoice*, *Contract*, or *Receipt*, it can automatically direct the document to a downstream pipeline or a field-extraction schema that is optimized for that specific category.

Classification can also perform document splitting, segmenting multi-document

PDFs or TIFFs into individual logical parts, each associated with a detected category. Unlike custom machine-learning models, The classifier of Content Understanding does not require training data. Instead, the user defines up to approximately fifty categories - each with a descriptive label that guides the reasoning process of the system.

Key characteristics include:

- The ability to categorize content based on semantic and visual cues without explicit model training.
- Support for multiple occurrences of the same document type within a single file.
- Optional "split" mode to automatically separate distinct document segments when different categories are detected.

In practice, the classification capability acts as the first logical layer of organization. It enables workflows to handle unstructured content efficiently by ensuring that each file or segment is processed using the correct extraction logic and validation rules.

By combining classification with field extraction, organizations can build intelligent document pipelines that are adaptive, transparent, and easily scalable.

Attribute Detection and Structured Data Extraction

The attribute detection and structured data extraction capability provides the foundation for transforming unstructured content into machine-readable, business-ready data.

It allows developers and solution architects to define a field schema, which explicitly describes the data elements to be identified in documents, images, or media–such as *Vendor Name*, *Invoice Number*, *Total Amount*, *Dates*, or *Line Items*.

Each field in the schema specifies its data type (string, number, object, or array) and its processing method:

- **extract** – for direct value extraction from the content,
- **generate** – for summarization or generative output,
- **classify** – for labeling or attribute categorization.

When a document is processed, Content Understanding applies the schema across the content and returns a standardized JSON structure containing the extracted fields.

Each field includes its recognized value, a confidence score, and evidence metadata (spans and source) that describe the exact position of the extracted text or visual region. This traceability supports auditability and transparency in enterprise workflows.

Unlike rigid, template-based systems, this schema-driven approach is flexible and resilient to layout variations. It enables consistent data extraction from diverse document formats and languages without retraining or template reconfiguration.

By combining field extraction with summarization and classification methods within a single schema, organizations can design comprehensive analyzers that not only extract key values but also generate contextual summaries and apply domain-specific tagging in one unified process.

Ultimately, the structured data extraction capability turns heterogeneous and unstructured content into consistent, verifiable data assets that are immediately usable for analytics, compliance, and automation.

Multimodal Analysis: Images, Audio, and Video

Beyond text and documents, Content Understanding supports multiple modalities through specialized prebuilt analyzers. These analyzers apply the same schema principles to visual and auditory data, enabling unified processing across diverse media.

Content Type	Capabilities
Images	Object and chart detection, caption generation, and attribute classification.
Audio	Speech transcription, summarization, speaker segmentation, and sentiment detection.
Video	Scene segmentation, key-frame extraction, and per-segment summarization.

Table 7.6: *Supported Capabilities for Multimodal Analysis*

Conclusion

Throughout this chapter, we have explored how knowledge mining and information extraction transform unstructured enterprise content into actionable intelligence. By leveraging Azure AI Search, Document Intelligence, and Content Understanding, we learned how to design scalable architectures that combine semantic enrichment, vector search, OCR, and structured data extraction. These capabilities enable organizations to retrieve, interpret, and operationalize their data efficiently–unlocking insights that fuel automation, analytics, and generative AI solutions.

We also emphasized the importance of hybrid retrieval and Retrieval-Augmented Generation (RAG) as bridges between traditional information systems and modern AI models. With proper provisioning, security, and observability, these solutions can operate reliably in production, supporting complex business workflows with grounded, explainable responses. The integration patterns discussed in this chapter form the technical backbone of intelligent search, document processing, and content understanding systems in the AI ecosystem of Azure.

In the next chapter, we will shift from implementation to preparation. *Chapter 8, Exam Preparation Strategies* equips you with practical guidance to succeed in the AI-102 certification exam. It breaks down the exam structure, question formats, and scoring model while offering study techniques, time management advice, and official learning resources. By consolidating the knowledge gained throughout this book, you will be ready to approach the certification with clarity and confidence.

Points to Remember

- Azure AI Search transforms unstructured and semi-structured content into a searchable knowledge corpus by using indexes, skillsets, and indexers that support keyword, semantic, and vector-based search.
- Index design determines how information is retrieved, as field attributes such as searchable, filterable, and retrievable directly influence query behavior and returned results.
- Skillsets enrich content during ingestion by applying AI-powered transformations such as text splitting, embeddings generation, and OCR before data is indexed.
- Vector search enables semantic understanding by allowing Azure AI Search to retrieve conceptually related content based on embeddings rather than relying solely on keyword matching.
- Hybrid and semantic retrieval improve search relevance by combining BM25, semantic ranking, and vector similarity through Reciprocal Rank Fusion (RRF).
- Retrieval-Augmented Generation (RAG) grounds large language model responses in enterprise data using classic or agentic retrieval patterns to improve accuracy and traceability.
- Azure AI Document Intelligence converts unstructured documents into structured data by extracting fields from forms, invoices, receipts, and contracts using prebuilt, custom, or composed models.

- Custom and composed models increase flexibility by combining template or neural extraction models with classifiers to support multiple document types within a single processing pipeline.
- Azure AI Content Understanding enables multimodal analysis by unifying OCR, summarization, classification, and structured data extraction for documents, images, audio, and video.

CHAPTER 8
Exam Preparation Strategies

Introduction

This chapter is designed to help readers approach the **AI-102: Designing and Implementing a Microsoft Azure AI Solution** certification exam with clarity, confidence, and purpose. It explains how the exam is structured, scored, and delivered; introduces official study resources from Microsoft Learn and Azure documentation; and outlines effective time-management and best-practice strategies for exam day.

While previous chapters had focused on building technical and architectural expertise, this one translates that knowledge into a preparation plan–turning your understanding of Azure AI into the readiness and composure required to succeed in a professional certification environment.

Structure

In this chapter, we will cover the following topics:

- Preparing for the AI-102 Certification
  - Exam Structure and Timing
  - Scoring and Evaluation
  - Question Types and Navigation
  - Understanding AI-102 Question Formats
- Building Your Knowledge Foundation
  - Microsoft Learn and the AI-102 Study Guide
  - Using Product Documentation Effectively
  - Recommended Study Workflow

- Succeeding on the Exam Day
  - Exam-Taking Strategies, Time Management, and Best Practices
  - Managing Time and Mental Energy
  - Using Microsoft Learn During the Exam
  - Environment and Stress Management

Preparing for the AI-102 Certification

The **Microsoft AI-102 Certification** validates the ability of a candidate to design, implement, and monitor AI solutions using Azure AI Services and Azure AI Foundry. The exam assesses not only technical proficiency, but also decision-making skills that balance innovation, governance, cost, and ethical responsibility.

For the most accurate and current outline of skills measured, consult the **official Microsoft Study Guide for Exam AI-102**, which details domains, weightings, and objectives.

You can review here: **https://learn.microsoft.com/en-us/credentials/certifications/resources/study-guides/ai-102**

Exam Structure and Timing

Most role-based Microsoft exams include 40–60 questions. For AI-102, Microsoft lists 100 minutes to complete the assessment; if labs are included, some role-based exams may extend to 120 minutes. The overall seat time (including instructions and the post-exam survey) ranges between 120 and 140 minutes.

The exam begins with a short navigation tutorial and concludes with an optional survey. Candidates may flag items for later review; however, sections such as **Case Studies** or **Labs** become locked after you leave them, so review your answers thoroughly before exiting each section.

The question pool spans five skill domains reflecting real Azure AI engineering responsibilities:

1. Plan and manage Azure AI solutions (20–25%).
2. Develop generative AI solutions (15–20%).
3. Implement an agentic solution (5–10%).
4. Implement computer-vision solutions (10–15%).
5. Implement NLP, knowledge mining, and information extraction solutions (15–20%).

The precise weighting may change as Microsoft revises the certification to reflect new Azure capabilities. Updated information is available in the official exam description:

You can review here:

https://learn.microsoft.com/en-us/credentials/certifications/azure-ai-engineer/

Scoring and Evaluation

Scores range from 1 to 1000 points, with a minimum passing score of 700. Microsoft applies a scaled-score model to account for differences in question difficulty across exam versions. Certain multipart questions allow **partial credit**, while unanswered items are always considered incorrect. But, since there is no penalty for incorrect answers, candidates should provide a response to every question.

At the end of the exam, the system automatically generates a performance report that visualizes the relative strength of each domain through bar indicators. This feedback enables targeted preparation for any future retake and supports continuous professional growth.

Question Types and Navigation

The AI-102 exam combines different types of questions to measure both conceptual understanding and practical reasoning. These formats include:

- Multiple Choice and Multiple Response items test theoretical knowledge and design judgment.
- Drag-and-Drop or Build-List questions, where you arrange processes or steps in logical order.
- Hot Area or Active Screen tasks that simulate configuration interfaces within the Azure portal.
- Case Studies presenting real-world business scenarios with multi-part questions.
- Lab Simulations (if included), in some versions of the test, assesses the ability to perform implementation steps in a simulated Azure environment.

Becoming familiar with these formats reduces stress and helps you manage time effectively. Paying close attention to the language used–words such as *must*, *should*, *can*, or *best*–is crucial. Similarly, understanding whether a service is in Generally Available (GA) or *Preview* can determine the correct answer.

Before the exam, it is worth practicing with the **Microsoft Exam Sandbox**, which replicates the interface and navigation experience. It allows you to see how "**mark for**

review," "**next**," and "**submit section**" functions behave–an advantage that prevents unnecessary hesitation on exam day.

The following image highlights a sample view of the Microsoft Exam Sandbox interface, illustrating how questions, navigation controls, progress indicators, and review options are presented during the exam. Familiarity with this layout helps candidates reduce cognitive load and manage time more effectively on exam day.

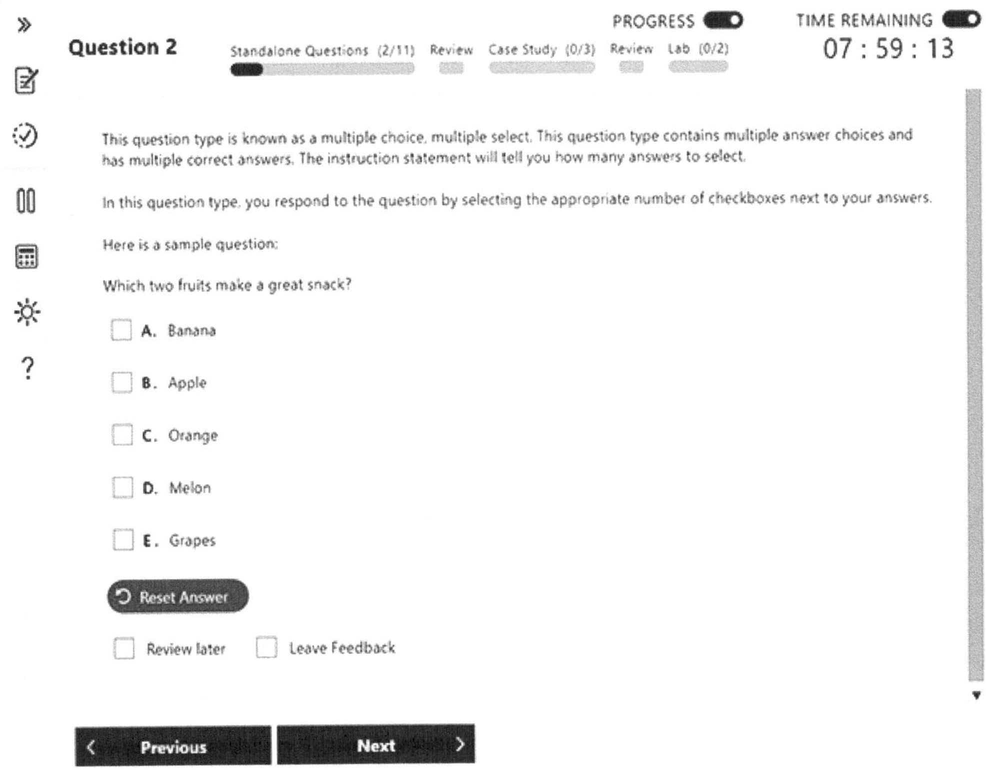

Figure 8.1: *Sample View of the Microsoft Exam Sandbox Interface*

You can review here: *https://learn.microsoft.com/en-us/credentials/certifications/resources/exam-sandbox*

Understanding AI-102 Question Formats

Each question type measures a distinct dimension of knowledge–from conceptual understanding to practical application. The following table summarizes common formats, their purpose, and effective response strategies.

Question Type	Purpose	Recommended Strategy
Multiple Choice / Multiple Response	Assess conceptual understanding and design judgment.	Read carefully for constraints. Eliminate options that conflict with requirements and choose the most secure, scalable answer.
Drag-and-Drop / Build List	Evaluate logical ordering or process knowledge.	Identify the first and last steps, then arrange the sequence logically. Visualize the workflow before answering.
Hot Area / Active Screen	Test familiarity with Azure interfaces and configuration choices.	Verify the correct scope (resource, project, or subscription) before selecting. Double-check before submitting.
Case Study	Measure analytical reasoning across multi-part business scenarios.	Read the overview, note constraints (cost, security, compliance), and review answers before leaving the section.
Lab Simulation (if present)	Assess the ability to perform practical tasks in a simulated Azure environment.	Complete high-value steps first, confirm permissions, and manage time carefully.

Table 8.1: *AI-102 Question Types, Objectives, and Recommended Response Strategies*

Building Your Knowledge Foundation

Official Study Resources - Microsoft Learn and Product Documentation: The learning ecosystem of Microsoft provides everything you need to prepare effectively–completely free and always updated alongside product changes. The following resources form the core of a serious study plan.

Microsoft Learn and the AI-102 Study Guide

The **AI-102 Study Guide** on Microsoft Learn outlines every skill domain, the percentage weight of each section, and direct links to recommended learning paths. Treat it as your primary roadmap; when Azure AI Foundry or service capabilities evolve, the guide is updated to match.

The **Practice Assessments** mirror the wordings and the logic style of Microsoft. Each question includes rationales for the right and wrong answers, allowing you to identify conceptual weaknesses. Schedule one assessment early to establish a baseline and another near the end to measure improvement.

You can review here: **https://learn.microsoft.com/en-us/credentials/certifications/practice-assessments-for-microsoft-certifications**

These tools ensure that your preparation reflects the recent exam updates by Microsoft, helping you focus your studying verified and authoritative content.

Using Product Documentation Effectively

Beyond Learn modules, the official documentation for Azure AI services, Azure AI Foundry, is of essential reading. A strong preparation routine weaves theory with small, practical exercises drawn directly from docs.

- **Azure AI Foundry** documentation explains projects, connections, and agent development. It also covers observability and cost-monitoring practices.
- **Azure OpenAI** guides you through deploying GPT and other models, managing tokens, and designing prompts that align with responsible AI guidelines.
- **Azure AI Search** explores index design, hybrid retrieval (BM25 + vector), and enrichment pipelines that form the backbone of RAG architectures.
- **Azure AI Document Intelligence** teaches how to use prebuilt and custom models for extracting structured data from complex documents.
- **Language, Vision, and Speech** service references present end-to-end examples for sentiment analysis, translation, image classification, and speech synthesis.
- **Responsible AI and Content Safety** resources explain transparency, fairness, and harm-prevention techniques fundamental to every solution.

The documentation of each service includes quick starts and sample code repositories on GitHub. Working through these examples in your own subscription will transform abstract concepts into real-world competence.

Recommended Study Workflow

An academically rigorous and practical preparation cycle might follow these stages:

1. Read the relevant official documentation for one domain or service.
2. Experiment by deploying a small Azure project that implements what you have studied.
3. Record findings, commands, and observed limitations in a structured study notebook.
4. Evaluate progress through a Microsoft Practice Assessment to verify comprehension and identify weak areas.

Repeating this cycle strengthens both theoretical understanding and applied expertise.

Succeeding on the Exam Day

Exam day is not only a test of technical knowledge, but also of judgment, composure, and decision-making under pressure. Even well-prepared candidates can underperform if they mismanage time, overlook constraints, or allow stress to disrupt their focus. This section bridges preparation and performance, outlining the practical strategies and mental frameworks that help translate months of study into confident, disciplined execution during the AI-102 exam.

Exam-Taking Strategies, Time Management, and Best Practices

While technical mastery provides the foundation, disciplined execution during the exam determines success. The AI-102 test rewards clarity, focus, and methodical reasoning under time pressure.

Managing Time and Mental Energy

Adopt a pacing rule of about two minutes per question. Use the first pass to answer straightforward items and mark uncertain ones. This ensures that you secure guaranteed points early. Reserve the final fifteen to twenty minutes for revisiting flagged questions.

In case studies, read the overview and identify non-functional constraints–security, cost ceilings, or regional data residency–before evaluating proposed solutions. Since these sections lock after submission, double-check your reasoning before proceeding.

If labs appear, complete the high-value tasks first and verify permissions and endpoints before performing long-running steps. Remember that accuracy matters more than volume; incomplete but correct work earns credit.

Cognitive and Strategic Techniques:

- **Pattern recognition**: Many items test the same underlying principles (governance, observability, or cost control). Spotting these themes quickly helps eliminate distractors.
- **Trade-off thinking**: Ask yourself which option best balances performance, security, and simplicity–a mindset identical to real solution design.
- **Situational reasoning**: Microsoft values production-ready logic over experimental shortcuts. If two answers work, choose the one that could scale safely in an enterprise setting.

Using Microsoft Learn During the Exam

For Associate- and Expert-level certifications, a built-in browser tab allows limited access to **learn.microsoft.com** documentation. It is a powerful but time-sensitive aid: use it only to confirm a parameter, API name, or command syntax. Time continues to run while browsing, so use it sparingly.

Environment and Stress Management

Before exam day, perform the official **system test** (for online sessions) or confirm ID and arrival procedures (for test centers). Prepare a quiet workspace, ensure a stable network, and remove distractions.

On the day itself, start with a few easy questions to build confidence, check the timer every 20 minutes, and practice deep-breathing techniques when your focus drifts.

Key behavioral guidelines:

- Read each question twice; subtle qualifiers change meaning.
- Trust first instincts but validate against explicit constraints.
- Never leave items blank; guessing cannot lower your score.
- Keep an eye on the progress bar—psychological pacing prevents panic.
- Apply the mindset of an engineer solving a business problem, not a trivia quiz.

By integrating calm focus with structured time allocation, you convert preparation into performance. Each question becomes an opportunity to demonstrate not only technical knowledge but also professional judgment—the hallmark of every successful Azure AI Engineer.

Conclusion

Preparing for the AI-102 certification exam is not about merely memorizing facts or reproducing documentation but rather is about developing the analytical mindset and confidence of an Azure AI Engineer. Through structured study, consistent practice, and the application of Responsible AI principles, candidates learn to connect technical implementation with strategic decision-making.

By mastering the examination structure, scoring, and question types, you gain the clarity needed to navigate complex scenarios under time pressure. Equally important is leveraging Microsoft's official learning ecosystem: the combination of **Microsoft Learn**, **Azure product documentation**, and **Practice Assessments** forms a powerful foundation for success.

Hands-on experimentation, reflection, and continuous evaluation transform knowledge into applied expertise. This preparation not only leads to certification but also sharpens the professional judgment required to design secure, ethical, and scalable AI solutions in real-world environments.

In the next and final chapter, you will apply everything learned through comprehensive **practice tests and sample questions**. This practical section mirrors the AI-102 exam experience, thereby, enabling you to test readiness, analyze performance across domains, and strengthens understanding through detailed explanations–a final bridge between theory and certification success.

Points to Remember

- The AI-102 exam typically includes 40–60 questions to be completed within 100–120 minutes. Sections such as case studies lock after exit, so review them carefully before proceeding.
- Refer to the official AI-102 Study Guide to align your preparation with the latest skills outline and percentage weightings.
- Scores range from 1 to 1000, with 700 required to pass. Some questions offer partial credit, and there is no penalty for incorrect answers, so always respond to every item.
- Practice Multiple Choice/Response, Drag-and-Drop/Build List, Hot Area/Active Screen, Case Studies, and Labs to reduce anxiety and improve pacing.
- Use Microsoft Practice Assessments to become familiar with Microsoft's wording and logic style. Each question includes rationales for correct and incorrect answers, helping identify conceptual weaknesses.
- Plan your study using Microsoft Learn by following the Study Guide, completing linked learning paths, and validating progress with Practice Assessments.
- Strengthen your understanding through official documentation and quick starts from Azure AI Foundry, Azure OpenAI, AI Search, Document Intelligence, Language/Vision/Speech services, and Responsible AI.
- Follow a structured study cycle: read official documentation, deploy a small Azure project, record findings in a study notebook, and verify comprehension with a Practice Assessment.
- Allocate time strategically by allowing about two minutes per question, securing easy points on the first pass, and reserving 15–20 minutes to review flagged items before locking case study sections.
- Prepare your environment and mindset by running the system test or confirming test-center procedures, ensuring a quiet setup, monitoring the timer, practicing deep breathing, and using Microsoft Learn during the exam only to confirm specific syntax or parameters.

CHAPTER 9
Practice Test and Sample Questions

Introduction

The **AI-102: Designing and Implementing an Azure AI Solution** certification exam validates your ability to design, build, and manage AI solutions using the Azure AI ecosystem. This advanced practice chapter simulates the real exam experience, reflecting both the **question style** and **technical depth** of the current AI-102 objectives of Microsoft.

You will encounter scenario-based case studies, realistic architecture decisions, JSON configurations, and command-line examples similar to those found in the exam environment. Each question is immediately followed by the correct answer and a concise explanation–making this a self-study mock exam to reinforce both conceptual understanding and practical implementation of skills.

This chapter provides a comprehensive set of practice questions designed to simulate the AI-102 certification exam experience. Readers will have the opportunity to test their knowledge across all domains covered in the book. An answer key with explanations is included to help learners understand the rationale behind each correct answer and to reinforce key concepts.

Structure

In this chapter, we will cover the following topics:

- Scenario-Based Case Studies
    - Contoso Retail – Vision-Based Product Automation
    - Fabrikam Finance – Document Intelligence and Knowledge Mining
    - Northwind Health – Generative AI and Agent-Based Solutions
- Standalone Questions (Q21 - Q35)

- Knowledge Checks (Q36 - Q40)
- Skills Coverage Overview

Scenario-Based Case Studies

The AI-102 certification places strong emphasis on scenario-based questions that assess your ability to design, evaluate, and justify Azure AI architectures under real-world constraints. Rather than testing isolated features, these questions measure how well you can interpret business requirements, apply the correct Azure AI services, and balance considerations such as security, cost, scalability, and compliance.

The following case studies are designed to mirror the structure and complexity of the exam's multi-part scenarios. Each one presents a realistic business context, clearly defined goals, and a set of technical and organizational constraints. You will be asked to make architectural decisions, select appropriate services, and reason about implementation details in a way that reflects how the AI-102 exam evaluates applied knowledge.

As you work through these case studies, focus not only on identifying the correct answers, but also on understanding *why* certain options are more appropriate than others. This approach will help you develop the analytical mindset required for the certification–where success depends on aligning Azure AI capabilities with business objectives, governance requirements, and operational best practices.

Contoso Retail – Vision-Based Product Automation

Contoso Retail operates 400 stores across North America. They plan to automate product image tagging, price extraction, and customer feedback analysis using Azure AI Services. Their existing infrastructure includes Azure Blob Storage, Azure SQL Database, and a .NET web app deployed on Azure App Service with Private Link.

Business goals:

- Automatically analyze product photos uploaded by store associates.
- Extract printed prices from shelf labels and associate them with SKU data.
- Perform real-time sentiment analysis on customer reviews.
- Ensure that the data remains within the U.S. region.

Question 1

You must design an image analysis workflow that can extract **tags**, **objects**, and **text (OCR)** in a single API call for efficiency. Which service and feature combination should you use?

A. Computer Vision v3.2 with the `/analyze` and `/read` endpoints

B. Custom Vision classification + OCR

C. Azure AI Vision Image Analysis v4.0 with the `features=tags, objects, read` parameter

D. Video Indexer with frame extraction

Answer: C

Explanation: Image Analysis v4.0 unifies tags, objects, OCR, captions, and more within one synchronous call–ideal for product catalog automation.

Question 2

Contoso must deploy the image-processing component **on-premises** due to low connectivity at some warehouses. Which design meets this requirement while staying supported?

A. Install the Vision SDK locally without Azure connection

B. Deploy Azure AI Vision in Docker containers connected to the cloud for billing

C. Export the model to TensorFlow Lite and run it offline

D. Use Logic Apps with the Vision API

Answer: B

Explanation: Azure AI Vision supports container deployment for offline or edge scenarios. The container authenticates periodically with Azure for metering and compliance.

Question 3

Customer reviews stored in Azure SQL must be analyzed daily for sentiment and key phrases. The data pipeline uses Azure Data Factory. Which integration minimizes development effort?

A. Data Factory Custom Activity with Python SDK

B. Azure AI Language Sentiment Analysis linked service in Data Factory

C. Stream Analytics job calling Cognitive Services

D. Web activity invoking a REST API manually

Answer: B

Explanation: Data Factory integrates directly with Azure AI Language for sentiment and key-phrase analysis through built-in connectors–no custom code needed.

Question 4

Management requests automatic masking of PII before storing text analytics results. What should you enable?

A. SQL Dynamic Data Masking

B. Application-level regex replacement

C. PII Entity Recognition API with `redactedText` output

D. Azure Information Protection policy

Answer: C

Explanation: The PII entity recognition API identifies and redacts sensitive data automatically, returning a sanitized text version ready for storage.

Question 5

To comply with data-residency rules, all AI services must remain in the **United States**. Which configuration ensures compliance?

A. Use the Global endpoint for redundancy

B. Deploy all resources in the EastUS or WestUS2 regions and restrict network via Private Endpoint

C. Use region-agnostic API keys

D. Set the x-location header in API calls

Answer: B

Explanation: AI services process data in the region where the resource resides. Private Endpoints ensure requests remain within Azure's regional boundary.

Fabrikam Finance – Document Intelligence and Knowledge Mining

Fabrikam Finance processes thousands of invoices, receipts, and purchase orders monthly. They want to implement a document understanding solution using Azure AI Document Intelligence and Azure AI Search with RAG (Retrieval-Augmented Generation).

Business goals:

- Automatically classify and extract fields from financial documents
- Store structured results in Azure SQL

- Allow auditors to query documents in natural language with grounded references
- Keep all data encrypted and private

Question 6

Fabrikam needs to extract invoice totals and IDs from standard invoices **without training a custom model**. Which feature should you use?

A. Custom Neural model

B. Prebuilt-invoice model with `queryFields=["InvoiceId","Total"]`

C. Prebuilt-layout with key-value pairs

D. Custom Template model

Answer: B

Explanation: Prebuilt-invoice can return standard fields and optional ones via `queryFields`, enabling dynamic schema extension.

Question 7

Some incoming files contain multiple document types (invoice + receipt). You need the system to automatically separate them. Which approach supports this behavior?

A. Batch analysis with multiple models

B. Composed model using a custom classifier with `split=auto`

C. Prebuilt-layout with OCR only

D. Manual routing by filename

Answer: B

Explanation: Composed models with an associated classifier can auto-split and route sections to the correct extractor.

Question 8

After extraction, Fabrikam wants to enable semantic search and question answering over all documents. Which Azure service should be added?

A. Power BI

B. Azure Data Explorer

C. Azure AI Search (semantic + vector index)

D. Synapse Analytics

Answer: C

Explanation: Azure AI Search supports hybrid retrieval and can power RAG-style question answering over indexed content.

Question 9

Developers must ensure sensitive information doesn't leave the private network. What configuration should be applied?

A. Use public endpoints with API keys

B. Enable Private Endpoints and disable public network access on all AI resources

C. Use a service principal only

D. Deploy resources in multiple regions

Answer: B

Explanation: Private Endpoints route traffic within the Azure backbone, ensuring isolation and compliance.

Question 10

Auditors require full traceability of model versions and extracted results. How can you ensure this?

A. Maintain logs in local storage

B. Use Document Intelligence model versioning and output metadata stored with each record

C. Delete intermediate results after extraction

D. Export models as static ONNX files

Answer: B

Explanation: Each build and analysis result in Document Intelligence includes version metadata for audit and reproducibility.

Northwind Health – Generative AI and Agent-Based Solutions

Northwind Health, a healthcare provider with clinics in multiple states, plans to deploy **AI-powered assistants** that can generate medical summaries, triage patient inquiries, and automate administrative reports. The organization must comply with

HIPAA, minimize exposure of sensitive data, and ensure every response is grounded in validated internal documentation.

Business goals:

- Build a **Generative AI Copilot** hosted in Azure AI Foundry using GPT-4 models.
- Integrate **agents** capable of using internal data, such as policies and treatment protocols, through Azure AI Search.
- Guarantee traceability and content safety for all model outputs.
- Monitor cost and performance in real time.

Question 11

Northwind wants to design a generative chat assistant that can access internal policy data securely. Which architecture provides both grounding and network isolation?

A. Azure OpenAI global endpoint with Internet access

B. Hub-based Azure AI Foundry project using Azure AI Search with Private Link

C. Stand-alone OpenAI API plus VPN

D. Azure Machine Learning online endpoint

Answer: B

Explanation: Hub-based projects in Azure AI Foundry integrate directly with Azure AI Search, thereby, allowing hybrid retrieval while staying within a private network through Private Endpoints.

Question 12

Developers must evaluate generative responses for **relevance** and **groundedness** before production deployment. Which toolset should they use?

A. Azure Monitor metrics

B. Azure AI Evaluation SDK with built-in relevance and groundedness evaluators

C. Manual spreadsheet review

D. Application Insights

Answer: B

Explanation: The Evaluation SDK automates testing of generative outputs for groundedness, coherence, and compliance, ensuring quality before go-live.

Question 13

The compliance team needs to verify that no unsafe or disallowed content is generated. What Azure capability should be integrated?

A. Azure Information Protection
B. Azure AI Foundry Content Safety with input and output moderation filters
C. Azure Defender for Cloud
D. Microsoft Purview

Answer: B

Explanation: Azure AI Foundry Content Safety provides configurable moderation for text and image prompts, including severity thresholds and blocklists.

Question 14

To handle high concurrency, Northwind wants the model endpoint to scale automatically and charge only for usage. Which deployment option meets the requirement?

A. Provisioned Throughput Units (PTU)
B. Dedicated managed compute
C. Serverless API endpoint
D. Batch Inference

Answer: C

Explanation: Serverless endpoints automatically scale based on demand and charge per token processed–ideal for unpredictable conversational workloads.

Question 15

The assistant must call an **external appointment API** to book visits when requested by users. Which feature allows this within an Azure AI Foundry agent?

A. Logic Apps connector
B. OpenAPI spec tool registered as an agent tool
C. External Function App via REST
D. Microsoft Graph API calls

Answer: B

Explanation: The OpenAPI spec tool lets an agent invoke operations defined in an OpenAPI schema, enabling secure, auditable integration with external APIs.

Question 16

Northwind plans to run multiple specialized agents (Medical Advisor, Billing Assistant, Compliance Reviewer) that collaborate under one orchestrator. Which orchestration framework should be used?

A. AutoGen only

B. Semantic Kernel (SK) Process Framework

C. Azure Functions Durable Tasks

D. Power Automate

Answer: B

Explanation: The SK Process Framework supports sequential, concurrent, and group-chat patterns for multi-agent orchestration with full traceability and hybrid connectivity to Azure AI Foundry.

Question 17

The compliance officer asks whether agent-to-agent communication is auditable and secure. Which statement is correct?

A. Inter-agent messages bypass logging.

B. Connected Agents (A2A) calls are logged and governed under the same RBAC and observability policies as other tools.

C. Only external logging captures agent communication.

D. A2A is unsupported in managed projects.

Answer: B

Explanation: Connected Agents in Foundry provide modular interoperability while maintaining built-in auditing, RBAC, and telemetry consistency.

Question 18

Developers need a **persistent conversation thread** that maintains context across multiple sessions for each patient query. Which component of the Agent Service stores this information?

A. Run Steps

B. Message History

C. Thread object within the Agent Service

D. Chat Session API

Answer: C

Explanation: Threads maintain long-term context and messages; each run executes against the current state of a thread.

Question 19

Executives want to monitor **token usage and latency** by agent to optimize cost. From where can this data be accessed?

A. Application Insights custom logs

B. Azure Monitor metrics only

C. Azure AI Foundry Agent Service metrics (Tokens, Runs, ToolCalls) via Azure Monitor

D. Azure Cost Management

Answer: C

Explanation: Agent Service exposes granular metrics for tokens, tool calls, and runs through Azure Monitor, enabling cost and performance analysis.

Question 20

Northwind will store logs of every interaction, including inputs and outputs, for auditing. Which privacy practice should be applied to protect patient data?

A. Encrypt logs manually after export

B. Enable `loggingOptOut` and store only anonymized metadata unless explicit consent is granted

C. Disable diagnostics entirely

D. Store full transcripts in Blob Storage

Answer: B

Explanation: Using **`loggingOptOut`** prevents sensitive payloads from being retained in diagnostic logs, supporting HIPAA and Responsible AI requirements.

Standalone Questions (Q21 – Q35)

The following **stand-alone questions** reflect the style and difficulty of typical items on the AI-102 exam that assess applied technical knowledge. Unlike the case studies, each question here focuses on a single concept or a decision–covering a range of real-world topics such as computer vision, Azure OpenAI, cost management, Azure AI Search, and network security. They are designed to validate not only your familiarity with Azure AI services, but also your ability to select the correct implementation or configuration under exam pressure.

Read each question carefully before reviewing the answer and explanation that follow.

Question 21

You need to capture **latency, success rate, and error codes** for all Azure AI resources in a solution. Which configuration should you implement first?

A. Enable metrics manually in Azure Monitor.

B. Create Diagnostic Settings on each resource and send logs to a Log Analytics workspace.

C. Add custom telemetry in application code only.

D. Use Azure Activity Log for data-plane monitoring.

Answer: B

Explanation: Diagnostic Settings collect platform metrics and data-plane logs from Azure AI services and route them to Log Analytics, Event Hub, or Storage for unified monitoring and alerting.

Question 22

A company plans to process large batches of audio recordings weekly for transcripts. Which Speech API option minimizes cost while supporting long files?

A. Real-time STT

B. Batch Transcription (Asynchronous)

C. Fast Transcription (Synchronous)

D. Streaming Transcription via WebSocket

Answer: B

Explanation: Batch Transcription is optimized for high-volume workloads, processes files stored in Blob Storage, and is cheaper than real-time modes.

Question 23

You need to build an **image-classification** model that identifies product categories and exports to TensorFlow Lite for mobile use. Which Azure AI service should you choose?

A. Face API

B. Image Analysis v4.0

C. Custom Vision (Classification Compact Domain)

D. Azure Machine Learning

Answer: C

Explanation: The compact domain models of Custom Vision can be exported to TensorFlow, ONNX, or CoreML for edge and mobile deployment.

Question 24

A developer must detect both **text and objects** in an image and return coordinates for each. Which API parameters should be used in Image Analysis v4.0?

A. `features=caption,people`

B. `features=read,objects`

C. `features=tags,denseCaptions`

D. `features=smartCrops`

Answer: B

Explanation: The read feature performs OCR while objects detect items with bounding boxes; together they return text and object coordinates in a single call.

Question 25

You are deploying Azure AI Search for enterprise documents. To implement **semantic and vector retrieval**, what must be included in the index schema?

A. Only searchable=true fields

B. A vector field with dimensions matching the embedding model, and a semantic configuration

C. Two separate indexes for text and vectors

D. Synonyms map for keywords

Answer: B

Explanation: Hybrid search requires a vector field aligned to the embedding dimension and a semantic configuration (title/content/keywords) for re-ranking.

Question 26

Your team wants to use Azure OpenAI models for internal development but **prevent public Internet access**. What should you configure?

A. Application Gateway with WAF

B. Private Endpoint and disable Public Network Access on the resource

C. NSG rules allowing HTTPS only

D. VNet service endpoints for Key Vault

Answer: B

Explanation: Private Endpoints securely expose Azure AI resources inside a VNet and blocking public access enforces network isolation.

Question 27

You need to estimate monthly costs for Azure OpenAI and set budget alerts if spending reaches 80%. Which Azure tool combination should you use?

A. Azure Advisor + Excel

B. Azure Pricing Calculator + Cost Management (Budgets and Alerts)

C. Power BI + Log Analytics

D. Application Insights Usage Metrics

Answer: B

Explanation: The Pricing Calculator provides forecast estimates, while Cost Management creates budgets and automated alerts for real spending.

Question 28

You need a Generative AI model that handles both text and images in the same conversation. Which model should you choose?

A. GPT-4.1

B. GPT-4o (Omni)

C. gpt-image-1

D. DALL·E 3

Answer: B

Explanation: GPT-4o is multimodal–it accepts text, image, and audio inputs and returns text or images in a single session.

Question 29

You need to generate high-resolution images and edit specific areas using masking. Which Azure OpenAI model supports this requirement?

A. dalle-3

B. gpt-image-1

C. GPT-4o-mini

D. text-embedding-3-small

Answer: B

Explanation: gpt-image-1 enables image editing (in-painting) and improves text rendering over DALL·E 3.

Question 30

You must evaluate a generative model to ensure it produces accurate and safe responses. Which three evaluation metrics should be prioritized?

A. Latency, Throughput, Uptime

B. Relevance, Groundedness, Safety

C. Creativity, Novelty, Style

D. Cost, Speed, Security

Answer: B

Explanation: AI-102 exam emphasizes evaluating LLM outputs for relevance (correctness), groundedness (source faithfulness), and safety (policy compliance).

Question 31

You plan to deploy a Custom Vision model for object detection in a factory with intermittent Internet. Which deployment method should you use?

A. Azure Functions hosting

B. Azure Kubernetes Service in the cloud

C. Containerized Custom Vision model on edge devices

D. Power Automate flow

Answer: C

Explanation: Exported Custom Vision containers run on edge or on-prem infrastructure with periodic license checks against Azure.

Question 32

You are designing a solution that summarizes transcribed meetings and emails. Which two Azure services should you combine?

A. Azure AI Speech (for transcription) and Azure OpenAI (for summarization)

B. Azure Monitor and Power BI

C. Azure Databricks and Azure Search

D. Cognitive Search and Custom Vision

Answer: A

Explanation: Speech transcribes audio to text, and Azure OpenAI (GPT-4 series) summarizes the resulting text.

Question 33

A user asks the AI assistant a question about internal HR policies. Responses must cite sources from indexed files. Which pattern should you implement?

A. Fine-tuned LLM

B. Retrieval-Augmented Generation (RAG)

C. Chain-of-Thought prompting

D. Azure Function Webhook

Answer: B

Explanation: RAG retrieves contextual information from Azure AI Search and injects it into the prompt so responses remain grounded and verifiable.

Question 34

You need to classify customer messages into intents and extract entities like dates and locations. Which Azure AI Language feature should you use?

A. Sentiment Analysis

B. Conversational Language Understanding (CLU)

C. Custom Question Answering

D. PII Recognition

Answer: B

Explanation: CLU recognizes intents and extracts entities from conversational inputs—key for chatbot and workflow automation.

Question 35

You are building an AI Search index for a document repository. The system must support **hybrid search**. What does hybrid search combine?

A. BM25 and spelling correction

B. Keyword (BM25) and Vector search merged by Reciprocal Rank Fusion (RRF)

C. Semantic and OCR search

D. Facets and filters

Answer: B

Explanation: Hybrid search runs lexical (BM25) and vector queries in parallel and merges results via RRF for balanced precision and recall.

Knowledge Checks (Q36 – Q40)

This final section provides a set of quick knowledge checks which are aimed at reinforcing critical facts, limits, and terminology frequently tested in the AI-102 certification.

These concise questions focus on details such as service endpoints, parameter names, quotas, and framework identifiers—elements that often appear in the real exam's shorter multiple-choice items. Use these to ensure that you have mastered the foundational knowledge that supports the broader, scenario-based questions presented earlier in the chapter.

Question 36

Which Azure AI service exposes the **`/documentModels/{modelId}:analyze`** endpoint?

A. Azure AI Vision

B. Azure AI Document Intelligence (v4)

C. Azure AI Search

D. Azure Machine Learning

Answer: B

Explanation: Document Intelligence v4 uses the **`/documentModels`** REST API for analyzing and extracting structured data from forms, receipts, and invoices.

Question 37

What is the maximum character length for a single document in **synchronous Text Analytics** requests?

A. 1 KB (≈ 1 000 chars)

B. 2 KB (≈ 2 000 chars)

C. 5 120 characters

D. 125 000 characters

Answer: C

Explanation: The synchronous Text Analytics API supports about 5120 characters per document; larger payloads require asynchronous batch jobs.

Question 38

Which Azure AI Vision feature returns **smart crop coordinates** instead of an image thumbnail?

A. `captionResult`

B. `denseCaptionsResult`

C. `smartCropsResult`

D. `peopleResult`

Answer: C

Explanation: Smart Crops generate bounding-box coordinates for adaptive cropping while preserving composition–useful for responsive design.

Question 39

Which Azure service provides speech translation in real time with optional voice synthesis?

A. Azure AI Translator

B. Azure AI Speech (Speech Translation API)

C. Azure AI Language

D. Cognitive Search

Answer: B

Explanation: Azure AI Speech performs real-time translation from one spoken language to another and can synthesize the translated output as speech.

Question 40

Which Microsoft framework is recommended for building **graph-based multi-agent workflows** interoperable with Azure AI Foundry?

A. AutoGen

B. Microsoft Agent Framework (MAF)

C. Durable Functions

D. Airflow

Answer: B

Explanation: MAF unifies orchestration and process modeling for multi-agent systems, providing checkpointing and direct deployment to Azure AI Foundry.

Skills Coverage Overview

The following table summarizes how the practice exam questions are distributed across the **AI-102: Designing and Implementing an Azure AI Solution** skill areas.

Each skill area aligns with the official *Skills at a glance* outline of Microsoft and reflects its relative weight in the actual certification exam. This mapping helps learners identify which sections of the book are to be reviewed when focusing on specific competencies.

Skill Area	Skills Tested	Number of Questions
Plan and Manage Azure AI Solutions	Governance, Cost Control, Networking, Monitoring	8
Develop Generative AI Solutions	OpenAI Models, Foundry, Evaluation, Safety	7
Implement an Agentic Solution	Agents, Connected Agents, SK/MAF Orchestration	5
Implement Computer Vision Solutions	Image Analysis, Custom Vision, Face API	5
Implement NLP, Knowledge Mining, and Information Extraction Solutions	Language, Speech, Search, Document Intelligence	15

Table 9.1: *AI-102 Question Distribution by Skill Area*

Conclusion

By completing this comprehensive practice exam, you have reached the final stage of your preparation for the **AI-102: Designing and Implementing an Azure AI Solution** certification. This book has guided you through every core skill required of an Azure AI Engineer–from designing secure and governed AI architectures, to implementing generative, agentic, computer vision, natural language, and knowledge mining solutions using the Azure AI platform.

You now possess the technical foundation and practical insight to design, deploy, and maintain intelligent solutions that are scalable, responsible, and aligned with enterprise standards. While the questions in this chapter mirror the format and complexity of the real certification, they also serve a deeper purpose: to reinforce your ability to reason, architect, and troubleshoot AI workloads in production environments.

Moving forward, continue exploring the Azure AI ecosystem–the evolving services, SDKs, and Responsible AI practices. One should Engage with the community, share what you have built, and stay informed through Microsoft Learn and official Azure updates. Remember that earning your certification is not the finish line–it is the starting point of a lifelong learning journey in AI innovation and ethical technology leadership.

Index

A

T

V

X